ALSO BY PETER EVANS

Nonfiction

Nemesis: The True Story of Aristotle Onassis, Jackie O, and the Love Triangle That Brought Down the Kennedys

Behind Palace Doors (with Nigel Dempster)

Ari: The Life and Times of Aristotle Onassis

Bardot: Eternal Sex Goddess

Peter Sellers: The Mask Behind the Mask

Goodbye Baby and Amen: A Saraband for the Sixties (with David Bailey)

Fiction

Theodora

The Englishman's Daughter

Titles

ALSO BY AVA GARDNER

Ava: My Story

AVA GARDNER

THE SECRET CONVERSATIONS

Peter Evans

AND

Ava Gardner

SIMON & SCHUSTER

New York London Toronto Sydney New Delhi

Simon & Schuster
1230 Avenue of the Americas
New York, NY 10020

First Simon & Schuster hardcover edition July 2013

Designed by Joy O'Meara

Manufactured in the United States of America

10 9 8 7 6 5 4 3

Library of Congress Cataloging-in-Publication Data
Evans, Peter.
Ava Gardner : the secret conversations / Peter Evans and Ava Gardner. — First Simon & Schuster hardcover ed.
pages cm
Includes index.
1. Gardner, Ava, 1922–1990. 2. Motion picture actors and actresses—United States—Biography. I. Title.
PN2287.G37E84 2013
791.4302'8092—dc23
[B] 2012048411
ISBN 978-1-4516-2769-5

Photo Credits

1: Courtesy of the Ava Gardner Trust · 2, 4: State Archives of North Carolina and *The News and Observer*, Raleigh, North Carolina · 3, 9: Everett Collection · 5, 8: Photofest · 10: Hulton Archive/Getty Images · 11, 13: © Sunset Boulevard/Corbis · 6, 7, 12, 14: © Bettman/Corbis · 15: © 1983 Tom Zimberoff.

For my family.

—Peter Evans

AVA GARDNER

THE SECRET CONVERSATIONS

Prologue

Her phone calls in the middle of the night had fallen into a habit. I picked up the receiver on the first ring, an old newspaperman's trick.

"Did I wake you, honey?" she asked softly, without preamble.

"It's 3 A.M.," I said, checking my watch. "Of course you didn't wake me."

"It's me," she said.

"I know it's you, Ava." No one else in the world sounded like Ava Gardner. Nobody I knew anyway. There was always a sense of weariness, a hint of a recent bender in her voice, even when it wasn't three o'clock in the morning, even when she was stone-cold sober.

"You said I could always call, no matter what time it was," she reminded me. "Were you sleeping, honey?"

"Just dozing," I lied. She sounded low. "Can't you sleep?"

"I miss Frank," she said after a small silence. "He was a bastard. But Jesus I miss him."

"*Was?* Is he dead?"

"Not as far as I know, honey."

Sinatra would outlive her, she said. "Bastards are always the best survivors."

We talked for a long time, as we always did when she called me in the night. We talked about the films she had made, her mistakes and missed opportunities, one of which, she said, was turning down the role of Mrs. Robinson in *The Graduate*. We talked about bull-fighters; John Huston, whom she adored; restaurants; her favorite dogs; her lovers. She told me about the days when she swam like a champion, played tennis, and could dance all night. She talked about the lousy prices secondhand dealers were offering for her dresses and couture gowns. "I could hoist the price if I put my name to them, but that'd be telling the world Ava Gardner's hanging on in there by the skin of her teeth," she said.

"You can sum up my life in a sentence, honey: She made movies, she made out, and she made a fucking mess of her life. But she never made jam," she said.

She could make me laugh even when she woke me up at three o'clock in the morning. She could make me laugh even when I would have liked to throttle her.

She had pulmonary emphysema, or feared she had, the lung disease that had recently carried off John Huston, and I knew that she was afraid of dying painfully and slowly as he had. So much of her life had been caught up with his. "Huston had all the courage in the world. I told him he should just put a gun to his head—he loved playing with fucking guns—and pull the trigger when the pain got too much. But the stubborn bastard wanted to die game. He always had a cruel streak in him even when the cruelty was directed at himself," she said.

I heard the clink of a bottle against a glass.

"You know this thing called Exit, baby?" she asked, after a long silence.

I said I had but she ignored me.

"They help you switch off the lights when you've had enough," she said. "There was an old lady, Mrs. Chapman, a neighbor of mine. She'd had a stroke and didn't like it one bit. She belonged to Exit. I'd go up and sit and listen to her once in a while. She was a classy old broad, full of piss and vinegar. She must have been quite pretty once, too. She said that when you get to the point you can't take it any longer, these people help you close your account, and make sure you do it right first time—they give you pills, a bottle of brandy, or Scotch, if that's your poison."

I didn't say anything. I didn't know what to say. Her mind was always full of surprising twists and turns but this was the first time she had told me that she wanted to kill herself. Not straight out like that anyway. No matter how smart you think you are, there are times when you don't know what to say, because there is nothing wise or comforting you can say.

"Ava, I hope you don't mean that," I said.

"I'm getting close to that point, honey. I'm so fucking tired of being Ava Gardner," she said.

There was pain in her voice. I still wanted to say something reassuring but I knew it would be a lie and she would spot it at once. I said nothing.

"When I don't want to be around anymore, I don't want any retakes. I don't want to recover next day and find myself the lead story on the six o'clock news. I'd like to do it in one take," she said. It was, she said, and began to laugh, something she had never managed in her whole movie career. "I never missed my mark but I didn't always manage a scene in one take either. It would be nice to finally break the habit of a lifetime," she said.

When the time came, she said, would I take her to the people at Exit? "I'm not afraid of dying, baby. I just want you to hold my hand, I want you to be there when I go, that's all," she said. "Will you do that for me, when the time comes, baby? Will you promise to be there for me, honey?"

"I won't help you die, Ava. I can't do that," I said. I knew she scorned cowardice as much as she despised disloyalty, and she made me feel guilty on both counts. I almost told her that I was a Catholic, but caught myself in time. "I'm sorry, Ava."

"I thought you were my friend," she said.

"I am, Ava," I said.

"I thought you loved me," she said.

"I do, Ava," I said.

"Obviously you don't love me enough. You don't understand friendship at all. If you loved me, if you were my friend, you'd help me die when I want to go. Fahcrissake, honey, my body's failing every which way, you know that. I'm falling apart here. And you refuse to help me the one way you can. You don't love me at all, baby."

She said that she wanted to go to sleep now. "Shit, I'm going to have a peach of a head in the morning, I know that," she said, perhaps to let me know she was angry at herself, too.

I told her that I loved her, whatever she thought.

"The thing is, honey, I'd have helped you. If you came to me and asked, I'd have done it for you, baby," she said, and put the phone down.

I went to my study and wrote down everything she had said, as I always did. I knew that she was always at her most honest at that hour.

1

In the first week of January 1988, Ava Gardner asked me to ghost her memoirs. Since I had never met Ava Gardner, the call, late on a Sunday evening, was clearly a hoax. "Sounds great, Ava," I played along. "Does Frank approve? I don't want to upset Frank." There was a small silence, then a brief husky laugh.

"Fuck Frank," she said with a faint but still unmistakably Southern drawl.

"Are you interested or not, honey?" she said.

Only Ava Gardner could have made the ultimatum sound both threatening and so full of promise. She had been called "the most irresistible woman in Hollywood," and "the world's most beautiful animal." Such encomiums were typical of the hype that was de rigueur in the Hollywood marketing machine of the 1940s and '50s, but they were not inappropriate. Ava Gardner's whole life had been defined by her beauty and the many and various lovers it ensnared—and she famously devoured. In another age, in another world, she would have been a *grande horizontale*. She had seduced, been seduced by, married to and divorced from, lived with and walked out on, some of the most famous names of the twentieth century. She had toyboys before Cher had toys, although it was unlikely that any of them remained boys for very long in her company. "Are you interested or not, honey?"

I should have said no right there. I wasn't a ghostwriter. I was working fifteen hours a day to finish my third novel; an interesting biography was on the stocks; I really didn't need this kind of distraction. But this was *Ava Gardner* calling *me*. Only a fool would say he wasn't interested. Or not be tempted. Although we had several mutual friends, the closest we ever got was the twenty minutes between my departure from, and her arrival in, Puerto Vallarta, Mexico, during the filming of Tennessee Williams's *The Night of the Iguana* in 1963. Richard Burton, who was playing the unfrocked minister T. Lawrence Shannon opposite Gardner's man-hungry Maxine Faulk, told me that I should stay on a couple of days and meet her. "She's not a movie star; she's a legend. She'll either love you or hate you. Either way, you won't forget her," he said. But I had to go.

Twenty-five years later, I still hadn't met her, and had no idea why she had asked me to ghost her story.

"It's okay, I checked you out, honey," she said, anticipating, but not answering, my unasked question. She gave me her London telephone number. "Call me tomorrow evening, after six, not before. I come awake after six," she said. She apologized for the late hour, said good night, and replaced the receiver. I made a note of the conversation, and the time: it was 11:35 P.M.

The following morning, before I called my friend and agent, Ed Victor, I read everything about her I could lay my hands on. "Ava Gardner has seldom been accused of acting," wrote the film historian David Shipman in 1972. "She is of what might be termed the genus Venus, stars that are so beautiful that they needn't bother to act. It's enough if they just stand around being desirable." But even after she had acquired a reputation as a neurotic drinker, with a pathological urge to self-destruct, her sensuality continued to animate nearly every part she played. Her taste for matadors, millionaires, and wholly inappropriate men had become notorious. She believed that sexual freedom was a woman's prerogative. Her affairs had brought her final husband, Frank Sinatra, to the brink of suicide, taken her lover Howard Hughes beyond the edge of madness, and provoked George C. Scott to bouts of near-homicidal rage.

She undoubtedly had a life worth writing about, and of course I was interested. Nevertheless, I knew that a couple of years earlier she'd had a stroke and hadn't worked since. The question was: how much of her tumultuous life would she be able to remember—or prepared to own up to, even if she remembered plenty? But by the laws of the game that publishers play, Ava Gardner was still a catch. It was not every day that a Hollywood legend offered to tell a story that was so full of history, scandal, and secrets.

I called Jack Cardiff, a friend of mine. He was one of the finest cinematographers in the world. He had photographed Ava in *Pandora and the Flying Dutchman* and *The Barefoot Contessa*. They had known each other for forty years and were Knightsbridge neighbors. I explained the situation.

"She's always sworn that she'd never write a biography. How the hell did you get her to change her mind?" he asked, with incredulity in his voice.

"I didn't get her to change her mind. I didn't get her to do anything. And I haven't agreed to write it yet," I said.

"Don't kid yourself, pal. If Ava Gardner wants you to write her book, you'll write it," he said.

I said that it could be a very short book, indeed, if the stroke had loused up her memory.

"She might occasionally forget where she put her car keys, but she'll remember what she needs to remember," he said. "But let me give you a word of advice. *Nobody* becomes a movie star by putting all their cards on the table—and there'll be plenty she'll want to forget. She'd be mad not to keep the lid on some of the things that have happened in her life. She'll give you plenty of problems, with Ava there are always problems, but sure as hell amnesia won't be one of them."

The timing of the book was a more immediate problem. The late hour of her phone call on Sunday evening might have given her offer a greater sense of urgency. I definitely had the feeling that she wasn't prepared to be kept waiting. A sexagenarian, in poor health, she had lived extravagantly, drunk to excess. It was unlikely that she had much of an income coming in from her old movies. It was rumored that Frank Sinatra, thirty-one years after their divorce, still picked up her medical bills, and maybe other bills, too. Even so she was probably still feeling the pinch.

I told Ed Victor what had happened, and about my talk with Cardiff. I'd still like to give it a shot, I said, but I didn't think I'd be able to stall her until I'd finished my novel.

He agreed. "But it would be a pity to let her go. She's got one of the greatest untold stories in movies. Her very name epitomizes Hollywood in its heyday," he said. "I think we should do whatever we have to do to move it on, don't you?"

To further complicate things, the heroine of my novel *Theodora* was a movie star of the same vintage as Ava. He advised me not to mention this to Ava. "Actresses are never comfortable knowing they have a rival, even if she's only a character in a book," he said. He proposed that I work with Ava in the evenings, and continue to write *Theodora* during the day—"or whichever way round she wants to play it, but it sounds as if she might be at her best after dark," he said cheerfully.

I CALLED AVA THAT evening, after six as she had suggested, and, as Jack Cardiff had prophesied, I got my first surprise.

"I have to tell you, I have a problem with this book idea, honey. I'm in two minds about the whole goddamn thing."

The sense of accusation in her voice, the implication that the book had been my idea, stunned me. Before I could remind her that she had approached me, she explained that she had remembered a conversation with John Huston when he was writing his autobiography, *An Open Book*. Her favorite director, Huston had cowritten *The Killers*, the movie that, in 1946, rescued her career after a dozen forgettable B movies (*Hitler's Madman, Ghosts on the Loose, Maisie Goes to Reno*) and set her on the path to stardom.

"I loved John. God, I miss him. He had a great life. He lived like a king, even when he didn't have a pot to piss in. His entire life was a crap shoot. He even loved foxhunting, fahcrissake! I hope to Christ there are hounds and foxes wherever the old bastard is now."

The problem was she had recalled that Huston once told her that writing his book was like living his life all over again.

"Second helpings was perfect for John. He even got a kick out of remembering the bundles he'd dropped at Santa Anita, the poor bloody elephants and tigers he'd shot in India—reliving all that stuff, the drunken brawls—was no end of fun for Huston. But do I want to go through the crap and mayhem of my life a second time just for a book, honey? The first time, you have no choice. Lana Turner says that life is what happens to you while the crow's-feet are fucking up your looks. Lana has a name and a story for every goddamn wrinkle in her face. I'm not saying my own looks don't give the game away. Nothing I can do about that anymore. A nip and tuck ain't gonna do it. The thing is: do I have to put myself through the mangle again?"

It sounded like something she had thought about a lot. I was only disappointed that she hadn't thought about it a lot before she involved me. Nevertheless, it was an extraordinary tirade: cynical and anguished as well as sad and funny. It made me want to write her book more than ever. I had no idea whether it was a game she was playing to test me. All actresses liked to be cajoled and wooed a little, of course; I remembered what John Huston had said when she was having misgivings about playing the role of Maxine in *The Night of the Iguana*: "I knew damned well that she was going to do it; she did, too—she just wanted to be courted."

If that was what she was doing now, I decided to play along. I told her that I understood her anxieties; her apprehension was normal. "I don't blame you, Miss Gardner," I said. "If you don't want to do it, don't do it. Writing about yourself must be like looking at your reflection in a mirror when you're nursing a God Almighty hangover."

To my surprise, she burst out laughing.

"Well, let's not beat about the bush, honey," she said. Her laugh became a racking cough. When she stopped there was a long silence. I heard a lighter click a couple of times, followed by a deep intake of breath as she drew reflectively on a cigarette. "How long would it take to write this stuff, honey?" she asked. I said that it would depend on many things—how long the interviews took, how good her memory was, how well we got on together.

"I'm told we'd get along fine, but who the hell knows? You've been a journalist; I hate journalists. I don't trust them," she said. "But Dirk Bogarde says you're okay. So does Michael Winner. Dirk said you deal from a clean deck, and you're not a faggot. Don't get me wrong. I get on fine with fags, I just prefer dealing with guys who aren't. Dirk reckons you'd break your ass to get the book right. That's what I need—a guy who'll break his ass to please me."

As she became more relaxed, her uncertainty about doing the book seemed to lessen. I asked whether she had read anything of mine. She said that she had read one of my novels and *Ari*, my biography of Aristotle Onassis. She had known Onassis, and been a guest on his yacht *Christina*. She said that my book was "on the money, but the horny little fuck had other attractions beside the dough."

What are they? I asked. I was genuinely curious.

"If he hadn't had a dollar he could have snapped a lady's garter anytime he liked. I understand what Jackie Kennedy saw in him besides the fortune. She never fell for him, like Maria Callas. He was a primitive with a yacht. Mrs. Kennedy would have appreciated that. A primitive with a yacht," she repeated. "For some ladies that's an irresistible combination.

"Did Ari ever tell you his views on Aristophanes' *Lysistrata*—about the morality of broads who bargain with their pussies? He might have said 'cunts' I can't remember. He probably said 'cunts.' He was always trying to shock me. It became a game between us. I tried to shock him, he tried to shock me. I don't think he ever shocked me, although I think I managed to surprise him once or twice," she said with evident satisfaction.

We talked for a while about Onassis, whom she clearly liked. "I never slept with him, although it was tempting, it would have been interesting. Are you taping this?" she suddenly asked sharply, with suspicion in her voice. "This is between the two of us, right?"

"Of course," I said.

"I'll tell you when the meter starts," she said.

I assured her again that I wasn't taping her, which was true; however, I was making plenty of notes. To change the subject, I told her that her first husband, Mickey Rooney, was coming to London shortly in his nostalgic Broadway success, *Sugar Babies*.

"Mickey, the smallest husband I ever had, and the biggest mistake I ever made—well, that year it was. Pearl Harbor in December [1941], spliced to Mickey in January [1942]. It was the start of the goddamnedest, unhappiest, most miserable time I'd ever had. He wasn't an easy man to live with, God knows. It was really a fucked-up marriage from day one. I was nineteen years old. Jesus! I was just a kid! *A baby!*"

She talked about her days with Rooney, losing her virginity to him on their wedding night, when he was the biggest star on the MGM lot, and she was a starlet. "But I do owe Mickey one thing: he taught me how much I enjoyed sex—in bed, I've always known I was on safe ground."

I said that was very funny.

"If I get into this stuff, oh, honey, have you got something coming."

There was a long pause in which I could sense her making up her mind. Finally, she said: "Well, okay, if this book is going to happen, honey, I guess I'd better see you up close and personal. I trust Bogarde, but I'm a gal who likes to buy her own drinks."

When shall we meet? I asked her.

"I'll call you," she said.

"DON'T THANK ME. SHE will eat you alive; you know that, don't you? I haven't the faintest idea whether I've done either of you any favors putting you together. Maybe it's a book she should never write, maybe she should remain an enigma," Dirk Bogarde told me over lunch at La Famiglia, a favorite Tuscan restaurant in Chelsea. I'd known him a long time; when I was starting out in journalism and he was a Rank contract player going nowhere, I ghosted an article for him in *Films and Filming,* a now defunct movie magazine. Although he could be caustic and touchy—bitchy even—I enjoyed his company and wicked humor, and could take his ribbing in my stride. Now in his late sixties, he had been a handsome and popular leading man in British films in the 1950s and early '60s. His performance as a working-class manservant who seduces and corrupts his aristocratic master in Joseph Losey's *The Servant* launched him as an international star. His reputation grew rapidly in such films as

Luchino Visconti's *The Damned*, and *Death in Venice,* in which he played the dying Mahler character; and as a masochistic concentration camp doctor in Liliana Cavani's *The Night Porter.* Then a film by Rainer Werner Fassbinder, for which he had high hopes, turned out badly and he stopped working for twelve years. When we met for lunch, he had semiretired from acting and was writing novels, literary criticism, essays, obituaries, and fragments of autobiography for the London *Daily Telegraph*.

He said, "Before you start with Madam, old chum, a piece of advice: remember that she is essential to the Hollywood myth about itself. You tamper with that at your peril. She is very dear and adorable. I am devoted to her. She can also be outrageous—Dom Perignon at 5 A.M. in Makeup: 'The only way to make filming fun,' she used to say—but she is terribly conflicted about herself, especially about her fame. Most well-known actors are, but she especially, pathologically so. She may never make another movie, that stroke has buggered up her career for good, I imagine, but if she lives to be a hundred she will never go into oblivion, she will never be forgotten. She will try to spin you the expurgated version of her life. She will often be evasive and capricious and sometimes bloody tiresome—the obstacles and diversions she will throw at your feet!—but you must persevere if you wish to get to the truth. Trust me, the truth is something else. You must already have heard that she's more fun when she's had a tipple or two. But when she's had more than a tipple or two, watch out! She can be rough, and bloody unpredictable. But always show her respect, yet not too much reverence. She's smart, she'll know the difference. And she will eat you alive."

When we said goodbye, he repeated with a bleak smile as he got into the cab in the King's Road: "Don't say I didn't warn you, chum: *she will eat you alive!*"

With slightly more trepidation, I continued to wait for her call.

2

It's true then what they say: the world is so full of madmen that one need not seek them in a madhouse," Peter Viertel greeted me when I arrived in Marbella, on the Spanish Costa del Sol, where he lived with his second wife, the English actress Deborah Kerr. Although they had come to meet me at the airport, I could see he was not happy that I had ignored his advice not to accept Ava's offer. "Don't even think about it, if you value your sanity; she was a ballbreaker then, and she'll still be a ballbreaker. But she's also beautiful and smart, and you're going to go ahead with her book whatever I say," he'd said when I called him from London to seek his advice on how to handle her.

Viertel had known Ava since 1946, when she was an MGM starlet and married to her second husband and Viertel's friend, the virtuoso clarinetist Artie Shaw. Each morning, Viertel had swum with Ava in the pool of the Shaws' Beverly Hills house while Artie, who had literary ambitions, discussed books and writing with Viertel's first wife, Virginia—known as "Jigee"—the former wife of novelist Budd Schulberg and onetime story editor for Sam Goldwyn. In 1956, Viertel was asked to write the screenplay for Ernest Hemingway's *The Sun Also Rises,* in which Ava was to play the aristocratic Lady Brett Ashley.

I knew that they had been close—"men are inclined to fall in love with Ava at sight," he admitted—although he denied they had been lovers. A disclaimer, if not said out of modesty and guile, uttered for the comfort of his wife, who sat next to him as we lunched at the Marbella Club.

The son of Berthold and Salka Viertel—she was Greta Garbo's friend and wrote several of her notable films of the 1930s—Peter had grown up in Hollywood and knew everybody. Over lunch he told lively anecdotes about Humphrey Bogart, Hemingway, John Huston, Orson Welles, as well as his parents' famous friends in the Los Angeles refugee community, including Bertolt Brecht and Thomas Mann, whom he had known as a child.

"Anyway, you want me to tell you about Ava," he continued seamlessly as the coffee was poured. "Let me tell you something: *nobody* handles Ava Gardner. Artie Shaw was a smart guy, a regular polymath—as well as a male chauvinist shit of the first order—and he couldn't handle her, and neither could Luis Miguel Dominguín, one of the bravest bullfighters in Spain." He looked at me pointedly, as if waiting for me to say something.

"What about Sinatra?" I said.

He shook his head. "Sinatra, the poor bastard, never stood a chance, and he loved her probably most of all. He was too possessive of her; that was the problem, or one of the problems—no one is ever going to possess Ava." He shrugged; he clearly didn't want to get involved in her marital problems. "Let's just say she's a complicated woman, courageous, difficult . . . well, you'll find out. She'll promise you anything. She'll be nice as huckleberry pie—until the day you get down to work. She'll take it as a personal affront if she can't seduce you, by the way—and if she does succeed, you'll have the time of your life. But you won't have the book you could have had, or Ava deserves."

I expressed my doubt that she would still be sexually active. "Don't forget she's had a stroke," I said, lamely.

"That won't have stopped her," he said, sounding very sure of himself. "The trouble will begin when you show her pages. She will hate them. She loathed my screenplay [*The Sun Also Rises*]. She sent it to Hemingway for his opinion, for Christ's sake. No author likes what a screenwriter does to his book. Fortunately, Papa went easy on me. Hollywood had screwed up every one of his books; he was getting used to it, he said. Anyway, he was my friend.

"But even so, what Ava did was unforgivable, and unkind. But she craves second opinions. A second opinion is always Ava's first weapon of choice. You'll have to fight her all the way, and I warn you now she's a money player. She knows what is good for Ava, or thinks she does, but that won't necessarily be good for you or your book. No matter what she promised to get you on board, when it comes to the point, Ava isn't going to condone a truly honest biography. Her language, using all the four-letter words, the booze, the scandals, the lovers she's had—okay, plenty of actresses put out, but few have been as eager or as beautiful as Ava Gardner. I'm telling you, I know her, and she's not going to admit to one tenth of that stuff.

"If only she would tell the truth about herself—or allow it to be told—my God, what a book that would be! But it's not going to happen, and that's a pity because everything she has ever done in her life, all that she has achieved, has been done and achieved on her own terms. I still love her, in spite of a couple of things she shouldn't have done to me, and to others. She is still the proudest, the most liberated, the most uninhibited woman I know," he said.

Deborah Kerr, who starred with Ava in *The Night of the Iguana*, and had been listening politely to her husband's stories, chipped in with a wan smile: "I think what Pete is trying to tell you is that Ava's a man-eater."

I RETURNED TO LONDON that evening feeling none the wiser about how to deal with Ava, whom I still hadn't met. She had canceled a couple of appointments, but we had talked on the telephone nearly every evening and despite her procrastination she talked eagerly about the book, throwing in ideas and opinions and some wonderful throwaway lines.

Eleven days after her first phone call, Ava invited me to her apartment, spaciously spread across the first floor of two converted fin de siècle mansions in Ennismore Gardens, Knightsbridge. There were four bells on a brass plate screwed to the red-brick wall by the front door, with names written on cards fixed in small plastic slots by each bell. Her bell had the name Baker. "It's my mother's maiden name. I live like a goddamn spy," she'd told me earlier.

I rang the entry phone and gave my name; the lock was released and I was told to go to the first floor, where her housekeeper, Carmen Vargas, met me and led the way to the drawing room. But before we reached it, Ava appeared in the hall wearing nothing but an angry scowl and a bath towel. "I loathe it when people spread bedtime stories about me." She explained her bad temper and the reason why she had been delayed getting dressed for our meeting. (Later, when we had gotten to know each other a whole lot better, she admitted that she also wanted to see how I would react to her state of dishabille; she never to her dying day lost her pride in her sexuality.)

"I was in the tub when a girlfriend called from L.A. She said that Marlon Brando told her he'd slept with me; he reckoned we'd had a little thing going in Rome. That's a goddamn lie, honey," she said. She had called Brando on it right away. "I told him that if he really believed that I'd ever jumped into the feathers with him, his brain had gone soft. He apologized. He said that his brain wasn't the only part of his anatomy that had gone soft lately. He said, 'Ithn't that punithment enouth, baby?'" she lisped, mocking Brando's speech impediment. "That's a funny line, isn't it? How can you stay pissed with a guy who comes up with a line like that?"

As I followed her into the drawing room, she pulled the bath towel more tightly around her; she was clearly wearing no underwear.

She held out her hand. "Mr. Evans, good evening," she said politely, as if remembering her manners. "May I call you Peter?" she asked, holding on to my hand and searching my face, slowly and quite openly.

"Of course," I said.

"Call me Ava," she said, releasing my hand with a nod of acceptance. "I must put some clothes on," she said. When she returned she was wearing a gray tight-fitting jersey track suit and horn-rimmed eyeglasses.

"I don't know about Jimmy Dean, Ingrid Bergman, Larry Olivier, Jackie O, and the rest of the names Marlon's supposed to have carved on his bedpost, but my name's definitely not one of them, honey," she said, casually picking up the conversation where she'd left it. She was calmer now that she had finished dressing. "Marlon ought to know better than to make up a story like that. I think the most vulgar thing about Hollywood is the way it believes its own gossip.

"I know a lot of men fantasize about me; that's how Hollywood gossip becomes Hollywood history. Someday someone is going to say, 'All the lies ever told about Ava Gardner are true,' and the truth about me, just like the truth about poor, maligned Marilyn [Monroe] will disappear like names on old tombstones. I know I'm not defending a spotless reputation. Hell, it's too late for that. Scratching one name off my dance card won't mean a row of beans in the final tally.

It's just that I like to keep the books straight while I'm still around and sufficiently sober and compos mentis to do it," she said.

"Is that why you want to write a book?" I asked warily. "You want to put the record straight?"

"I'm broke, honey. I either write the book or sell the jewels." Although it was what I had suspected, I was surprised at the frankness with which she admitted it. "And I'm kinda sentimental about the jewels," she added.

She tapped a cigarette out of a half-empty pack on the Adam mantelpiece, lit it with a gold lighter, and inhaled deeply. It was a slow, well-practiced performance—a routine I had seen her go through a dozen times on the screen—during which I got my first good look at her. Her luminous beauty had faded with age and hard living although good bone structure and a strong jawline still gave her face a sculptural force. The stroke she'd had two years earlier had partially paralyzed her left side and froze half her face in a rictus of sadness. It would have been a hard blow to bear for any woman, but for an actress who had once been hailed as "the world's most beautiful animal," it was a tragedy. And yet her sensuality hadn't completely deserted her; in her composure, in her stillness, it was still there.

I tried not to stare, but she must have guessed my thoughts. "As if getting old wasn't tough enough," she said, with no sense of self-pity at all. She carried her limp left arm across her chest, holding it at the elbow. "Actors get *older*, actresses get *old*. Ain't that the truth. But life doesn't stop because you're no longer a beauty, or desirable. You just have to make adjustments. Although I'd be lying to you if I told you that losing my looks is no big deal. It hurts, goddamnit, it hurts like a sonofabitch."

She crushed out the cigarette with an irritable gesture.

"The thing is, I've survived; I dodged all the bullets that had my name on them. I have to be grateful for that. But it does remind you of your mortality when you hear them whistle by. You go on living knowing that from now on in, death is always going to be somewhere about. But I've had an interesting life; I've had a wonderful time, in parts. I'd be crazy to start squawking now."

It was six o'clock.

"Tea—or something else? I'm a something else kind of woman myself." She grinned at me.

Peter Viertel had warned me that she didn't trust men who didn't drink, and I suspected that this was more of a challenge, some kind of test, than an invitation. "Something else would be fine," I said. She handed me a bottle of wine and a corkscrew. "You do the honors, honey," she said.

"One thing you must understand about me from the get-go is that my vices and scandals are more interesting than anything anyone—including Mr. Limp Dick Brando—can make up about me. If we tell my story the way it should be told, maybe I won't have fucked up my life completely," she said, watching me open the wine.

I sensed that she was judging me as much by the measures I poured as by my reaction to what she was telling me. "Last month I was sixty-five years old. I've had a stroke—a couple of strokes, actually. I got both barrels," she said as I handed her the drink. "But before they put me to bed with a shovel, we've got to finish this book, honey. I've lived an interesting life, goddamnit. I want an interesting book, one that tells it the way it was."

"It'll be a great book," I said.

"And let's make it a fast one, because pretty damn soon there's gonna be no corn in Egypt, baby," she said. She saw the look of surprise on my face, and laughed. "We might as well be honest with each other, baby; we are going to be spending a lot of time together."

She held out her glass in a toast.

"Movie stars write their books, then they are forgotten, and then they die," she said.

"You're not going to die for a long time yet, Ava," I told her.

"If our book doesn't replenish the larder, honey, dying's going to be my only hope."

It had been my intention that first evening simply to break the ice, to discuss the areas of her life we would need to explore. Instead, we talked about a lot of things. I was not prepared for her frankness, or her wicked sense of humor. ("I saw Elizabeth [Taylor] on TV. *'Yes, I had a little tuck under my chin.'* A little tuck! Jesus Christ! She's such a wonderful actress." And, "I liked to fuck. But fucking was an education, too." And, "Who'd have thought the highlight of my day is walking the dog.")

At the end of the evening, she asked how I wanted to handle the deal. Before I could answer, she said she'd like Ed Victor to deal with the publishers ("I'm told he knows all the questions and all the answers."), and she would have her business manager, Jess Morgan in Los Angeles, talk to Ed about our split. I said fine; it was as simple as that.

"So how will we do this thing with us, honey?" she asked. "I don't like interviews."

"I prefer conversations," I said.

"I can handle conversations," she said, seriously. "I never played a woman who was smarter than me."

It was time to go. At the door, she shook my hand in a very English manner. Then she kissed me on the mouth—"the only real way to seal a deal," she said. "Now that the meter's running, let's not waste any more time."

I said I would call in the morning and fix a meeting as soon as possible.

"We're gonna have fun, but don't think it's not going to be a bumpy ride, honey," she said with a smile.

It was a smile I would get to know very well, for it conveyed a warning as well as warmth.

3

At five o'clock the following morning Ava phoned and said she wanted to start work on the book that afternoon. "I can't sleep," she said, when I mentioned the time. She suggested that we meet at four o'clock at her apartment. "It's not my best hour, Jesus knows. I'm a night owl. Let's make it five, okay? I don't want to waste any more time, honey. We've frittered away too much of it already. Now time is of the essence, as they say." She laughed wickedly at the trite phrase. "When you get to be my age, baby, you have to pay time more respect."

Her enthusiasm was reassuring, and I said that five was fine with me. It would give me another hour to work on my novel, *Theodora,* only Ava still didn't know about that yet. It was part of her attractiveness that she showed no interest in my life beyond our working relationship.

"How do you want to start the book, by the way?" she asked.

To be honest, I hadn't given it a lot of thought. I'd imagined that we'd begin with her childhood in North Carolina. That's what I suggested.

"Jesus, honey, that's so boring. *It's* so goddamn . . . *boring*, baby, don't you think? We can come up with something a little better than that, can't we?"

"Where would you start, Ava?" I was curious.

"I think we should begin with the story of my stroke—how I had to learn to control my bladder again; that was fun, having to train myself not to wet my goddamn pants every time I sneezed, or got excited?"

It was a funny idea and she made it sound outrageous, but I wasn't convinced that it was the best way to begin her book, although her ebullience gave me a warm feeling toward her, a reminder of the moxie she had needed to get her through a stroke, which left her half paralyzed, temporarily speechless, and with a form of glaucoma that threatened permanent blindness at any minute.

"You don't think people might find it a little too downbeat to open with that?" I said.

"Come on, they'll love it. The irony of a screen love goddess peeing her pants, and having to learn to walk again. We start the book with my *second* childhood?" she said, and laughed again. "That's funny, isn't it? That would work."

There was an edge of obstinacy in her voice, as if she had already made up her mind that this was how the book would begin. I'd planned to use her stroke as a set piece—but not in the opening chapter, and certainly not in the way she suggested. "You really think that's a good idea, Ava?" I asked cautiously. Both Dirk Bogarde and Peter Viertel had said that she could take offense for the most abstruse reasons, even when she was sober, and I knew I might be on tricky ground.

"You don't think so, honey?" She sounded surprised, but still perfectly friendly. "We start the book with me back in diapers, a sixty-something old broad back in diapers?" Her voice had a cajoling quality. But the idea conjured up a troubling image. I still couldn't think of a more inappropriate way to begin her story. Perhaps she was testing me, perhaps I hadn't got the joke—it was, after all, five o'clock in the morning, and I was still half asleep.

"I don't want a book that's downbeat; I don't want a 'pity me' book, honey. Jesus, I hate those kind of books."

I agreed that that would be a mistake.

"Let's at least start off with a few laughs," she said.

The stubbornness in her voice had hardened. I knew that she wasn't joking.

"It had its funny side," she said. "I fell down in Hyde Park with a friend who'd had a hip operation and neither of us could get up again. People must have thought we were a couple of drunks rolling around and walked on by. Tell me that's not funny? Thank God, nobody recognized me. Or maybe they did and thought, There she goes again!"

Of course it was funny. It would make a wonderfully funny piece; it would win the reader's sympathy, and her fans would identify emotionally with her dilemma. But it was a question of balance. The stroke had been the most desperate and demoralizing episode of her life, and the idea that we treat it in such a trivial, lighthearted way in the first chapter was not only perverse and illogical, it was plain stupid. She didn't seem to understand—or even want to acknowledge—the seriousness of the stroke she had suffered, or the courage she had displayed in her fight to overcome it.

Even if I wrote the episode as black farce rather than in the lunatic Lucille Ball fashion she suggested, it would still diminish her mystique, it would destroy her legend; all the things that she was admired for, the qualities that had sustained her box office appeal for so long, would be jeopardized. It would deprive her book of its heart.

I knew there would be arguments—she had been a movie star for forty years; getting her own way was in her DNA—and times when I'd simply have to roll with the punches. I decided to say as little as possible and hope that eventually she would see reason and change her mind. The one thing I didn't want to do was trade shots with her at five o'clock in the morning when I was still half asleep.

"You don't like that opening?" she pressed me impatiently.

"It's a funny idea, Ava. I think it could be quite poignant, too. But I wonder if it's the best way to begin your story?"

"You really don't like it, do you?"

"No, I really don't. But maybe I'm missing something," I said, in spite of my determination not to get into an argument with her so early in the morning. "Maybe you could persuade me to change my mind, but I rather doubt it."

"Then how should we begin it? You're the writer."

I tried to think of what I could say that might divert her, and undo the damage I had obviously done with my last remark. Had she read J. D. Salinger's *The Catcher in the Rye*? I quoted Holden Caulfield's opening line: "If you really want to hear about it, the first thing you'll probably want to know is where I was born, and what my lousy childhood was like . . ."

"I didn't have a lousy childhood. I had a happy childhood—well, it definitely wasn't lousy anyway," she said. "I don't think childhood is an interesting place to start anything, honey. Where I was born, what my childhood was like! Jesus! It has no *come-on*. I made over a hundred movies in my time, one thing I learned was that the opening scene has to have sucker bait, honey. I learned from the best . . . John Huston, Tennessee Williams, Papa Hemingway, John Ford, Joe Mankiewicz, the sonofabitch. I worked with them all. They knew how to tell a story. You want to second-guess Hemingway, Tennessee Williams? You know how to tell a story better than those guys? I'm sorry, I don't think so."

I had obviously been put in my place but let it pass. I remembered Dirk Bogarde's warning that "she can go from solicitous to savage in three seconds flat." I must always ignore her when she's in that kind of mood, he said.

"You have to show the bait, honey," she repeated. Why didn't I want to start with the story of her stroke? Didn't I think that was interesting? "I almost died fahcrissakes! That's interesting to *me*, goddamnit. It was one of the most frightening things that ever happened to me in my entire life," she said. "I almost *bought it*, honey! I almost died."

She was not being rational. I knew that she couldn't defend that argument and continue to justify the case for beginning the book in the bright-eyed and bushy-tailed way she proposed. But I knew that it would be futile to attempt to point that out to her in her present mood. I was wide awake now and had the sense to bide my time, and try to change her mind later.

"Ava, I'm not saying it isn't interesting. I'm certainly not saying it wasn't frightening. Of course it was. It must have been terrifying. I just don't think it's the best place to start, and it would deprive us of a really compelling ending," I said in an attempt to preserve at least the appearance of reasonableness. "But it's your book."

"You're damn right, honey, it is *my* book, and that fucking stroke ruined my looks and put paid to my career, that's why I'm having to write the fucking thing in the first place. I can't believe you said it isn't interesting."

"That's not what I said, Ava," I said, hoping we could finish the conversation, and I could catch up on a little more sleep before it was time to get up.

I heard her light a cigarette. "You know what? I think you just want to call all the plays, honey. And I won't have it."

She sounded so petulant, it was almost childish, and I wanted to laugh, only I still didn't know her well enough to risk offending her any more than I already had. I suggested that we talk about it at a less ungodly hour.

"Five A.M. is not an ungodly hour, baby. I call it studio time, although it's been a while since I got up at that hour to make a movie," she said in a more agreeable tone. "We'll finish this conversation later. I'll see you at four."

"Five," I reminded her, but she'd already hung up.

I ARRIVED AT FOUR, to be on the safe side. Ava, in bare feet and blue jeans, wearing a man's black V-neck sweater over a white linen shirt, was waiting for me in the drawing room. She wore no makeup, or very little I could see, and that must have taken a lot of confidence two years after suffering a stroke that had frozen half her face. She lit a cigarette and inhaled deeply. She was standing in front of the Adam fireplace on which stood a near-empty glass of wine. I thought she was still angry with me. Nor was I sure that she would go ahead with the interview, or even the book, after our conversation that morning.

Weeks had passed since she asked me to ghost her memoirs. We'd had dozens of telephone conversations, and three or four "script meetings" as she called them, but we still hadn't gotten down to a serious interview. We would discuss ideas and the subjects we needed to cover but her manner would change abruptly the moment I suggested that we switch on the tape. She became cautious; the spontaneity went out of her voice. She would even attempt to clean up her language, and I missed the profanities that enlivened our private conversations. It was like Bogart without the lisp.

I knew that she was only doing the book for the money; the fact that her heart wasn't in it didn't really surprise me. But I still hoped that if I could persuade her to let me tell her story in the same uninhibited way she talked to me privately, her book would have an edge and a humor that no other movie star's biography had. No other actress's memoirs anyway. Little by little I was beginning to understand her, and I'd be disappointed if she pulled the plug on the book now.

"Have you thought any more about where you'd like to begin, Ava?" I was determined to be positive.

She poured a little more wine into her glass, filled another glass and handed it to me. "Not too early for you, is it?"

It was but I said no.

She said: "I've been thinking about what you said this morning. Maybe there's some truth in what you say. But maybe you're wrong, too. But what the hell—we'll start with my childhood, okay? That's what you want, isn't it? What the fuck difference does it make where we start? We can always change it if it doesn't work, right?"

I knew that she would at least want an option on the last word. "It makes sense, doesn't it—to start at the beginning?" My relief felt like a shot of adrenaline.

She said, "Maybe it's the only way people are ever going to make any sense of my fucked-up life. My God, it's probably the only way *I'm* going to make any sense of it. It's the later years that get me mussed up. Sometimes I can't even remember the movies I was *in*, but some of the ones I saw as a kid come back clear as daylight." She sipped her wine. "I'm sorry I lost my temper this morning. I shouldn't have made such a song and dance about it. But you did provoke me," she said.

I said it was obviously a misunderstanding. I was sorry, too. "It was too early in the morning. We should never discuss serious matters before breakfast." I hoped that she would take the hint, although I knew she probably wouldn't.

"This isn't going to be easy for me, honey. My memory isn't all it used to be. I will lose the combination a few times. You'll have to help me out with the dates and a lot of the names and places."

I said I'd sort out those details with research.

She had an air of wanting to get on with it, and that was encouraging. I told her that I would run two tapes, one for her to keep and play back later to remind her of what she'd said, forgotten to say, or would like to add. I would give her a copy of the transcripts as soon as I'd typed them up. Later I would write draft chapters for her comments and any corrections she wanted to make.

Did she really make over a hundred movies? I asked her. I was curious.

"I don't know, honey. Eighty, ninety, a hundred maybe. I don't have a clue. I did a lot of hokey movies when I was starting out at MGM. Good and bad, mostly bad. Maybe it's a blessing I lost track. A lot of my stuff ended up on the cutting-room floor. A lot more should have. You'll have to help me out with that stuff, honey. We might even discover some lost Ava Gardner masterpieces. That would be fun. It would be a goddamn miracle, too."

I reached for the Sony VOR microcassettes and switched them on. "Shall we start?" I said. That was usually the signal for her to find some excuse to delay the interview: a further question about the ground we intended to cover, a need to visit the bathroom . . . but before I asked my first question she was off.

4

I was born in Grabtown, North Carolina. I was named after Daddy's spinster sister, Ava Virginia. She lived with Mama and Daddy all her life. I guess she never had the marrying gene—but neither did I. You only have to look at my record to figure that one out! I gave it a shot three times, but none of them stuck. The marriages to Mickey Rooney and Artie Shaw were hit-and-run affairs, both of them were over and wrapped up in a year. The marriage to Frank Sinatra . . . well, that did a little better. Anyway, on paper it did. On and off it did. It lasted seven years on paper—if you counted all the goddamn splits and the injury time we played. And there were plenty of those, honey, believe me. I tried to be a good wife. I tried to be any kind of wife; the plain fact is, I just wasn't meant to ride off into the sunset and live happily ever after. After Frank—we married in '51, separated in '53, divorced in '57—I knew that a happy-ever-after marriage was never going to happen for me. The marriages to Mickey and Artie were easy come, easy go. I called them my 'starter husbands'! You only had to sneeze and you'd have missed both of them. My marriage to Artie Shaw might have lasted a little longer if I hadn't asked John Huston for advice. John was the last person in the world anyone should go to for advice of *any* kind—let alone advice about their marriage. Although what Huston said didn't matter a damn one way or the other. Artie was determined to get rid of me anyway. He already had my replacement lined up, fahcrissake. You know how many times John Huston was married? *Five times*. Jesus, I needed my head examined asking Huston for advice about my marriage. Although it's true I was pretty sloshed at the time, and so was he. The pair of us, sloshed to our bloody eyeballs. It was the first time he invited me to his place in the [San Fernando] Valley. They were thinking of using me in *The Killers*, which he'd written [with Tony Veiller].

"God, I was beautiful then; that was the first time I looked at myself on the screen and didn't want to hide with embarrassment. Huston clearly fancied me—although he struck out with me that night. I was a married lady, I told him—but I also knew he had his hands full with Olivia de Havilland and Evelyn Keyes at the time. He was screwing a lot of women in those days. He knew how to give a girl a good time. He had plenty of stamina, but his romances never lasted. Actually, the following weekend he went off to Las Vegas with Evelyn and married her. I'm not saying he married her because he struck out with me but that's what he did. Anyway, when he'd got tired of chasing me around the bushes, I asked him what I should do about Artie."

The marriage was not that good but it was not that bad either. She and Artie Shaw had been married for less than a year and it could have gone either way, she said. But Huston, aged forty, with all the gravitas and cunning of an older man—"he wanted to get into my pants, honey," she said with her own measure of wisdom—told her: "You know damn well that it's not going to work, kid—just get the hell out while he's still got the hots for you."

Although she knew that Huston had no feelings about it one way or the other—"John loved giving mischievous advice; causing trouble always gave him a kick in the pants," she said—"I picked up my shoes and shuffled out of Artie's life. He didn't seem to have minded too much, I have to say."

It was entertaining stuff, she could always make me laugh, she could always do that, but the narrative was a mess, the continuity nonexistent. It was clear that the strokes she'd had a couple of years earlier had affected her ability to concentrate—the wine obviously didn't help—and she was all over the place, lost in the debris of her past.

Rather than try to dig her out, I just shut up and listened. The material was all grist for the mill, nothing would be wasted; her tone, her cynicism and ribald vocabulary, would be invaluable when I attempted to reproduce her voice on the page. But, first, if she was going to deliver the goods, she had to come clean about herself; she had to stop sidestepping the interesting truths, and ducking the painful ones. I already suspected that, in spite of her promises, she never intended to be totally frank with me about her life. ("Do you think I'm crazy? Of course I'm not going to tell the whole truth," I later learned she admitted to Michael Winner the day she told him she was going to write her autobiography. "I'm going to say things that leave the impression with people that I want left with them," she said.)

It was a deliberate betrayal of our deal but I wasn't surprised, and it didn't disturb me. She was broke, she sorely needed the money, and I was convinced that I would get to the truth when I started asking the hard questions once we got into the stuff that sold books.

What concerned me right now was that she still expected the book to be wrapped up in a couple of months. *"Pretty damn soon there's gonna be no corn in Egypt, baby,"* she had warned me, but she had no idea, and I didn't want to be the one to tell her, how long a good book—the book she deserved, paying the kind of money she needed, the book I knew it could be—was going to take to write. I'd leave it to Ed Victor to break that news to her when he'd worked out a deal with the publishers. He was good at that sort of thing.

Ava shook a cigarette out of the pack and sighed as she began to search for her lighter among the cushions on the sofa. There was a small silence. Now that I was beginning to know her better, I knew that this wasn't an invitation to interrupt.

"Okay, concentrate, Ava. *Concentrate*," she said to herself sternly.

She turned to me: "You've got to help me, baby. I'm struggling here. Tell me exactly what you want to know."

"I'd like to know more about your childhood," I said. "Can we go back to that?"

"Jesus, that Holden Caulfield crap again, Peter," she said. "You don't give up, do you?"

"People are fascinated with the childhoods of famous people," I told her.

"You really think so?" She didn't seem convinced. "Why don't we start with my first husband, Mickey Rooney?" she said. "Why don't we start there? I was still practically a child anyway."

"You were nineteen," I said.

"Only just," she said defensively. "I was still a virgin. That would be a good place to start, when I was still chaste?"

"Fine. Let's start there," I said. I made no attempt to argue with her. I just wanted to get on with it. There would be plenty of time for arguments when we stopped being polite to each other, which would happen when I started asking about the intimate stuff that publishers would want to know when a sizable advance was being asked.

"Well, I laughed a lot with Mickey Rooney," she said slowly, as if searching for a tone of complete candor. "I laughed with Artie Shaw, too—but not so much, and sometimes when I shouldn't have, I guess. It needled him when he couldn't figure out why he made me laugh. He was smart as a whip, about politics, about communism, about jazz, about all sorts of things, but he wasn't smart about women at all—although he's had other wives since then, including John Huston's old ex, Evelyn Keyes, so maybe he's learned a thing or two about ladies since my day in the hay with him."

I was amused at how quickly she had lost the Mickey Rooney thread. "But I have to say, what education I got, I got from Artie—the schoolroom kind of education that is," she said. "He was always trying to improve me and I always wanted to learn stuff. He definitely got me into reading books, which I'm grateful for."

Did she still read a lot? I asked.

"Not so much since my stroke," she said. "I haven't done a lot of things since the stroke."

It was a stupid question.

"Where were we?" she said.

"Mickey Rooney?" I told her.

"Mickey. Well, I got another kind of education with Mickey. Going to the fights every Friday night in L.A., that was an education. We'd go along with George Raft and Betty Grable. Betty loved the fights as much as Mickey did, but I dreaded those Friday nights. Mickey always insisted on sitting ringside; he could never get close enough. I used to cover us with newspapers, to keep us from being smothered in blood. Those little bantamweights were the worst; they'd cut each other to pieces—they'd nearly kill each other to entertain us. That fact bothered me more than any of the rest of it—the things people would do to please you if you were famous enough, and there was nobody more famous than George Raft, Betty G, and Mickey in those days. They were legends.

"'You're walking in the shadow of giants,' Mickey used to tell me. He was an egotistical sonofabitch, but he was right about how famous they all were. Not me so much, Jesus, not me at all, I was just starting out—I was just famous for being the first Mrs. Mickey Rooney—'Arm candy' they'd call me today. You have to remember Mickey was bigger than Gable in those days. At least, his pictures took in more money than Gable's, although they each earned the same five grand a week when five thousand dollars was real money," she said. "Movie stars were gods and goddesses in those days."

She stopped looking for her lighter and slipped the cigarette back into the pack. "Filthy habit anyway," she said, shaking her head. "I can go on all day long about the mistakes I've made in my life. I'm a real expert on the saddles I've put on the wrong gee-gees. That the kind of stuff you want, honey?"

"All I have to do is listen," I said.

"Good. I hate smart-ass questions," she said.

I was still keen to get her to tell her story in some kind of chronological order, if only to make it easier for me when I came to put the jigsaw together. I again suggested that when we completed the Mickey Rooney section, I'd like to go back to her childhood.

"Why?" she said, with fresh irritation in her voice.

"Among other things, you said it would help you to make sense of your life," I said.

"To make sense of my *fucked-up life*," she recalled her exact words with glee.

"Well, to begin with, I was a way afterthought," she said slowly. "Mama, you know, poor baby, she'd had her family all finished: four daughters and a couple of sons, and suddenly I arrived in her midlife on Christmas Eve 1922. Mama and Daddy must have thought they were all through with babies! What a Christmas present I must have been! That little bundle of joy must have fucked up everything. I've been fucking up other people's lives ever since. Mama and Daddy needed me like a hole in the head."

"Money was tight?" I said.

"You could say that. Daddy was a sharecropper, a tenant farmer.

There aren't many more precarious ways of making a living than that, honey. There was *never* enough money. Daddy's ass was always in some kind of sling or another. It was a struggle for them but they got by and I always felt loved. There was always milk on our doorstep. If you're going to be poor, be poor on a farm, that's what I say. I remember when I started out in movies, in the forties, one of the Hollywood papers said we had been dirt poor. It was a story some MGM press agent must have put out to make my life sound more interesting than it was. That pissed me. *Dirt poor!* It made it sound as if we were white trash. I didn't even mind being called a *hillbilly* but *dirt poor* crossed a line. There were plenty of hard times, no question. We were often broke, but never in our lives were we *dirt poor.* I resented it when reporters put it in their stories. It made me mad."

It was the first time since I'd known Ava that we'd talked about her family to any degree, and I was surprised at how strongly she cared about her past.

"I want to get this right in the book," she said deliberately.

I said I did, too.

"I might have worn hand-me-down frocks, and had dirty knees, maybe I didn't always scrub them as often as polite little girls should—but we were never *dirt poor.* I was the goddamnedest tomboy you ever met. In the summertime, I went barefoot, that was what farm kids did. Of course, we were poor. It was the Great Depression, *everybody* was poor. It cost you just to breathe. But being hard-up didn't make us *dirt poor,* fahcrissake."

I could see that the subject was upsetting her. "Tell me about your dad, Ava," I said, moving off the subject just enough. "Were you close to him?"

She said, "I was probably closer to Daddy. Little girls usually are. I have his green eyes and the same cleft in my chin. I also inherited his shyness, particularly when I'm sober. When I was married to Artie

Shaw, Artie complained that I was drinking too much, and made me go to a shrink. He was right, of course. I *was* drinking too much, but I didn't need a shrink to tell me why—Artie was the reason why! After six months of seeing me every day the shrink said I had an Oedipal complex. Artie had to tell me what the hell an Oedipal complex was! So, yeah, I guess I was Daddy's girl more than Mama's."

She had always spoken of her father with great affection, and I knew that he was some kind of icon for her. I was still trying to figure out how to phrase my next question diplomatically when she said: "Did I get my weakness for booze from Daddy? Is that what you want to know?"

The thought had occurred to me, I said.

"Daddy's drinking is hard for me to picture. I don't think I ever saw him drunk, which would have registered, I imagine. Bappie [her sister Beatrice] says he drank quite a bit though; she says he sometimes went off on benders. If he did, he kept it from me. He did disappear from time to time, I remember that. Once he was gone for weeks and I got upset; Mama said that he was looking for work in New York. I just don't know, honey. I'm a drinker and my grandpa enjoyed a glass or two so they say, and drink is supposed to run in families."

Did she know her paternal grandfather? I asked.

She shook her head. "His name was James Bailey Gardner. A good old Irish name. He was an ornery sonofabitch by all accounts, but hardly up there with the Kennedys' old man, old Joe Kennedy. Grandpa Gardner died before I came along. I didn't know any of Daddy's side, except for Aunt Ava, but I must have inherited some of their Irish temper. Frank reckons I did. He was probably right."

I asked about her mother's family.

"Mama's daddy was David Baker, David *Forbes* Baker."

Did the middle name suggest a touch of class somewhere down the Baker line?

"I doubt it, honey. Grandpa Baker was a Scot—a hardworking cotton hoer," she said. "He never amounted to much more than that."

Her maternal grandmother, Elizabeth, died when Ava's mother was a young girl. "Mama took over the running of the house for Grandpa while he went marching on, doing what he did," Ava said. "The old boy ended up with eighteen or nineteen kids between Grandma and his second wife. He was a randy old boy. He obviously enjoyed peddling his wares."

"You never met any of your grandparents?"

"They had all passed before I was born," she said. "Mama talked about her family, but Daddy never did. But he was never much of a talkin' man. I do know that Grandma Gardner and my Aunt Ava, the one I was named for, lived with Mama and Daddy when they moved from Wilson County to Johnston County, where I was born."

She became thoughtful.

"Grandpa Gardner was a drinker, which is probably why he and Grandma Gardner were not together," she said. "That was not the usual scene in the South. In those days people didn't get divorced, they didn't split. No matter how bad things were between you, you just stuck it out, lived out your miserable existence together until the day one of you kicked the bucket."

The pause was a little longer this time. There seemed to be sadness in there somewhere.

"But Grandma and Grandpa Gardner split," she said eventually. "That tells us something, huh?"

"What does it tell us, Ava?" I was deliberately obtuse. I didn't want to have to guess, I wanted Ava to tell me what *she* made of it. It was her story I was going to tell.

"It tells me that Grandpa was a lush," she said.

"Would you like to deal with that in the book?"

She shrugged. "If you think it's interesting."

"I think it would interest readers," I said. I also thought it might throw a light on Ava's drinking problems, although I decided not to mention that just yet.

"Here's something else that might be interesting for the book," she said. "My sister Elsie Mae told me that as a small child she remembered going with Daddy to Wilson County to visit an old man. She said she remembered the building because it was so gloomy and unfriendly. She said it wasn't a prison, but she remembered going through passageways of locked doors, and she heard screams, and people crying.

"The story used to scare the pants off me. Elsie Mae said she used to visit an old man there, an old man with white hair. I don't know how old I was when Elsie Mae first told me that story, maybe seven or eight, but I remember thinking to myself, Yeah, Wilson County, the old guy must have been Grandpa Gardner. The more I think about it now, the more it makes sense to me. The old guy had been committed."

"Your grandpa was insane?"

"It was a bat house, honey."

She saw my puzzled look.

"That's what we called insane asylums as kids." She made a dismissive motion with her hand. "I'm sure plenty of serious drinkers in those days were put away as crazies. Some of them might have lost their marbles, but plenty were probably suffering from depression, or just couldn't cope. People didn't understand depression back then. If they didn't know so much about it today, a lot of people around here would be locked away. Me included. Grandpa Gardner had black Irish moods. He'd split from my grandmother, and his family—that was enough to depress anyone."

"And you think that he was the old man Elsie Mae used to visit in that place in Wilson County?"

"It figures, wouldn't you say? Madness is the last stage of human degradation. Who said that?" she asked.

I said I didn't know.

"Neither do I," she said. "But I think that madness runs in my family, honey. Booze and depression definitely do. That's close enough."

Madness in the family! It was the kind of story that can send a celebrity memoir flying off the shelves. But I didn't attempt to pursue it right then. She had a habit of retracting some of the most intimate things she told me if she thought I showed too much interest. I would have to think about how I would handle this one. I said casually: "You said your grandfather was a drinker, but you didn't think your father was."

"No, I said it was hard for me to picture."

"But he might have been?"

"Bappie reckons he was. I know he had deep depressions, and got terrible headaches. 'Sick headaches,' he called them. Whether they were suicidal hangovers or genuine depressions, I was too young to know, and he was too proud to talk about anything personal.

"According to Bappie, he started getting the headaches really bad when he was around forty-five, a year or so after I was born, which is interesting because my depressions started at the same age. I was lying in bed at my sister's house in California, recovering from my hysterectomy, which does jumble up a woman's mind, and I saw the assassination of Robert Kennedy on television. That night I had a terrible sort of vertigo, and by morning I was in a black depression. The deepest, blackest cloud descended on me; it completely engulfed me. The gynecologist didn't know what the hell was wrong. I was finally hospitalized."

She was put on a drug called Elavil, called Tryptizol in England.

"I've been on the same drug for over twenty years. It brings temporary comfort but no cure." She looked at me solemnly. "My life's a fucking train wreck," she said. She found her lighter among the cushions, shook a cigarette from the pack. "Who the hell is going to be interested in this stuff anyway?"

It was a familiar question when she was getting tired. I asked whether she'd like to call it a night.

"When I was making *The Sun Also Rises*, Hemingway asked me my Daddy's name," she said, ignoring my offer. She lit the cigarette, and exhaled smoke through her nose. "I told him Jonas Gardner. Hemingway said he sounded like a character in a John Steinbeck novel. I loved that. What was the name of that Steinbeck book, the movie James Dean was in?"

East of Eden, I said.

"There was something about Daddy that I never understood as a child, but I think it was the same sense of loneliness Jimmy Dean had in that movie. It makes me sad when I think of how hard Daddy's life must have been, the disappointments he'd suffered. He always called me Daughter. It was to distinguish me from his sister Ava. I loved being called Daughter. It sounded so possessive, and to be possessed when you are a child is just a wonderful feeling. It makes you feel safe. It makes you feel loved. But later if anyone tried to possess me—oh boy, I was outta there. That was something Frank never understood. He just couldn't deal with it, and I couldn't explain it to him. Probably because I couldn't understand it myself," she said.

"But it was a happy childhood?" I said.

"I was spoiled. I was the baby of the family. Mama and Daddy kept the tougher side of being tenant farmers from me. But it was plain to me early on that sharecropping was never going to be any way to make a fortune. Daddy built the wood-frame house I was born in with his own hands; he cut and hauled the timber, dug the well, built the outhouse."

"Were you aware of how hard your life was when you were growing up?"

"No running water, no electricity, the privy at the bottom of the backyard—yeah, I probably had a suspicion of how horse-and-buggy life was for us." Her smile took the edge off the sarcasm.

"But you don't care about those things when you are a small child and your Daddy's the best lemonade maker in the whole world. And Daddy had plans. He always had plans. He built a tobacco barn, and he opened a little country store across the way—Grabtown was just a crossroad in the middle of *nowhere*, really; God knows where the customers came from, there can't have been too many of them; I hope to God they were loyal—but the buildings caught fire and burned to the ground one night and that was the end of that little enterprise. Rumor had it that my brother Melvin Jonas, everybody called him Jack, started the blaze when he slipped into the barn to roll a ciggy and dropped the match.

"I remember that night—I must have been about three—somebody holding me at the window to see the flames from Mama and Daddy's bedroom, where my sister Myra and I also slept together; Daddy wept that night."

"You remember your father weeping? You were only three."

She said, "I remember the flames. I remember Daddy crying. You don't forget things like that. They stay in your mind, honey. Maybe I didn't understand the *significance* of his tears that night until I was older—the fact that he had *nothing* socked away. No insurance. We were broke, really and truly broke, not just poor, out on the sidewalk broke, honey."

Jonas Gardner was used to tragedy in his life. His first son, Raymond, was killed when he was two years old, twelve years before

Ava was born. Jonas had been using dynamite to clear a parcel of land of rocks and tree roots; the explosive caps he used to ignite the sticks of dynamite were kept in a kitchen cabinet. One dropped onto the floor one morning when Jonas was handing them out to the blasters; unnoticed, it was swept up and thrown into the fire with the rubbish. The explosion caught baby Raymond full in the face. He died on the way to the doctor in Smithfield.

Ava lifted the hand of her paralyzed arm onto her lap. "Anyway, somebody up there must have taken pity on us. After the barn burnt down—God bless the kindness of strangers, honey—Mama was offered a job, and a place for us to live, running the Teacherage, the boardinghouse for women teachers at the school down the road in Brogden. Whoever had the idea of getting Ma to run that place was wise as a hoot owl. It definitely saved our skins."

Mama's full name was Mary Elizabeth but everybody called her Molly. "She was always up and doing, she never stopped: she took to that job like a duck to a water pond—she washed sheets, cleaned toilets, scrubbed the floors, and cooked three meals a day for about twenty boarders. We took in field workers as well as the teachers. She was always ironing; the guests paid extra for that, and eventually I got to help. I picked up some pocket money ironing the shirts; I'm still one hell of an ironer. Frank used to say I pressed his collars better than any laundry service. I damn well did, too."

I asked about her sisters.

"Mama was thirty-nine when she had me—that was seven years after Myra was born. Growing up, I was closest of all to Myra. All the others, Bappie—she was pregnant the same time Mama was pregnant with me, only she jumped out of a peach tree and lost the baby—Elsie Mae and Inez were all married and away by this time. I remember Daddy holding me and waving goodbye to Inez and her husband, Johnny, as they drove away in a Model T Ford after their wedding."

She stopped and gave me a look. "Is this really interesting, honey?" she asked me again. "I'm skipping. I don't know what the fuck I'm talking about. Is this really the sort of stuff people want to read about?" she asked again.

I told her that it was *exactly* what they wanted to read about. There was nothing wrong with her memory, I told her.

"I've been thinking about it a lot, honey."

"How old were you when you started school, can you remember that?"

"I was three—not to study, to visit. I would just sit there until I fell asleep, and a teacher would take me back to the Teacherage, and put me to bed. The teachers always made a fuss of me. I was a pretty little thing; I had platinum blond curls. I started school proper when I was five, which was a year before most kids in Brogden, probably because I was a familiar figure around the place. But I was never a great learner. When I was eight, there were other distractions—I started to hang out with boys. It wasn't a sexual thing; at least I don't think it was. I was a regular tomboy. I could climb any tree a boy could climb, and higher, too—I've still got the scars to prove it. I could run as fast as any of them, and cuss even better. The one thing I didn't catch on to was smoking. It made me sick as a dog. I didn't start smoking until I was eighteen, when I got to Hollywood. I saw Lana Turner sitting on the set holding a beautiful gold cigarette case and lighter. She looked so glamorous. I went straight out and bought myself an identical cigarette case and lighter, just to carry around."

She shook another cigarette from the packet.

"From there to sixty a day!" she said ruefully.

She played with the cigarette between her fingers but didn't attempt to light it this time. "We had two Negro maids living with us at the Teacherage," she continued after a while. "One was my best friend, Virginia. I slept with her more than I slept with Mama and Daddy, or my sister Myra; blacks were like family in our house. Sometimes when Mama went in to Smithfield to do the big grocery shop on a Saturday, Virginia and I would go to the movies. She wasn't allowed to sit downstairs, that was whites only, so I was the only little white thing, a white blond child, up in the balcony with the blacks. I remember seeing one movie with Bing Crosby and Marion Davies. You'll have to check what it was called and what year that was. [*Going Hollywood*, 1933.] I must have been ten or eleven years old. Virginia and I came home and acted out the whole thing; one time I'd be Davies and she would be Crosby, then we'd switch around.

"I loved the movies, but I never had any interest in being an actress. One time, I tried out for a play in high school. I was the first kid to be eliminated. *Out! Don't call us! We'll call you!* Fuck, I was bad. I was so bad, honey. But that was after the Teacherage closed in the Depression. Mama had found a job running a boardinghouse in Newport News, Virginia. It was a big navy base and shipbuilding town in the North."

She began massaging her arm, a sign that she was getting tired. "Honey, I don't want to talk about me anymore. Not tonight. I'm exhausted." She finished her wine and put the glass down. After a small pause, she tapped the empty glass with her forefinger. "Okay, just one more," she said, and began to laugh. "Just one more—Jesus, how many times have I said that in my life?"

"I'm not surprised you're tired. You've been up since dawn," I reminded her, and poured the last of the wine, which wasn't very much, into her glass.

"Did I wake you this morning? Oh Christ, I woke you, didn't I? I'm sorry about that, honey," she said, and laughed again.

"You should laugh more often," I said.

"When I was young I laughed a lot—that's because I liked to laugh in bed," she said.

"We got through a lot of good stuff today," I told her.

"Thank you," she said.

"You did all the heavy lifting," I said. "My turn comes when I've typed up what we've done today, and I can start work on the manuscript."

"Did any of it make sense, honey?"

"It will have to be expanded in places," I said truthfully. "But basically I'm thrilled. You covered a lot of ground."

"I can remember all those things a hundred years ago, yet I can't remember what I did yesterday. When I called you this morning, I was going to call the whole thing off," she said. "I had one foot out the door."

"I'm pleased you changed your mind," I said.

She asked me what plans I had for the next day. If I were free, we could have another session, she said. "I'll be ready to talk about me, if you're willing to listen," she said.

Absolutely, I said.

"I like working with you, honey. I like having somebody to dance with," she said.

5

Ava canceled our appointment the following day, and was incommunicado for several days after that. I caught up on my reading, including a slim, skin-deep biography of her written in the early 1960s by a film unit publicist. I transcribed several of the interviews I had taped; I wrote up the notes of our telephone conversations, including her nocturnal calls, which were often the most interesting and were becoming more frequent. She seemed to have forgotten the argument we'd had the night I told her I wouldn't help her to die. At least she hadn't mentioned it again, and neither had I.

It was over a week before I finally reached her on the phone, and my euphoria, following the promise of the last interview, had turned to a sense of unease again.

"I'm sorry I haven't returned your calls, honey. I promise you, you've been in my thoughts," she said, as soon as she heard my voice.

"I hope the book's been in your thoughts, too," I said, and regretted it immediately. A Sinatra record was playing in the background, one of his slow numbers, a sure sign that she was feeling low.

"I had a real bad week, honey. I felt just godawful. I wouldn't have been any good to you."

"What was it? Flu?" There had been a lot of it about.

"I don't know, honey. I had blinding headaches, like the worst goddamn hangovers *ever.* And not just in the mornings either—*before you ask.* How is Ed Victor making out? What's happening there? Any sign of a deal yet?" She ran the sentences together, in the same tone, closing off one subject and starting a new one before I could ask another question about her headaches.

It was the first time Ava had asked what was happening with the publishers. She had shown no interest in the business arrangements since her acceptance that Ed would handle the book for both of us. I told her truthfully that I didn't know what the current situation was, although I understood the proposal was attracting a lot of interest in New York. I also knew that Ed was talking to a couple of the major publishing houses in New York, but I didn't want to tell her that; he liked to announce those developments to a client himself. "Are you ready for some good news?" was his favorite opening line when he had a deal lined up. I didn't want to spoil his surprise.

"Ed's such a good agent," I told her. It was no more than a casual remark, an en passant comment, but she picked up on it.

"You think so? *Really?* Better than . . ." She hesitated as if thinking of a suitable agent with whom she could compare him. ". . . Swifty Lazar, for instance?"

In his day, Irving Paul Lazar—Humphrey Bogart dubbed him "Swifty," a name Lazar detested, after he arranged three deals for Bogie in a single day, on a bet—was considered one of the best agents around. He had made deals for Noel Coward, Cole Porter, Clifford Odets, Truman Capote, Neil Simon, Lillian Hellman, and dozens of other big-name celebrities of the past. He sold ideas and people as well as books and plays. He put together a lucrative television deal for Richard Nixon with David Frost when Nixon was still in the wilderness after Watergate. He would move in on any deal that took his fancy—"with or without the author's permission."

("Everybody who matters has two agents: his own and Irving Lazar," a Hollywood wit once said.) But, according to Michael Korda, Simon & Schuster's editor-in-chief, who knew him well and dealt with him many times as a publisher, Lazar never claimed to be an agent at all. "He described himself as a deal maker and thus did not feel bound by the normal rules of agenting. Sometimes, he took his 10 percent from the buyer, sometimes from the seller—sometimes it was rumored, in the old days, from both," said Korda in amused awe at Lazar's legendary chutzpah.

By this time, however, Lazar was over eighty years old and clearly past his outrageous prime. I didn't want to say that to Ava. They were old friends—he had known her since before her marriage to Sinatra—but surely it must have been as obvious to her as it was to me.

"Swifty Lazar! That's a name from the past," I said.

"He's still in the game, honey, believe me," she said. She told me about the fabulous deals he had done, his amazing energy, the money he had made for his authors! "He knows about our book, by the way," she said, eventually coming to the point. "He loves the idea of it. He thinks it'll make a fabulous movie. He's *very* interested."

"I bet he is," I said as noncommittally as I could. "How does he know about the book, Ava? Have you talked to him?"

"He called me last night from New York. He said Peter Viertel told him about it. He knows you, by the way. Has he called you yet? He said he was going to. He said he had lunch with you at Claridge's."

"It was a long time ago. I'm surprised he remembers."

"He remembers everything. He doesn't forget a thing. So what do you think, honey? He says he got $350,000 for Betty Bacall's book and that was ten years ago [*Lauren Bacall: By Myself*, published in 1979]. We should talk to him, don't you think?" The question was wary, testing; she obviously sensed my unease. "At least let's find out what he has in mind. It can't do any harm, can it? He's still full of piss and vinegar."

Whether Ava wanted Lazar, or thought she needed him, or whether her suggestion was to test my loyalty to Ed Victor—or perhaps Lazar's intrusion had raised questions in her mind about Ed—I had no idea. Maybe I was becoming paranoid, but Ava's suggestion that I call Lazar seemed to me to be dangerous. Apart from the fact that his intervention in a deal was always likely to cause complications—later to be told as hilarious anecdotes by Lazar himself—apart from that, Ed was my friend as well as my agent, and I wouldn't go ahead with the book without him.

But was Ed a better agent than Lazar? That was what Ava had asked. Both were *über*-agents—one past, one present, one chalk, one cheese, one a straight arrow, the other Swifty Lazar. In their own way, both were giants. Ava knew all this perfectly well. She was too smart not to have checked out Ed before she agreed for him to represent her in the first place. So what more could I say about him that she didn't already know?

Finally, I said, "Ava, there are *three* things you must remember about Ed Victor. One, he's a big fan of yours; two, he loves to make money for his clients; and three, he's determined that your book is going to make you very rich, indeed."

"Has he put a figure on that, honey?" she asked quietly. "I'd like him to get a little more than Swifty got Betty Bacall for her book. Can Ed do that for me?"

I'd heard a figure of half a million dollars mentioned, and if she delivered the goods, especially about her time with Sinatra, I'd also heard that it could go as high as $800,000, even more. But I didn't want to tell her that. Instead, I said: "A *fourth* thing you must remember about Ed Victor is that he likes to see the look of surprise in an author's eyes when he tells them what the offer is. I think you're going to be *very* surprised, Ava."

There was a long silence on the line before she said in a low voice: "I like surprises, honey."

Her suggestion that I contact Irving Lazar was forgotten. At least, she never brought up Swifty's name again, and naturally neither did I.

A WEEK LATER, AVA asked me to go for a walk with her in Hyde Park Gardens. I picked her up at her flat in Ennismore Gardens and we walked through the quiet afternoon streets of Kensington. She leaned into me as she held on to my arm; her weight made me aware of her limp. She wore a gray woolen coat and hat; a Burberry checked cashmere scarf was pulled high across her mouth as if she was determined not to be recognized. Although, in black horn-rimmed glasses, and her eyes devoid of makeup, she looked more like a smart Knightsbridge matron than the Hollywood icon she was. We crossed the busy Kensington Road into the quiet of Hyde Park Gardens.

"Before the goddamn stroke, I often used to run around this park before breakfast, the whole nine yards," she said. "It was the best cure for a hangover there was. I used to run a lot in those days," she added with a sly smile.

"I'm impressed," I said.

"You should be. It's no spitting distance. I once bet Grace Kelly that the park was bigger than her spread in Monaco. I had no idea whether it was or wasn't but I bet her twenty dollars it was. She got one of her palace flunkies to check it out—and I was right! The park's bigger than the whole of her old man's principality."

"Did she pay up?"

"Grace was tight with a buck but she always paid up. She sent over the twenty dollars—with a magnum of Dom Perignon from Harrods, and a note pinned to an almighty pack of aspirins saying they were for the hangover I was going to get! She knew me too damn well. I do miss her. There aren't many people I miss, but I do miss Gracie Grimaldi."

"Who else do you miss, Ava?"

"I miss John Huston—especially now the sonofabitch is across the river. He knew me better than anyone alive, better than I knew myself. The world is an emptier place not having him at the end of the line."

"You said he made a serious pass at you once," I said.

"More than once, honey," she said, with a nostalgic smile.

"Do you want to talk about that?" I said.

"It might make me cry," she said. "God, I miss him."

"Well, you knew him a long time," I said.

"Since 1946," she said, "just after the war. John had written *The Killers,* which was based on Hemingway's short story. They would call it my 'breakthrough movie' these days. John had written the screenplay with Tony Veiller, although John's name wasn't on the credits. He was still in the army. He'd probably been moonlighting, I guess that was the reason they didn't use his name. Anyway, I'd been invited to dinner at his house near Tarzana in the San Fernando Valley. I went with a friend of his, Jules Buck, who'd worked on *The Killers,* and Jules's wife, Joyce.

"John must have been forty then, I was twenty-four, he was already a successful screenwriter at Warner Brothers. He was tall and rangy. He had a craggy, Irish face—one of his wives said it was full of cruelty. I don't think cruelty was the right word, although he did have a cruel streak in his humor. He had women eating out of the palm of his hand. He was divorced, and on the prowl the night I went out to his place at Tarzana. I fell for him at once."

"At the dinner party?"

"Yeah, pretty much. But he made a pass at me first. I was twenty-four, I had divorced Mickey Rooney after only a year, I'd had an affair with Howard Hughes, and was in a bad marriage to

Artie Shaw—I couldn't blame him for thinking I'd be a pushover. He chased me around the bushes. I was as stewed as he was. But I didn't sleep with him."

"Do you mean that evening—or you *never* slept with him?" I said. It was probably the most direct question I had asked her about her intimate relationships.

She stopped and gave me a long quizzical look. "I was still married to Artie Shaw," she said, then smiled. "John was pissed when I wouldn't stay the night with him. We'd been fooling around. But I wasn't going to jump into bed with him on our first date, as much as I wanted to. I don't think many women said no to Johnny. He was a spoiled sonofabitch."

We continued walking slowly, her weight leaning against me. "Anyway, Artie hadn't discarded me at that stage. I was loyal to my husbands." She was good at ducking questions she didn't want to answer.

After a while, she stopped and we sat on a park bench. "Actually," she said, catching her breath, "John had invited Evelyn Keyes to dinner that evening. She'd played Scarlett O'Hara's younger sister in *Gone With the Wind.* He was dating her at the time, but the way John told the story it wasn't anything serious. But she was pretty—and smart. When she heard I was going to be at dinner, she wouldn't come. 'I'm not going to compete with Ava Gardner,' she said. 'I'm not that dumb!'

"Anyway, a few days later John ran off to Las Vegas with her and they got hitched! John said it was all her idea. He did seem a bit bemused by it, I must say. Naturally, the marriage didn't last more than five minutes. And listen to this, Miss Keyes later became Artie Shaw's eighth wife!" She laughed softly. "A small world, huh?"

She stood up, she took my arm, and we resumed our walk.

"But I made three good movies for John. They can't take those away from me," she said sadly.

"Peter Viertel says Huston was a great joker," I said.

"The best. Did I tell you the time I played Lily Langtry in *The Life and Times of Judge Roy Bean*? John had set up a complicated tracking scene for Lily's arrival in Langtry, Texas, the town named after her by Judge Bean. I looked piss-elegant, I have to say. I was about fifty then. It might have been the last time I looked truly beautiful on the big screen. Lily is met at the railroad station by a grizzled old-timer, played by Billy Pearson. Pearson was an ex-jockey, one of John's cronies. John collected characters. Billy takes Lily's hand and helps her down from the carriage and they start to walk up the high street with the camera tracking ahead of them. It must have been a four-minute take. The train had stopped where it was supposed to stop, right on cue, with the sun going down. I didn't want to fuck it up. I was hitting my marks and feeling good. We'd almost got to the end of the take, when Billy Pearson says: 'You don't know how nice it is to welcome you, Miss Langtry. How'd you like an old man to go down on you after your long journey?' That was John's idea of a joke. It broke me up. God knows what it cost the studio. It was half a day's work done for."

We continued our walk very slowly toward the Round Pond.

"Who else do I miss? Well, Frank—or rather I miss my fights with Frank. We'd better not say that. I miss a lot of things: playing tennis; Spain I miss, of course, and dancing to flamenco music late at night." She smiled sadly. "Those days are over, baby."

We walked in silence for a while.

"I'm not a quitter, honey. I just get tired, that's all," she said apropos of nothing I had said, but I suspected it was to let me know that she understood what was bothering me. "I just felt so awful last week. I couldn't have worked. I thought I was going to die."

"You wouldn't do that to me," I said. "We have a bestseller to write."

"I'm not a quitter, honey," she said again. "We'll finish the goddamn book if it kills me. I was just so low, baby. I brought Morgan [her Welsh corgi] for a walk in the park to try to clear my head. That didn't work. I had a memory lapse that was terrifying. I couldn't remember Morgan's goddamn *name*. He ran off into the shrubbery, I couldn't even remember what the hell he *looked* like, what *color* he was, nothing. My mind was a total blank."

I could understand her forgetting Morgan's name. I couldn't get my head around her failure to remember what he *looked* like, I said.

"I remembered fuck-all, honey. It was a *complete* memory loss. My mind was a complete blank," she said again.

"Did you tell your doctor what happened?"

"I didn't bother. I've been forgetting things for years. Anyway, next day I was fine. There are still some things I can't remember—names, faces, what I had for dinner last night. But for a few hours, I thought my whole memory had been wiped out."

"A memoirist without a memory would be a problem for both of us," I said.

"I know quite a few people who'd be damned pleased to hear that news, honey."

I urged her to talk to her doctor. "You should have a brain scan, at least get a checkup," I said.

"Dirk Bogarde said it was hysterical amnesia. He reckoned the same thing happened to him in France last year. He said it was nothing to worry about. He said it was a temporary condition."

"For God's sake, Dirk's not a doctor, Ava."

"Yeah, what the fuck does he know?" She grinned.

"Ava, I'm serious. You should get a checkup."

She squeezed my arm reassuringly. "When he fell down the stairs, he told people he'd had a stroke. He was just pissed out of his skull. I love Dirk, he is such a drama queen."

"Will you talk to your doctor? I think you should."

"We'll see. Let's not talk about this anymore, honey. Let's talk about something else."

"When I couldn't reach you last week, I was afraid you might have changed your mind about the book again," I told her, obediently changing the subject, and immediately regretting it.

"That's still a possibility," she said dryly.

Ava never made it easy, and I didn't want to be goaded into another argument about whether she should go ahead with the book or not. "You know how to keep a fellow guessing," I said.

"You can't teach an old broad new tricks, honey."

I laughed but I knew that she probably meant it—her throwaway lines, especially the funny ones, always contained a grain of truth.

"Anyway, I've been beating my brains out trying to think of things that'll make my childhood interesting for you. Maybe that's what started off the goddamn headaches," she said, giving me an accusing look.

I said that I didn't want the book to make her ill. "Writing an autobiography should be fun." I lied, of course. An autobiography is never easy and always painful to write truthfully.

"Well, I'd enjoy it a whole lot more if . . ."

She didn't finish the sentence.

"If *what,* Ava?" If I had been wise, I wouldn't have pressed her. She had, after all, a gift for getting to the point when she needed to. But her hesitation made me curious. "It's important. *What* would make you enjoy it more?"

"Honey, we're getting in awful deep with some of the personal stuff," she said, after a long pause, as if she were still trying to sort out her feelings. "Is it really necessary to put down exactly what Mickey Rooney said, what I said, what Frank Sinatra did next, and all the rest of that stuff? My own bad behavior, I can live with that—some of it, anyway. I have no choice. I'd just rather not have to remember all the shitty things people have said and done to me. I'm happier not remembering, baby. Little of it seems pertinent now, anyway. Why can't we settle for what I *pretend* to remember? You can make it up, can't you? If I had lost my memory, you would have to have made it up, most of it, wouldn't you? The publicity guys at Metro did it all the time. Who the fuck knows the difference anyway? The difference can just be our little secret, can't it, baby? Let's make it easy on ourselves. We can do that, can't we?"

"Are you serious?"

"I'm tired, honey."

"It's a terrible idea, Ava."

I was astonished at the suggestion, especially after our last session a couple of weeks earlier which had gone so well. So far, I had gone easy on her. I hadn't pressed her about Mickey Rooney, I never had to. That stuff just flowed out of her; she needed no prompting at all. Since my faux pas about Frank Sinatra the night she first called me, I had barely mentioned his name. He was always going to be a tricky subject and, unless she brought him up, I'd decided to leave that phase of the book until I had the rest of it pretty well wrapped up.

I said, "I thought you wanted a truthful book, Ava. I thought that was the deal."

"The truth is trickier than I thought, honey."

"You've had a great life, Ava, an incredible life—the men you've loved, the incredible people you've known. You are more than just a movie star—"

"Being a movie star's only half of it, honey," she said.

"That's my point, Ava. You shouldn't settle for just another Hollywood bio, full of lies and hype. You deserve better than that." I was surprised at how passionate I felt about it, and how protective of her I had become.

It was nearly closing time in the park when we reached Rutland Gate, where we came in. She held on to my arm tightly. "Trying to cross this road is about the most exciting thing left in my life," she said.

6

The Barefoot Contessa," she said when I picked up the phone. There was no "hello," no "good morning, honey." Just the peremptory question: "*The Barefoot Contessa*—you saw it, didn't you?"

"Of course," I said. I was still half asleep. "You and Humphrey Bogart."

"And?"

"And *what,* Ava?"

"And did you *like* the movie, honey?"

Being woken from a deep sleep at three in the morning, I found it hard enough to recall the plot, let alone give a critique of it. Nevertheless, it was the movie—or maybe it was simply the title—that her fans remembered best. "I haven't seen it in a while. It's one we'll have to see again when we write about it," I said cautiously. "They called you *The World's Most Beautiful Animal,*" I said, remembering the advertising slogan.

"Thirty goddamn years ago I was, honey."

"You were stunning," I said. I felt on safer ground talking about her beauty than the merits of the picture. I had reservations about Joe Mankiewicz's script; I suspected that its literate, cynical banter would have dated badly. His attempt to do a similar hatchet job on the movie business as he had done three years earlier on the theater in *All About Eve*—which won six Academy Awards including Best Picture—was not as incisive, or nearly as witty. "You were beautiful," I repeated dully.

"It didn't hurt to be photographed by Jack Cardiff. That's the God-honest truth. I could be having the worst goddamn period, the worst goddamn hangover in my life, and Jack could still make me look good at six o'clock in the morning. He was a fucking magician."

"John Huston said he could photograph what you were thinking," I said.

"He'd photograph your soul if he could find enough light, honey." She laughed softly at her own joke.

"Mankiewicz always got great crews around him, people he could count on," I said.

"Mankiewicz was a sonofabitch," she said. She nearly always said that whenever his name was mentioned. "I didn't like him, he didn't like me. [Costar] Ed O'Brien said it was a failure in our chemistry. It was more than that, baby. The sonofabitch hated me."

There was a long pause on the line. I switched on the reading lamp, found my notepad and pen on the bedside table. You never knew what she was going to say from left field—that was part of the excitement of her calls, especially those in the middle of the night.

"But the sonofabitch was some writer, I'll give him that," she said, ending the silence on a forgiving note. "He wrote great parts for women; his women were up there with Tennessee's and Papa's. All those guys—Williams, Hemingway, Mankiewicz, the sonofabitch—they all wanted me to play their women. I played three of Papa's—Lady Brett Ashley in *The Sun Also Rises*; Cynthia, the ex in [*The Snows of*] *Kilimanjaro*; and that lapful in *The Killers*. I was Maxine Faulk in Tennessee's [*Night of the*] *Iguana*. I really brought that broad to life. And then there was Maria Vargas for Mankiewicz.

"Maria was a part we both knew I could kick into the stands. That role fitted me like a goddamn glove. I understood Maria Vargas"—the promiscuous café dancer who ended up as the Contessa Torlato-Favrini and a movie star—"I knew that lady inside out, in bed and out of bed. Especially in bed." She started to laugh. "Why the hell wouldn't I? The sonofabitch based the dame on me."

The next hour seemed more like a debriefing than an interview. I barely said a word or asked a question. She told me stories about Mankiewicz, *The Barefoot Contessa,* Humphrey Bogart—another sonofabitch, apparently—and the first time she met Howard Hughes. She told me about her short-lived marriage to, and divorce from, the constantly unfaithful but passionate Mickey Rooney, and what fun Hollywood was in the 1940s if you ran with the crowd who could afford to frequent Chasen's, Romanoff's, Mocambo's, where she loved to dance, and the Brown Derby, preferably the Beverly Hills branch. She said she loved to swim, and play tennis at the Beverly Hills Tennis Club. She talked about the mobster Benny Siegel, a regular at the movie colony restaurants in those days. She said, "I dated him once or twice, so did Lana [Turner]. But she liked gangsters. I mean, she *really* liked gangsters." A lot of young actresses and starlets did, she said. You couldn't avoid them if you were young and cute and worked in movies. Siegel was tall, nattily dressed, and a member of the toney Jewish Hillcrest Country Club. She said, "He could have been a movie star. But he didn't get to first base with me." George Raft introduced her to Siegel at Santa Anita, the track out at Pasadena, when they were making *Whistle Stop* in 1945. She said, "George loved to play the horses. All those guys did—George Raft, John Huston, Mickey, Spencer Tracy, Jimmy Durante, Errol Flynn. Louis Mayer stabled his horses at Santa Anita. So did Fred Astaire."

Higgledy-piggledy, she covered a lot of ground. She recalled scenes from her school days in Newport News, juxtaposed them with memories of her father's death, and her awe at Artie Shaw's intellectualism. She said, "I fell in love with Art's mind in a heartbeat. We made a damn fine-looking couple." It was a pity that he was a lousy dancer, but so was Frank Sinatra. Mickey was the best of the three. "But you can't dance with a midget!" She was telling me stories I knew I could never have winkled out of her in normal interviews. She told me things I didn't know enough even to suspect, let alone ask about. I must have had enough material for four or five chapters.

I switched to speakerphone, went into the kitchen, and made myself a pot of tea while she continued to talk. All of it was good stuff, some of it was priceless. I continued listening, sipping my tea, making notes.

Gradually, the humor, then the vehemence, started to go out of her voice.

I knew the signs.

I said, "You must be very tired now, Ava?"

She admitted she was.

I said it was late. She should try to get some sleep.

"Isn't this interesting, honey?" It was a familiar question when she was losing the thread of a story, or the point of an anecdote. Or when she simply wanted an interview to end.

I said, "Ava, it's very good. I just think you must try to get some sleep."

"You don't think people will think I'm settling old scores, telling tales out of school?"

"Some might," I said. I stopped myself from saying, I hope so.

She said, "I'm just trying to be honest."

"That is why your book is important, Ava. It *is* honest. It's Hollywood history."

"That puts me in context, baby," she said dryly.

It was daylight outside. I knew she'd still be in bed with the curtains drawn tight, total darkness being the only way she could sleep at night.

"So you think *The Barefoot Contessa* was shit," she said. There was accusation as well as amusement in her voice.

"I didn't say that, Ava. I don't think that at all. It's flawed but it's still an interesting picture. I'd like to see it again before we deal with it in the book."

"I thought it was a piece of crap," she said.

"You just don't like Mankiewicz," I said, and we both laughed.

She said, "Okay, *Barefoot Contessa, The Killers*—which do you prefer?"

I preferred *The Killers*, I said.

"*The Killers* was a better movie, you're right. Making it was more fun, that's for sure. We must say that in the book somewhere. Make a note to say what a good script it was and what fun I had making it." After a long pause she said, "What did you think of the way Mankiewicz started *Barefoot Contessa*?"

I knew what she was getting at. I said that the opening scene of her funeral in a rain-drenched Rome graveyard was beautifully shot, but it was a cliché. Anyway, didn't she think it would be a bit surreal to begin her *auto*biography with the narrator's death?

She said, "We don't start with my *death,* honey—we start with my *stroke,* and the death of my career. We both know I'm never going to work again. Not in movies. Not in television. You could make that work in a book, couldn't you?"

It wasn't the first time Ava had acknowledged her professional decline, nor was it the first time she had suggested starting the book with her near-fatal stroke—although this time her proposal was more sensible than the Lucille Ball episode she had come up with earlier.

"We can think about it, Ava," I said. I was tired, too, and as irritable with her as I knew she was with me.

"What the fuck is there to think about, honey. My career's finished. It's over, baby. Now I'm exhausted and I want to try to catch some shut-eye. Good night, baby," she said and replaced the receiver.

7

I would sit by his bed and read the newspapers to him but poor Daddy was so weak from coughing, he couldn't stay awake. But the moment I stopped reading he'd say, 'Go on, Daughter, don't stop, I'm listening. My eyes are closed that's all.' He'd squeeze my hand and I'd continue reading, and I'd read till my eyes burned a hole in my head. He loved to hear stories about President [Franklin] Roosevelt. Roosevelt was his hero. How I wish Daddy could have lived to see the day the president invited me and Mickey to the White House on our honeymoon. Everybody wanted to know Mickey in those days. I was a nobody, an MGM starlet, not even a nobody. He was such a star. Mickey Rooney was the biggest star on the MGM lot—and about five inches shorter than me! That never stopped him. Mickey was always on, and loving every minute of it. Everybody wanted to know Mickey. But nobody wanted to know Daddy when he was dying. He was so alone. He was scared. I could see the fear in his eyes even when he was smiling. I went to see the preacher, the guy who'd baptized me. I begged him to come and visit Daddy, just to talk to him, you know? Give him a blessing or something. But he never did. He never came. God, I hated him. Cold-ass bastards like that ought to . . . I don't know . . . they should be in some other racket, I know that. I had no time for religion after that. I never prayed. I never said another prayer. Not like I meant it anyway.

"I was sixteen years old. At that age, when you're poor, it's easy to believe that nothing's ever going to change; life is just going to keep heading the same way till it's your time to go and push the clouds around. That was just the way it was. I watched my Daddy dying, not complaining, just accepting, that was the way it was always going to end up for people like us. People like us, my Daddy and Mama, Bappie, my whole family, we sweated and slaved and made ends meet our whole goddamn lives, and for what? Nothing! Fuck-all, honey. Just sweet fuck-all."

She spoke with an intensity that was almost hypnotic. In our previous interviews, she had shown little instinct for what mattered in her life; she always struggled to find threads and meanings to her stories. But her story about reading to her father in his dying days in a public ward of a Newport News hospital in Virginia was deeply moving.

"I remember Newport News for three things: it was where my Daddy died, where I had my first period, and where my family went bust." It was a Sunday afternoon and we'd been for a walk in Kensington Gardens, her favorite London park, exchanging childhood memories and recalling things our parents had said. It was a game I had devised to get her talking about her past. "Nothing good ever happened to us in that goddamn town, except that Mama and I survived," she said.

"To this day, when people talk about the Depression, that's what I think of: Newport News, my Daddy dying, having no money," she said, and started to smile, "—and my first goddamn period!"

Whether the stock market crash of 1929 brought on the Depression or the Depression brought on the crash is a question that economists and historians still argue over today, but either way her family's move to Newport News had been tragically predictable as the American economy ran downhill at a disastrous pace. Steel companies, small businesses, big corporations toppled like dominoes. Thousands of cotton and tobacco farmers were forced off the land either by foreclosure or sheer destitution. By the winter of 1932–33, Jonas Gardner, increasingly beset by ill health and bouts of depression, joined the army of unemployed.

And there was worse to come. The following year, the Brogden school authorities decided that they could no longer afford to provide housing for the teachers. The Teacherage, the home where Ava had lived since she was three years old, was closed down. There was no other work for her mother in Brogden. "I knew how serious things were. I knew from Mama's whispered conversations with Daddy, and their awkward silences whenever I walked into the room, that something bad had happened. I always pretended I hadn't noticed. I hoped the problem, whatever it was, would go away," said Ava.

She was devastated when her mother finally explained what had happened and that they were moving to Newport News, Virginia, where she had found another job. "I knew that it was supposed to be wonderful news, and of course it was, Mama had found work, but I wept when she told me. It meant saying goodbye to my friends in Brogden. It probably meant never seeing them again. It seemed like the end of the world to me," she said.

Seeing how upset she was, her mother told her that if she didn't like it there, in a year or so, they could return to Brogden. The promise comforted Ava. But that night after she had gone to bed, Ava heard her mother's racking sobs and Daddy's voice trying to comfort her.

"I was twelve when we left Johnston County. Me, Mama, Daddy, and our Negro maid Virginia. She was two or three years older than me. I still didn't want to go to Newport News; even so, it was a big adventure for me. I could handle the move, and Mama could, too. But poor Daddy was a country boy clean through and he didn't like the city life one bit. But, as he said, you go where the work is—but the only available work was Mama's work, running another boardinghouse. That was tough, but she had done it all her life."

The house at Newport News was nothing like the Brogden Teacherage, where the boarders had all been women. Polite, respectable, elementary school teachers, they loved Molly Gardner, the small, plump, bubbly, *energetic* woman who treated them like her own family. In Newport News the lodgers were all men: shipyard workers, longshoremen, merchant seamen, crane drivers. They were a rough-and-ready lot but Molly treated them the same way she had cared for her ladies back in Brogden.

"'They put the food on our table, baby, never forget that,' Mama would remind me whenever I complained about them. What can I say, the woman was a fucking saint? I remember one evening, when I was pinning up her hair in paper curlers—she loved me doing that; she had never been a beauty but she loved me curling her hair, she loved to be fussed over a little bit, especially when she was tired—I said something about the way some of the longshoremen smelled. They smelled just godawful, especially when they'd just come back from their night shifts.

"Mama said: 'That's what money smells like, honey. You still wanna be rich?'"

"That was an interesting question, Ava," I said. "What did you say?"

"I don't remember what I said. I knew I was never meant to be rich anyway. I don't know why she asked the question, but I've never forgotten it."

She remained quiet for a while. "At least, none of those lecherous bastards ever touched me," she said. "They got a mouthful if they tried. Sure, a few tried, when Daddy wasn't around, but I could turn the air blue when I needed to. None of them tried a second time."

Newport News was a big upheaval in all their lives. Unable to find regular work, her father went to stay with Bappie and her second husband, Larry Tarr, a photographer, in New York, and try his luck up there.

"Poor Daddy, poor darlin', by this time he was in his late fifties. I'd say his chances of landing a job in New York, even if he'd been fit and well, were zilch. He'd been a cougher all his life, certainly all my life. Whenever I woke in the night, I'd hear him coughing somewhere in the house. He said it was a smoker's cough, it was nothing to worry about, he always said that. But it grew worse in New York, and he had to come back to Newport News, where Mama could look after him. I told you, he wasn't much of a talker. His silence was okay when I was a kid, but it makes me sad now, the conversations we never had. He liked to listen and nod, so I never even knew what he was thinking. But he was thin as a stick, and even I could see that his health was crashing downhill fast.

"It was a bad time for all of us. I hated school. Newport News was my first high school. The girls were smart and into nice clothes. Some of them seemed to have new outfits practically every week. I wore the same skirt for a whole goddamn year. Bappie gave me a couple of her old dresses to take in. They were nice dresses—when it came to fashion, Bappie was a pistol; she'd been given her own handbag and accessory section to run at I. Miller—but I was a lousy seamstress. Believe me, nothing is more humiliating than wearing your big sister's cast-offs when you're a kid.

"My teacher at Newport News was a patronizing bitch," she said. "My first morning, she made me stand up in front of the class and answer her questions: *Ava, that's an unusual name, where are you from Ava, what does your Daddy do for a living, Ava?* She should have done that quietly, not in front of the whole damn class. She made me feel like the entertainment. 'My Daddy's a farmer.' Well, that brought the house down. The minute I opened my mouth it was obvious that I was from tobacco country. Flat-ass country, they called it in those days. And *nobody* was a farmer in Newport News. Nobody there spoke the way I did. I dropped my g's like magnolia blossom. I must have sounded like a cotton picker in *Gone With the Wind.* I wanted the ground to open and swallow me up. There are so many reasons for my shyness I can trace back to that time."

She looked angry, but then slowly she began to smile. "Oh my God, the embarrassment of being young!" she said. "Mama had all those kids and didn't say a word to me about where babies came from. Isn't that the strangest thing? She didn't say a word about puberty, about menstruation. She said nothing at all about those things. Not a word. Can you believe that?"

"It's unusual," I said.

"The subject must have embarrassed her, I guess." She smiled forgivingly.

But physiologically, a girl of thirteen or fourteen must have had some awareness of the changes happening in her body? I said.

"I knew my body was changing, honey. I knew about periods. Of course, I did. Some of the girls in my class had started theirs. They talked about it all the time. That's how I learned about sex, and '*doing it*.' Not that I ever did anything until I did it with Mickey. I had a few boyfriends at Newport News High, and I was interested—and damn pretty, too—so there was plenty of interest, believe me.

"There was one boy I particularly liked. He was a senior, a football player. He came from a good family, his people were terribly conservative, it was such a cliché, but I knew it mattered—I was the girl from across the tracks! I was very conscious of that, although it didn't stop me having lewd thoughts about him.

"But I was shy and Mama was strict . . . so, anyway, that probably explains, in case you're wondering, how I was still a virgin when I married Mickey Rooney! Then I did it all the time! I'd been holding back a lot of emotions, honey. We screwed each other silly for the whole year we were married. We did it for a bit longer than that, actually. I was making up for lost time. We screwed on and off, right up to the time he went into the army in 1944. Shit, we made love the night he enlisted. We had dinner at the Palladium for old times' sake and then we . . ."

She hesitated, and I sensed what was coming.

"I'm not sure that we should say that in the book, honey," she said.

"Say what?" I said innocently.

"That Mick and I screwed all the time."

"You were married, for God's sake."

"We were separated, we were getting a divorce. It didn't stop us doing it. It makes me sound like a nympho, doesn't it, doing it when we were in the middle of a divorce?" she said.

"No," I said.

"You don't think it makes me sound like a goddamn nympho?" she persisted.

"It's the kind of thing readers want to know, Ava."

"Is it?" she said.

"It's a great insight," I said.

"Into *what*, honey?" she said.

"Into *you*—the person you were before you became a movie star," I said.

"How do you know that?" she said.

"I just do," I said. I didn't want to argue with her—at least not at that moment. One always had to choose one's moment with Ava.

"I'll think about it," she said.

I knew that wouldn't be the end of it. I knew she wouldn't want to leave it alone. She would go back to a subject again and again until she got what she wanted. She couldn't help herself—that was the movie star in her. But she needed different things from the book than I did. "My truth isn't necessarily your truth, honey, but let's forget this is *my* book and compromise—we'll make it my truth," she told me once. By this time, we both knew of the struggle we were in, yet still believed that we could get our way.

It was now past eight o'clock on a Sunday evening, and we had been talking since 4 P.M. when we returned from the park. I was ready to call it a day, but we had opened the second bottle of wine.

"Anyway, going back," she said, showing no signs of wilting. "When I had my first period, I was afraid to tell my mother. It was something I didn't want to talk about with her, and she most definitely didn't want to discuss those things with me. My first period started in the morning, before I left for school.

"I told Virginia what had happened. Well, bless her heart, she did the best thing in the whole world. She said, '*Lordie, you is a little woman now.*' I thought, *Well, that's rather nice. I'm a woman!* Virginia fixed me up with a Kotex. I asked her to tell Mama. I was too shy to tell her myself. Whether she did or not, I have no idea because Mama never said a word to me about it. But neither did she say a word when my white cotton shift became transparent when I was soaked with holy water at my baptism. I was thirteen. I was just beginning to grow pubic hair, you can imagine! I was mortified. My hair, which had always been blond, was beginning to darken. Especially down there," she said. "The whole congregation could see everything!

"This was about the time I started wearing a bra—and noticing boys. I remember I hung a picture of Clark Gable from one of the movie magazines on the inside of my wardrobe door. I was a sassy little bitch. One day I was in the kitchen, sassing Mama about something. She started to slap me when she noticed that my little breasts were just beginning to sprout out. She said, 'Yeah, and

I'm going to put a bra on you!' I guess she thought it was time she stopped slapping this young lady because she never slapped me again.

"Bappie wrote Mama from New York and said don't buy her a bra in Brogden. I'll get her a good one from here, which is what she did. I've worn good bras ever since. But I've never had large breasts. My sister Myra and I were normal but my other sisters were enormous. Mama, too. In the twenties, when flat chests were the thing, they used to tie diapers around each other and pull as tight as they could to flatten themselves out. I'm sure they must have torn every muscle in their breasts."

The conversation had run its course, and it was time to go.

At the door, she said: "I hope you can make sense of this, honey. I know it's muddly. And, oh, make a note of this when you get home: in the years we lived in Newport News, I never once asked a girlfriend back to the house, and no boys ever came there, not inside anyway. The boy I was sweet on, the boy in his senior year, he lived in a nifty-looking house. He had a little car and sometimes he'd pick me up at the house but I was out of the door like a shot before he'd even pulled to a stop. Shit, he must have thought I was keen! It was just that I didn't want anyone to know that I lived in a goddamn *boardinghouse!* I didn't want my friends to see any of those people who put the bread on our table. I was such a fucking snob—even if I was a girl from across the tracks."

8

"I don't want Ava to get hurt, Peter," Spoli Mills said.

We were having dinner at my London home a month after I had embarked on Ava's book. A year younger than Ava, although she looked older, Spoli was her closest woman friend I knew. A former German actress—Irmgard Spoliansky—the wife of Paul Mills, a movie producer and onetime publicity director at MGM's Elstree Studios in London, she had known Ava since they met in India during the production of George Cukor's *Bhowani Junction,* more than thirty years before.

Her comment puzzled me. "You think I might hurt her?"

"There's always a line in things," she said. "Sometimes people cross that line without even knowing it's there."

I assured her that Ava and I understood the terms of our deal. There would be no reason for me to cross any lines, I said.

"We both know movie stars are endlessly lied to," she said.

"Don't you think they know that?" I said.

"Not after a while," she said.

I was fond of Spoli, I liked her cynical wisdom and dark humor. I had known her for twenty years, and I was used to her frankness, which would have been brutal were it not for our friendship. "I won't let her down, Spoli," I said.

"I just want you to know how I feel about it," she said.

"We both have Ava's interests at heart," I told her.

"Let me ask you a question, Peter," Paul Mills said. "Why do you want to tell Ava's story?"

"If I don't write it, others will go on trying," I said. "Somebody will write it eventually."

"The grave robbers, you mean?" he said.

"Look what they've done to Marilyn," I said.

"Maybe nobody else will be as clever at sniffing out things as you are," Paul said.

"All it takes is time," I said.

"I know the book is Ava's idea. I know she needs the money, but her stories can be bloody alarming sometimes. I think the book is a terrible idea," Spoli said. "You can probably do it as well as anyone. But I want you to know that I've tried to talk her out if it." It wasn't news to me—Ava had told me, several times, as she continued to vacillate over whether to take her advice—but I was pleased at Spoli's honesty. "Her heart is my heart, Peter. I'll do whatever it takes to protect her happiness," she said.

"If you don't talk her out of it, will you help me get it right?" I said. I knew how useful she could be to me, how important it would be to have her on my side.

"Will I be a good loser, is that what you're asking me?"

"I'm not going to fight you, Spoli. We're on the same side. We both want what's best for Ava," I said.

"I hope so," she said.

I'D SPENT THE MORNING working on various transcripts, going backward and forward in time, piecing together Ava's reminiscences—of her childhood, of Hollywood, of her husbands and lovers—trying to make sense of her life. I was grateful for the interruption when the phone rang.

"Are you ready for some good news?" Ed Victor asked when I picked up.

"All you've got," I said.

"Dick Snyder's *very* interested in the book. He wants to meet Ava." Richard E. Snyder was the chairman and CEO of Simon & Schuster, the New York publishers. I'd never met him but I knew of his reputation: his astuteness along with his imperial style and epic temper tantrums were legend.

"He's coming in from New York next week and wants to sit down with her as soon as possible. Can we fix a date? How about lunch at the Savoy?"

I said that might not be such a good idea; it was where she had often stayed with Frank Sinatra when they were married. "I think they had some of their famous disagreements there," I said.

"You mean fights," he said.

"I was being polite," I said, but I also knew she probably wouldn't step outside the front door to have lunch with a man she'd never met, even if he were Richard E. Snyder, warrior-king and moneybags of Simon & Schuster.

"Can we meet at her apartment?" Ed said. "Dick would love that."

I wasn't too sure that she would agree to that either, but said I would ask her.

"Her apartment would be perfect," Ed said in his let's-get-rolling voice. "How is it coming? Is she behaving herself?"

"She's definitely got a book in her, Ed. Although she tends to repeat stories she's comfortable with. She's like someone learning to swim but still doesn't trust herself in the deep end," I said.

"It's important you win her absolute trust as soon as you can," he said. I could tell by his tone that my swimming analogy had disturbed him. I decided not to tell him about the sessions she had canceled, or her doubts about whether she should go ahead with the book at all.

"It's early days yet, Ed," I reminded him. "I won't have any pages to show Dick by next week."

"That's not important. He just wants to meet Ava. He wants to get some idea of what she's offering, how much she's prepared to talk about the Sinatra years."

"He wants to *interview* her?"

"He wants to hear what she has to offer—from her own lips. Is that going to be a problem?" He must have sensed my disquiet.

"It could be delicate," I said.

"How delicate?"

"She's pathologically shy with strangers. She's practically a recluse."

"Dick will be gentle with her," Ed said.

"It's not going to be easy for her to open up to a guy she's meeting for the first time. She's more relaxed after a glass or two but I don't think that would be advisable either."

"Dick really wants this book. Trust me, he can handle the situation."

I said I'd talk to Ava and get back to him.

AVA WINCED. "WHAT'S THE fucking point, honey? I thought Ed Victor was handling the money side of things?" she said when I told her that Dick Snyder wanted to meet her. Dressed in sweatpants and a gray wool sweater she looked bulkier than usual. "Didn't anyone tell you? I stopped auditioning a long time ago, honey. No, I don't think so. I don't think so. I hate dealing with suits. Tell Ed he can forget it."

I poured a couple of glasses of wine and handed one to her.

"Ava, he doesn't want to audition you, I give you my word. But he is buying your book, we hope for a lot of money. It's perfectly reasonable that he should want to meet you. He is the head of Simon & Schuster. He's the guy who signs the checks."

She lifted her glass. "Down the hatch, baby," she said, and sipped her wine. "I hate talking to suits," she said again.

"You said you wanted to redeem your life for a little cash," I reminded her.

"How about a lot of cash? A lot of cash would be better," she said, and burst out laughing. "Jesus Christ, I'm such a whore!"

"No, you're not," I said. "You're Ava Gardner, you're a legend, and you've got a wonderful story to tell. All you have to do is have tea with the man."

I told her how good our last interview was, and how moved I was reading about the death of her father.

"It's hard talking about those times, honey. Those times still hurt. Talking about the past makes you realize how many of those you've loved are dead. You know, you love people far more when they're gone," she said. She was calmer now but she still hadn't agreed to the meeting with Dick Snyder. I didn't push her. We talked for about an hour, reviewed our progress, and discussed ideas for the next couple of chapters while I made notes and asked questions that would keep her on track.

"When Daddy died in 1938, we were still living in Newport News. Daddy passed in the hospital there but we laid him to rest in the Smithfield graveyard back in North Carolina. I don't know whether he asked to be planted there but that's where his family had been buried for generations, so I guess he had said something about it, and that's where Mama said he belonged. 'He's done his purgatory in Newport News,' she said, and she was damn right. Then Mama took sick. We didn't know it then, but she had cancer.

Anyway, the following year, we shipped back to North Carolina—I reckon because she wanted us to be closer to Daddy, but she had never warmed to Newport News."

She stood up and walked across to the French window and looked down into the square. Her feet were bare. "I guess he will have to come here," she said. She put down her glass. "We don't need a butler, do we, honey?" My mind seized up—who was she talking about, what butler? Then I realized she was discussing Dick Snyder.

"I think a butler would be a bit over the top," I said.

"You can take care of the booze," she said.

"Why don't we invite him for *tea*? He will appreciate that," I said, remembering Dirk Bogarde's stories about her unreliable behavior after a glass or two. "I'll tell Ed you'll see them here for tea. If we say Wednesday at four o'clock, you and I can get in an interview session afterward. It'll be a productive day."

"You think tea rather than champagne?" she said. She sounded disappointed. "Really, honey, *tea*?"

"Absolutely," I said.

THE FOLLOWING MONDAY SHE phoned me at 2 A.M.

"What the hell should I wear for this guy on Wednesday? I guess a dress, huh? Jeans would be too casual, you think?"

"I think so," I said, clearing the sleep from my head.

"I think so, too. Why don't you come over this afternoon and help me choose one? There's a darling little dress shop near here. I saw a black dress I liked in their window the other day."

I was working on *Theodora* during the day; I didn't want to traipse around Knightsbridge looking for a dress for Ava. "You know, Ava, I wouldn't go to all that expense. You look great in anything, and you'll be more comfortable in something you've worn before."

"Maybe," she mused. "Get back to sleep, honey. I'm sorry I woke you."

No more was said about what she should wear for the meeting on Wednesday, and on Tuesday there was another crisis. "I look terrible, honey. I look as if I've been in a fucking train wreck. That fucking stroke," she said. She wanted to cancel the meeting with Snyder. I reminded her that he was only in London for a few days. "It would be a pity to miss this opportunity," I said. "He really wants to meet you."

"But he can't see me looking like this—we'd never get a deal if he sees me looking like this. I've got more lines on my face than Lana Turner."

"Do you want me to call Ed? Shall I tell him and cancel the meeting?"

That got her attention. "I don't know. What do you think?"

"It's your call. I'll do whatever you want me to do," I said. It was ten o'clock in the morning; an unusual hour for her when she wasn't filming. "Have you put your makeup on yet? I'm sure you'll feel much better once you've put your face on," I said.

"Call Jack Cardiff," she said after a silence.

"What can Jack do, Ava?"

"Call him now and explain the situation. Tell him I desperately need him," she said, and put the phone down.

I rang Cardiff and told him exactly what Ava had said. That afternoon, the world's finest cinematographer rearranged the lamps in her drawing room—and placed a key light above the chair on which she'd sit for her meeting with Snyder.

He called me that evening. "It's the best I can do discreetly," he said. "When she sits in that chair tomorrow, keep telling her how beautiful she looks. Keep on saying that. How beautiful she looks. Lay it on thick. She won't believe you, she's too smart to fall for blarney, but it's what she wants to hear. It's the tribute you must always pay to great beauties when they grow old. Remember, it's always the cameraman who grows old, never the star."

• • •

I ARRIVED EARLY. I wanted to go through some lines with Ava before Snyder and Ed Victor got there. A bottle of Louis Roederer Cristal champagne rested in a silver bucket packed in ice. There was another one in the fridge, she told me. She clearly mistook what must have been a look of deep apprehension on my face for one of approval. "And I hope they like quails' eggs and caviar," she spoke softly into my ear. "They cost a fucking fortune at Fortnum's."

"I'll go easy on the champagne," I said. I was determined we wouldn't have to open the second bottle.

"Don't make me look mean, honey. Jesus, I hate people who pour small measures."

"I won't," I said. "But don't forget who we're dealing with."

"Is it too late to back off?" she said.

I checked my watch. "Definitely," I said.

"It's just that I have to get a little pie-eyed to talk about myself, honey," she said.

I knew that was true. "Just don't overdo it," I said.

"Time will tell," she said mischievously, but I knew she understood what was at stake, and let it go.

"I'm just not happy having strangers digging around in my panties drawer, honey."

She sat in the chair Jack Cardiff had lit for her and slowly moved her face around, feeling the warmth of the key light on her cheekbones . . . tilting her head so the light made her eyes shine. "Tricks of the trade," she said.

I took her through some questions Snyder might ask her, and rehearsed her possible replies. She wore black silk stockings and high heels, which showed her legs—of which she was still extremely proud—to advantage. She had settled on a little black Jean Muir dress she'd worn before. She smoked several cigarettes, not finishing any of them.

"They're here," she said when the doorbell rang. She stood up and waited by her chair. It was as if somebody had called "Action." She was on.

"Hello, I'm Ava Gardner," she said, holding out her hand, the model of sobriety. She wasn't the first movie star these men had ever met, and she was no longer in her prime, but they were bowled over. She sat down, crossing her long legs. Carefully catching Cardiff's key light, which put the frozen side of her face into shadow, she exuded elegance and sensuality with all the composure of Lady Brett in *The Sun Also Rises.* I opened the champagne and began to fill their glasses. To my surprise, and relief, Ava discreetly lifted the neck of the bottle with her little finger before I'd poured little more than a taste into her glass.

"I guess my first and most important question, Miss Gardner, is why do you want to write your book?" Snyder asked pleasantly.

Ava was ready for that one. "Well, Mr. Snyder, my business manager, Jess Morgan, in Los Angeles, told me I either had to write the book or sell the jewels,"—she spoke in a tone so dulcet and Southern that Max Steiner could have set it to his score for Scarlett O'Hara—"and I'm kinda sentimental about the jewels," she added with a small sensuous smile. She even made it sound like the first time she had said it. Restraining her usual ribald language, she continued to talk easily and convincingly about herself. She made wicked remarks about the famous people she had known—a few of them "intimately but not well, honey." She smiled at Snyder knowingly. "Elizabeth Taylor is not beautiful, she is pretty—*I* was beautiful," she said, describing her looks in the past tense. It gave her self-appraisal a sense of reality and acceptance. She went on like this for more than an hour, her stories sometimes funny, sometimes indiscreet, but always interesting. There was no question that she made an impression. Ed and Snyder were beguiled.

"You were great," I congratulated her when they had left. She had drunk very little; the second bottle of Cristal remained unopened in the fridge.

"Aa-vah Gahd-nuh," she mimicked herself. "That was pure Tobacco Road, Johnston County, honey. But God, I so wanted a pee," she said.

"Why didn't you just go to the bathroom?"

"But they would have seen my limp," she said.

"That was silly, Ava," I told her.

"Sure it was." She clapped her hands. "Now let's open that other bottle of Cristal before I die of fucking thirst."

9

Newport News has bad memories for me. It's where Daddy died. He was so weak and so hurt from his coughing at the end. In the mornings, before I went to school, I would go to the hospital and comb his hair, and shave him with his own cut-throat razor, which I think had been his Daddy's. He loved watching me soap up the shaving lather in his old mug. 'You make a good barber, Daughter,' he'd say. He was fifty-nine years old—born 1878, he was younger than I am now, fahcrissake. Some men can still be young in their fifties, even in their sixties—I've had leading men as old as Daddy was when he died; even Clark Gable was up there, he was fifty-something when we made *Mogambo*. And he could still get the girl! But the years weren't good to Daddy, they just ground him down physically. I would follow his progress on a chart above his bed in the hospital, and it sank a little more every day. The last day I went in to shave him, he waved me away. It was a very little wave. He managed a weak smile. He said he wanted to sleep but I knew he meant he wanted to die. When I went back after school that day, the nurses were putting screens around his bed. And that was that. He passed in a goddamn public ward in a town he hated. Nothing can be sadder than that, fahcrissake."

THAT EVENING I SHOWED a draft of this material to Ava. Was there anything she wanted to add, or change? She read it quietly without saying a word. She closed her eyes and remained silent for a while. I didn't say anything, and waited. She read it again more slowly. Then read it a third time.

"You think the stuff about Gable being old is okay?" she said eventually. "It isn't too cruel, is it? It doesn't make me sound too bitchy?"

"You do say that he could still get the girl," I said.

She didn't smile.

"Do we have to say 'fahcrissake'?" she said. "It makes me sound like a fucking fishwife."

"We can take it out but it's what you said, Ava."

"I said 'fahcrissake'?" she said.

"Twice," I said.

"Screw you," she said.

It was the first copy I had shown her and I tried not to let her see how anxious I was. Would she like it? Was she going to be difficult? I hadn't put words in her mouth but I had turned her answers to my questions into prose, and sometimes I'd cut together quotes and ideas from separate interviews about her father's death to make a convincing whole. Was she going to understand why I'd had to do that? I'd also done my best to imitate her voice but would she recognize it on the page? More importantly, would she accept it? Her reaction to the relatively mild "fahcrissake" was a worrying start, although it did amuse me.

She removed her glasses, and looked at me quizzically. "What do you think, honey?" she said.

I remembered Peter Viertel's warning that she could make a writer's life hell if he showed any weakness. "Never let her get the upper hand, kid," he'd said. If she senses uncertainty in a writer, his life won't be worth living, he'd said.

"I think it's a good start," I said firmly.

"It'll be better when you take out the second 'fahcrissake,'" she said.

"Okay," I said. It seemed like a reasonable compromise to me.

It was seven o'clock. Was I going to open the wine, or were we going to sit and look at it all evening? she said.

"You know, when Daddy was alive I had no problems. I had a charmed childhood. Life was sweet," she said as she watched me open the bottle of Good Ordinary Claret that I had brought from Berry Brothers in St. James's. "The worst thing that had happened to me was failing a sewing exam! I'd made myself a little dress—that was the exam, to make a dress. I bought some brown linen and made a little princess style dress, with a round collar and round cuffs in pink. I made it as easy as possible for myself. That sewing teacher bitch hated it. Maybe she just didn't like pink and brown. Anyway, she failed me, the bitch. It hurt my pride but I'd already decided I wanted to be a secretary anyway."

I poured the wine and handed her a glass. She sipped it thoughtfully, and said it was good.

"When Daddy died I thought nothing as painful as that could ever happen to me again. He'd made me feel special, although I'm sure my life was no more special than any of the other kids brought up in the Depression. I didn't expect very much from life but Daddy made me feel loved. He made me feel safe. No daddy can do more than that for his daughter. It would be nice if you could work something like that into the story somewhere. Have you got enough material to do that, honey?"

"I think so. I'll come back to you if I need more," I said.

She asked me to leave the new pages with her. "I'll read them again tonight, when I can't sleep—instead of waking you up at three o'clock in the morning," she said. She smiled and asked what ground I wanted to cover that evening.

I suggested that we take it from when she returned to Newport News after her father's funeral.

She thought about that for a moment, and sipped the wine. "Well, Daddy was my favorite, but I loved Mama, too. Daddy's death brought Mama and me closer," she said. There was another long pause as she pondered where to start.

"After Daddy died, when he was no longer around to give her a hand, that was the time I realized how tough running the boardinghouse had become for her. We can begin there. When I suggested I quit school and get a job. Well, she just about went through the roof at that. 'Doing what?' she said. 'Bringing in a wage, Mama. Doing my share. I want to pull my weight,' I said. 'You finish your schooling first. I want you to make something of yourself, something your Daddy would be proud of.' I loved her dearly but she could still be fucking annoying at times. She still wanted to control my life. I was fifteen, for God's sake!

"Shortly after that, she was offered a job back in North Carolina—running another Teacherage in Rock Ridge, Wilson County. It was practically next door to Brogden. I remember Mama saying, 'We're going home, baby, where we belong.' I don't think I had ever felt happier in my life. It was sad Daddy didn't live to see that day. I remember Mama grabbing hold of me and both of us crying, the tears streaming down our faces."

"What year was this, Ava?" Pinning her down on dates was never easy.

"Well, Daddy died in '38. It was shortly after that. Mama was never the same woman after Daddy passed. That miserable, fucking boardinghouse was killing her. She looked worn. She looked the way I sometimes feel now."

She lit a cigarette while she thought about it.

"I think she might already have had cancer at that stage. It was a sneaky one, one of those insidious bastards that kill you slowly. Cancer of the uterus. Mama never talked about it. At the end she did, when she couldn't hide it any longer. I was so upset.

"I told Howard Hughes about it. He'd started calling on me while I was still married to Mickey. He had a great sense of entitlement, Mr. Hughes. He sent one of America's top cancer specialists to see her. But it was too late. She died on May 21, 1943—the day I got my divorce from Mickey. Mama was fifty-nine, the same age Daddy was when he died. Who was it who said that a mother's death is a girl's first tragedy without her sympathy? Baby, they sure had that right.

"I'm jumping, I'm skipping," she said irritably to herself. She stubbed out her cigarette without finishing it, as she often did. "Concentrate, Ava. *Concentrate,*" she said.

She nodded slowly for a moment without speaking.

"Okay," she began again. "Mama and I were back in North Carolina, right next door to the place where I was born. I was eighteen. Just. Taking life as it comes, the wind as it blows. My brother Jack came back into my life. He was a real go-getter. He was the one who accidentally burnt down Daddy's barn. I watched it go up in flames when I was a baby. Another time, when he was thirteen, a year after I was born, he set up a stall selling shots of corn whiskey he had bartered for fish. North Carolina was a dry state in those days, and Jacko was doing a roaring trade—until Daddy found out, and put a stop to that! Jack must have been a handful, but he obviously had great entrepreneurial skills. Anyway, he was sufficiently well-heeled by the time we returned to Rock Ridge to be able to afford to treat me to a year's tuition at the Atlantic Christian College in Wilson. I had started a secretarial course at Newport News. I got my shorthand up to 120 words a minute, and my typing to sixty. I was all set for an office career, and started searching for some kind of shorthand-typing job in Wilson. I was willing to settle for that."

But what happened next sounds like a script for a bad Hollywood B movie—"a *very* bad Hollywood B movie," Ava conceded. Her sister Bappie was on to her second husband, a photographer named Larry Tarr, a brash, dapper son of the owner of a chain of photographic studios dotted over New York in the 1930s and '40s. Impressed by Ava's looks, Tarr told her that she "oughta be in pictures."

In the spring of 1941, he displayed her portrait in the window of his Fifth Avenue store. The enlarged black-and-white print of Ava, wearing a floral-patterned dress and a wide-brimmed straw hat tied beneath her chin with a ribbon—"Larry must have been trying to copy that early Mary Pickford look," Ava later mused—caught the eye of Barney Duhan, an office boy at Loew's Inc., the parent company of Metro-Goldwyn-Mayer studios in Hollywood. Hoping to finagle a date with the shop-window beauty, Duhan called the store and, posing as an MGM talent scout, asked for Ava's telephone number. The manager refused to give it to him but agreed to pass on his query to Larry Tarr, who, believing it to be a genuine inquiry, promptly sent Ava's pictures to MGM's New York office on Broadway.

Since the studio hadn't requested any pictures, and nobody there had heard of Ava Gardner, there was some confusion and delay at the MGM offices. "Larry Tarr chased them up, he was a real little hustler, but he was getting the run-around. I had never figured on being a movie star anyway. I dreamed of being a singer with a big band one time, that would have been nifty, but I never saw myself as a movie star. Even so, I was disappointed when the interest appeared to disappear in a hurry. You know, I was a kid and it was *MGM! Metro-Goldwyn-Mayer.* The most famous movie studio in the world! *Where Clark Gable* worked! I must have voted for him twenty times to play Rhett Butler." She laughed. "He fucking well *owed me,* honey!"

Whether it was Larry Tarr's persistence that finally paid off or whether Ava's photographs alone were enough to persuade an executive called Marvin Schenck, a relative of Nicholas M. Schenck, the president of Loew's, to invite her in for an interview, isn't clear.

She said, "I was eighteen. The summer of 1941. I was eighteen, I knew I was pretty, nobody had to tell me that, and I loved visiting New York. I used to go up and see my sister Bappie every opportunity I got. I'd call in to see her at I. Miller and the other salesgirls would say, 'God sake, Dixie, put your sister in the back. She'll scare off all our customers.' I was a bit behind the parade for New York tastes.

"Mama came with me to New York for the interview with Mr. Schenck. We had to make our own way to New York City; nobody offered to pay our expenses or train fare. But Mama was all for it. She was a great movie fan. The idea of me being interviewed by MGM was the greatest thrill of her life. I have no idea how she got hold of the piece of change that trip must have cost her. But since the Depression and Daddy's illness, Mama was used to being the breadwinner. She was the one who always made the pot boil.

"Fortunately, in New York, we could bed down at Bappie and Larry Tarr's place. Even so, we still had to travel steerage to and from North Carolina. In the summertime that was something, believe me, especially for Mama. I still didn't know how ill she was, I don't think any of us knew, and the trip was too much for her. On the day, she was too exhausted to come with me to meet Mr. Schenck. Bappie came with me. But can you imagine how disappointed Mama must have been? She made me promise to remember *everything,* what he said, what his office was like. 'Darling, baby, he is going to love you,' she said when she kissed me goodbye. 'You are going to be a movie star.' From that moment on, that became her mantra. She had such confidence in me, it was embarrassing.

"Anyway, Mr. Schenck was very sweet. He said he liked my shoes. I was wearing my favorite oxford saddle shoes with white leather straps across the front, which your friends used to autograph. He couldn't help but notice them; I always wore my shoes too big—that's why I've got big feet now. But I was flattered when he admired them. I told him about each of the girls who had signed their names on the straps. I told him their whole goddamn histories. He seemed very interested, although I don't think he understood a damn word I was saying. My accent was as Tarheel as it gets. That's incomprehensible to anyone who lives more than two whoops and a holler outside the state of North Carolina. For years I woke up in cold sweats about that interview!"

Eventually, Marvin Schenck gave up trying to work out what she was talking about. He rose from his desk, and held out his hand. "I think we should test you, Miss Gardner. At least let's see what you *look* like on the screen," he said. Ava didn't miss the irony. "To be willing to tune out that goddamn accent, shit, I owe that guy plenty," she told me nearly fifty years later. "He really stuck his neck out for me."

Ava was tested at a small studio on Ninth Avenue the same day they tested Vaughn Monroe, a big band singer, and Hazel Scott, a singer and pianist. Again Bappie accompanied her because their mother was too unwell to make it in the sweltering New York City heat. This time Ava borrowed a pair of Bappie's high-heeled shoes and wore a pretty print dress with a long flared skirt that her mother had bought her in Wilson for sixteen dollars. "It was not a color most women would wear but I loved it. I felt like a real fashion flash," Ava said.

The test was basic: stand up, sit down, look this way, look that way, smile, be sad, look happy. She was asked to walk back and forward a couple of times, then they did a voice test: what's your name, when's your birthday, where do you live? It seemed like a waste of time to Ava. "I wasn't dumb. I knew that my looks might get me through the studio gates but the moment I opened my mouth that accent was going to do me every time."

Nevertheless, Marvin Schenck saw something in her. He shrewdly sent the test to Hollywood—minus the soundtrack. Meanwhile, Ava returned to Wilson, North Carolina, with her mother, convinced that her Hollywood adventure was over.

On that journey home Ava learned how sick her mother was. "She was eating aspirin by the fistful. She could barely walk. It was only when my sister Inez persuaded her to see a doctor in Raleigh that she learned the truth. She was riddled with cancer, although I didn't know that until later."

A few weeks later, to her astonishment, MGM offered Ava a seven-year contract. "Thinking back, it's hard for me to remember exactly how I felt. I was very confused. I had convinced myself that I wouldn't hear another word from them. I was sure the dream was over. But I do remember that my heart was thumping when I read the letter asking me to come to Hollywood. The idea had been, *if* they offered me a contract, Mama would come with me to California. She had been strict with me all my life, her word was law, and even then, when I was eighteen, she still saw me as a child. But by this time we all knew that she was in no fit state to come with me to the end of the road, let alone to the West Coast."

But the evening Ava got the MGM offer, Mama announced that of course she must accept it. "She said it was too good to turn down just because she was under the weather—I loved that 'under the weather.' She had cancer for fuck sake! Mama declared that Bappie would go with me instead, and she would stay with Inez and her husband in Raleigh."

The morning Ava left for New York to pick up Bappie and take the Twentieth Century Limited to Chicago and the Super Chief to Los Angeles to seek her fortune, her mother took her in her arms. "Enjoy yourself, my darling baby. You are going to be a movie star."

10

When I arrived the following evening, Ava kissed me—a little reward kind of peck on my lips. "Thank you for yesterday, honey," she said.

"What did I do yesterday?"

"You were nice, that's all. Talking about Daddy's death and Mama's cancer was hard for me. You understood. It's tough having to talk about how your parents died. Neither death was easy for them. I didn't know so much of it had stayed with me."

"Moments like that never go away," I said.

"Like guilt, honey," she said. "Like goddamn fucking guilt."

She had gone to Hollywood when she knew that her mother was dying. Her sister Inez had taken on the burden of caring for their mother in her last months. And although Molly had encouraged her to accept the MGM deal, and encouraged Bappie to accompany her to Hollywood, I knew that Ava's sense of guilt about that time still ran deep. She had married and, after only a year, was in the middle of divorcing Mickey Rooney and already dating Howard Hughes when her mother died.

"What a fly-by-night lady I must have seemed to poor Mama,"

she said, pouring the first drink of the evening before we began our session. "*A season in Hollywood does so change a girl!*" she mimicked Elizabeth Taylor, whose refined, rinky-dink delivery was one of Ava's favorite party pieces. I'd heard it before, and acknowledged it with a polite grin. Ed Victor and Dick Snyder were talking serious money now, and I wanted to get on with it. The previous evening, as we always did, we had discussed the areas we wanted to cover—her arrival in California, her early days at MGM, her first meeting with Mickey Rooney. It was rich and promising stuff, and she seemed okay with it.

A few days earlier I had written to Greg Morrison, an old friend of mine—and Ava's—telling him that I was working with her on her autobiography and asked whether he had any "laundered reminiscences" about her that he would like to share. Although I had never inquired, I suspected that they had once been lovers. I never expected him to break the publicists' *omerta* code of silence but anything he cared to say would be useful, I told him. An insider's insider, he knew where more bodies were buried than Ted Bundy. But that morning, I had received a scrawled note from Morrison in California:

> *She's 17 or 18 with one pair of shoes, cardboard suitcase, leaving everybody in her life to enter the MGM University. They teach her to walk, talk, sit, sleep, shave her legs, shake hands, kiss, smile, eat, pray. Her ass is great, fine tits, short but good legs, great shoulders, thin hips, fix the toes, do the hair—clean it, but don't touch the face. Everybody and every camera is drawn to that face. That town is jammed with pretty, but not like that—the eyes, the mouth, are from another world. She becomes the "armpiece du jour," learns what they want. Learns how to do it without giving her soul away, and learns everything but how to Act. In her whole shitkicking, barefoot*

> *life she never really learned to pretend, nor did poverty give her much humor, certainly none about herself, so she went to work on the Men—Lancaster, Gable, Huston, Douglas, Hughes, and the "suits" that needed her. And so she went to her last and most important school, the U. of Sinatra. In essence, by fucking, fighting, and forgetting with him she inhaled the gangster outlook of the world. Take what you want. Don't let them use you. They only understand tough. And all of her days became nights.*

Written in obvious haste, with affection and understanding, its prose simple and uncorrected, it had a frankness, a darkness, and a beauty that said more about her than anything I had ever read before—her shyness, the careless one-night stands, her love affairs, and disloyal passion for Sinatra—it was all there.

It was a priceless briefing note. I thought it insightful and sympathetic, but I wasn't sure how Ava would take it and decided not to show it to her straightaway.

"HONEY, THAT EARLY STUFF in Hollywood we talked about yesterday is so fucking boring. I think we should start the next part of my life with *Whistle Stop,* the picture I did with George Raft. It was my first leading role. It got me the part in *The Killers*, with Burt Lancaster. Nobody remembers the shit I did before that. *I* barely remember it myself, fahcrissake."

I was shocked. It was a terrible idea. It would mean eliminating much of her early life in Hollywood, and probably a good deal of her marriage to Mickey Rooney. Why would she want to do that? It didn't make any sense at all. But I made a show of giving it some thought.

"What about the stuff we talked about last night? It would be a great shame to lose the story of your start at MGM, and we can hardly ignore your marriage to Mickey Rooney. We already have some wonderful stuff on that," I reminded her.

"I don't mean we cut it out completely, honey," she said.

That sounded better, but I was still cautious. "What *do* you mean?" I said.

"I just don't want to dwell on it, honey. Mick has already written his book. All the stuff about our marriage and the divorce is in there. I don't want to go over that ground again. It's old hat, honey. Ancient history. Nobody cares about that stuff today. We've all moved on from there, fahcrissake."

"When you say you don't want to dwell on it—"

"I mean I don't want to dwell on it, period," she said flatly. "We can say what we need to say in a few lines."

"A *few* lines?"

"It's worth no more than that, honey, believe me," she said serenely.

"But it's a transitional part of your life—the end of your hillbilly days, the start of your Hollywood career. So much was happening. I don't think we can skate over it like that, Ava. No one else can talk about that time more knowledgeably, more entertainingly, than you can—especially about your marriage to Mickey Rooney."

"This book is about *me*, Peter. Not about fucking Mickey Rooney."

"Dick Snyder will definitely expect us to cover it," I said.

"Mr. Snyder can whistle for it," she said.

I knew that one rule of ghostwriting is that you must never let the star make the rules. But I also knew that now was not the time to argue about it. I suspected that somebody had put ideas in her head since we discussed our schedule the previous evening. "I don't see how we can avoid it," I said reasonably.

"You don't like my idea?"

"Not really, Ava. No."

"Fuck you," she said.

"Don't beat about the bush, Ava. Tell me what you really think," I said. I wasn't trying to be a smart-ass. I just thought it would make her laugh and ease the tension that was growing between us. Instead, it made her very angry. I'd forgotten another rule of ghostwriting: never tease a movie star.

"I'll tell you what I really think, baby," she said. "I think you want me to get into the whole fucking thing about my drinking with Mickey. You want me to say I was a teenage piss artist. If that's what you want, you can forget it right now. You're not going to lead me down that path, baby."

"Baby" was a dangerous word. "Honey" was fine, but "baby" usually meant trouble.

"People have warned me about you, baby," she said.

"Who?" I asked. I was curious, although I could guess.

"Lots of people," she said.

"Do you want to give me a name?"

"Friends of mine."

"Then why did you hire me, Ava?" I said.

"Because I figured I couldn't shock you. I felt I could say anything to you, and we could talk it through. I thought we were going to decide together what goes in the book," she said.

"Isn't that what we're doing?" I said. I now realized who she had been talking to. They were Spoli Mills's anxieties, not hers. I decided not to make an issue of it. "We can still talk things through," I said. "I don't want to put words in your mouth, Ava."

"Then what the fuck are you here for, baby? I thought putting words in my mouth was your job. The whole point of you."

"But they will be your words, Ava. I just have to clean them up a little."

She still didn't smile.

She said, "I thought we had a deal—if I don't mention it, you don't ask about it, right?"

"I don't remember that deal, Ava," I said.

"Well, I'm reminding you of it now, baby. And I was never a fucking hillbilly, by the way," she said. She seemed to have no idea how much of her life was already in the public domain. But I didn't reply. I didn't want to start another argument about the contents of the book, about what she would say, what she wouldn't say. I wanted to stay clear of that debate for the time being.

"And you were never a piss artist," I said as reassuringly as I could manage.

"Well, I was certainly having a damn good time giving the impression of being one," she conceded, and that made her laugh, although it was more mirthless than I would have liked.

"Is that what's worrying you?" I said.

She stared at me, frowning. "That story's been told a thousand times, honey. It doesn't worry me. The scandal magazines write about it every goddamn week," she said.

That wasn't true anymore, of course. Forty years ago it might have been so, and for a moment I had a flash of Gloria Swanson in *Sunset Boulevard* telling William Holden she was still a big star, it was only the pictures that got smaller. That made me sad, but I think I understood her a little better.

I reminded her that Mickey Rooney had been an important figure in her life—"at least for a year he was," I said. I thought it might make her smile again. It was worth the risk.

"He stuck around longer than that, honey," she said, but didn't smile. "I didn't shake him off until he joined the army."

I agreed that Rooney had written his own book, and he'd covered their marriage and divorce in that, but people were going to want to hear about that time from her perspective, I said. The publishers would certainly expect her to deal with it, I added.

"I've already told you about him, honey. If you want more, you'll have to make it up. Go ahead, Mick won't mind. Just give him some good lines. He's not going to complain. He's an old hambone."

It was impossible to reason with her when she was in this mood. But at least we were back on "honey" terms.

"I'm not going to make it up, Ava. It's your book, not mine," I said.

"I've told you all I know about Mr. Rooney, honey."

"I don't think so, Ava."

"It's all you're going to get, honey."

"You've told me some funny anecdotes, some funny bits. But we haven't gotten to grips with your life together at all, Ava. I haven't a clue how that relationship develops. Unless you give me a little more, I have no idea how I'm going to handle this chapter," I said.

"Howard was kindness itself to Mama when she was dying. I nearly killed the fucker once but he was marvelous to Mama when she was dying," she said. "All her life she had to roll with the punches. I got my survival instincts from her. But Howard got her the best palliative care money could buy. I could never have afforded the things he did for her. He sent two specialists from New York. Another from L.A. When I think of Howard Hughes now, I think of his kindnesses to Mama, his sweetness, not the fights we had."

The startling change of subject made it clear that she was bored with the subject of Mickey Rooney, and was not going to discuss it anymore. We had clearly gotten off on the wrong foot, and I knew that I had to let it go for now. I was grateful that the storm had passed.

"Anyway, we had a good session yesterday," I told her.

"That's because I trust you," she said. "I do, you know?"

I said I hoped so, although I suspected it was her way of apologizing for what she had said earlier. Yesterday's session was good because she had said something important about herself. She had seen her faults, and her sense of guilt as she prepared to leave home, knowing that her mother was dying, was genuinely touching.

"You convey your feelings very well, Ava," I said.

"These interviews are difficult for me, honey. I have to think very hard before I can find a sentence that will say even a little bit of what I feel. I'm not good at answering questions. I don't want to give you a hard time. The truth is, I hate being fucking interrogated," she said.

Interrogated? I thought I'd treated her with kid gloves. After all, we both wanted the same thing: a good book, as quickly as possible. I thought that was the best way to get it. "I didn't mean to grill you. I apologize," I said.

"I have to choose my words carefully when you keep asking me questions. I've been tripped up so many times by reporters," she said.

"I have to ask questions, Ava. I don't want to trip you up. We're on the same side, for God's sake."

"I know we are, honey. I know you have a job to do. I know you want to do it and never have to put up with me again. I know I can be a bitch sometimes. Most fucking times. But I prefer it when we can just chat. Conversations are more fun. Anyway, I'm happy you think yesterday's session worked out. I'm pleased we did it. I'm pleased it's over and out of the way. I do want this book to work for both of us," she said.

Her moods came and went all the time and I was pleased that she seemed keen to get on with the book again. Nevertheless, I decided to avoid the contentious area of her early days in Hollywood and Mr. Rooney. At least for the moment.

"Maybe, if you could explain—" I began.

"I can only tell you what happened, honey," she interrupted at once. "I leave the explanations to you."

I felt she'd pushed me away again but she laughed. "You have to earn your crust sometimes, honey," she said.

"I'm doing my best, Ava."

"I feel relaxed with you, honey." She really did trust me, she said. "It's just that you're not what I'd expected."

What did she expect? I took the bull by the horns. "Is Spoli still saying you shouldn't trust me?"

"She's never said that. She says I shouldn't trust *journalists*. You're not a journalist, are you honey?" she said in mock alarm.

"Once a journalist," I said.

She smiled. "Spoli doesn't think I should do a book—with you or anyone else. Books are dangerous, she says. She does like you, by the way."

"And I like her, too, Ava. But she can be a pain in the backside sometimes."

"She frets you will persuade me to say things I shouldn't say . . . when I drink too much."

"I know that. She told me."

"She thinks a book, any kind of book, will hurt me."

"I think she's wrong. Her husband is Paul Mills. Need I say more?" Paul Mills ran MGM's publicity in Europe for years on the basis that all publicity was bad publicity. "He is the most *cautious* publicist I ever met. He thinks it rather vulgar if stars see their names in newspapers," I said.

That made her smile. "I like Paul," she said.

"I know you do. And so do I. But you do see my point? They are both paranoid about publicity," I said.

"People write all kinds of shit about me. They misinterpret everything I say. Nobody knows what is true and what is false about me anymore. I'm not sure that I know myself anymore. Anyway, I've come to the realization that all journalists are cunts," she said.

It seemed as if she was about to put me back in the "baby" class.

"Are you still trying to pick a fight with me?" I said.

"Of course, I am," she said. "Fighting's fun."

The bottle of wine was almost finished. I should have said, Fine, if she wanted to back out she should tell me now. But I was in too deep for such gentlemanly gestures. And I really wanted to do the book.

"This will be your book, written by you, Ava! I promise you," I said.

"You will still be carrying the ball, honey. You will always have an input," she said. "I will have to watch you, honey."

"Ava, I want a good book, an honest book, a book that will set the record straight, and make us both a lot of money. What's wrong with that?"

She thought about it for a moment. "And you think the truth will set me free?" she said.

I laughed, she could always make me laugh, and she laughed, too.

"Okay, no more talk of casualties in the mess, gentlemen," she said. It was a phrase she had picked up from Papa Hemingway. It was the line he used when he wanted to end an argument, or bury the hatchet.

"Let's just get on with it, honey. Before I change my goddamn mind again. I think we should open the other bottle, don't you?" she said.

To my astonishment, she started talking about her journey to Los Angeles in 1941, her first days at MGM. And her meeting with Mickey Rooney.

11

The journey from New York to Los Angeles took four days and three nights, coast to coast. It was maybe the most exciting journey she had ever made in her life, Ava told me. It was definitely the longest. Accompanied by Bappie, she took the Twentieth Century Limited to Chicago, and picked up the Santa Fe Super Chief to the West Coast. Old Hollywood hands usually left the train at Pasadena—to avoid the fans, or the writs, or irate spouses at Union Station. "Only that was a trick I still had to learn," she said.

In New York, they were met at Grand Central Terminal by a young man from MGM with their tickets, twenty-five dollars pocket money for the train journey, and a copy of Ava's executed contract. "Here's something for you to read on the journey, but better take a couple of aspirins first," he said.

It was the standard deal but it was the first time she'd taken a good look at it. "That's how goddamn naive I was. Bappie went through it with a fine-tooth comb, not that that did any good: the deal was done! I was to be paid fifty dollars a week for seven years—except it never was fifty dollars, and it never was for seven years either. The studio had the option to let me go after the first three months. If I didn't measure up in the first quarter, after they'd had a good look at me, I'd be out on my ass. After that, they could get rid of me at regular six-month intervals. That took some of the wind out of my sails," she said.

The standard contract was a one-way bet for the studio. The small print was full of surprises and traps for the unwary. A "morals clause" demanded that Ava promise "to conduct herself with due regard to public conventions and morals," and that she would not "do or commit any act or thing that will degrade her in society, or bring her into public hatred, contempt, scorn or ridicule, that will tend to shock, insult, or offend the community or ridicule public morals or decency, or prejudice the producer or the motion picture industry in general."

The morals clause didn't bother Ava. "I was eighteen years old. I was still a virgin. I wasn't planning to perform a sex act with Clark Gable singing 'God Bless America' in the middle of Hollywood Boulevard. What shocked me was the fact that they were entitled to use a twelve-week layoff each year—and you can bet your boots, the bastards would make sure they always did, and they always did.

"So, instead of getting fifty dollars a week for the first year, it worked out at thirty-five. Out of that you always had to be well groomed and shell out for your food and a place to live. That's why many of the starlets and contract players had to put out, plenty of them thought nothing of giving a little bit away when the rental was due," she said.

She talked in a steady stream of recollection. She remembered the date—August 23, 1941—and the name of the MGM publicist—Milton Weiss—who met them at the train at Union Station and took them to the Plaza on Hollywood and Vine, which was known in those days as the Times Square of the West.

"Don't get too comfortable, ladies," Weiss told them. The studio would take care of the first week's accommodations and meals at the hotel—after that they were on their own, he said cheerfully. He was full of good advice. The sooner they got themselves a used car the better, he said: Hollywood is a surprisingly big small town if you didn't have your own wheels. Meanwhile, he gave her the details of the bus routes she would have to take to get to the studio each day. "Allow yourself at least ninety minutes, you have a couple of changes," he said.

"That was fine. I didn't mind that. When you're young, it's natural to be broke. I never had much money in my purse but it never worried me. I traveled in with the early-morning shift people, the cleaners, the stagehands, and maintenance people. They were a nice crowd. Even so, it was no fun getting up at 5 A.M. to get to work on time. But neither was being put on suspension. I didn't mind not working, I never did mind that, but the fact that I wasn't going to get a pay packet for twelve weeks of the year was a real body slam. Fortunately, Bappie got a job on the handbag counter at I. Magnin. I think the people at I. Miller in New York had recommended her. Bappie was a great saleswoman. That kept our heads above water. It also showed how smart Mama was, bless her. If she hadn't insisted on Bappie coming with me to Hollywood, I'd have been fucked. I couldn't have found my way to first base if Bappie hadn't been around to hold my hand."

Bappie's wages allowed them to move into a tiny walk-up on Wilcox Avenue, south of Hollywood Boulevard. It was within ten minutes walking distance of the buzziest part of town, including Musso and Frank's restaurant, and Don the Beachcomber's, which was more famous for its drinks than its food; and an array of ornate movie palaces including the Egyptian, Grauman's Chinese, and the Pantages, which turned movie premieres into an art form.

"That stretch of Hollywood Boulevard became our regular Saturday afternoon stroll. Every weekend we'd catch a movie, sometimes a couple. I remember seeing *Random Harvest* with Bappie's favorite actor, Ronald Colman, and *Mrs. Miniver* with Greer Garson. God, that was before history, honey.

"Money was tight but I don't ever remember going hungry. We had a two-ring gas cooker. We could always rassle up a meal. We shared a pull-down bed, but it was no great hardship. I'd shared beds for most of my life, sometimes with my sister Myra, but mostly with our black maid, Virginia. I'll tell you, honey, when you're sharing, there's nothing to choose between a brass bed in North Carolina and a bed that pulls out of the wall in Southern California. But I was young and optimistic. I had no trouble sleeping anywhere in those days. That's one of the best things about youth," she said.

Ava talked about her first days in Hollywood. She described the Roman columns that stretched for over half a mile along the front of the MGM studios on Washington Boulevard. She remembered her amusement and disappointment when she discovered that they were made of plaster and wood, and not marble, as she had imagined, and her excitement at being introduced to Mickey Rooney on the set of *Babes on Broadway*. She was funny about the commissary, known as the "Lion's Den," with its huge mural of Louis B. Mayer—"his weasel eyes behind those round wire-frame glasses watched every spoonful you ate."

Ava had been in Hollywood barely twenty-four hours and was being hauled around the studio by a publicist whose job it was to get her photographed with the stars. "It was a ritual all new contract players went through, and if the new girl was pretty enough and the star big enough, the pictures sometimes made the small town newspapers and occasionally even got into the Hollywood trades. Those fuckers never missed a trick. I'm told the photographs of my meeting with Mickey Rooney appeared in newspapers all over the world. But I still went on suspension after the first month!"

She'd talked for a long time. Suddenly she stopped and looked at me quizzically. "What's the matter? The cat got your tongue, honey?" she said.

"I'm listening. It's fascinating. You're doing fine," I said.

"You know I hate monologues, honey. My mouth gets dry," she said.

It was after 8 P.M. I knew what she wanted. "Would you like a glass of water?" I said.

"Fuck you, baby," she said.

I opened the bottle of red wine that was on the small table by her side. I didn't mind her drinking when we worked. "I drink to *remember,* honey," she often said, and to a point it seemed to work. I poured two glasses. "A Chilean Merlot with aromas of blackberries and a hint of vanilla," I said facetiously, handing her the glass.

"As long as it's wet, honey," she said. She lifted her glass. "*Prost*, honey."

"To you," I said.

She tasted the wine, holding the glass to her lips with both hands. "That's nice," she said.

"Okay, here's a question," I said, getting back to business. "Can you recall your feelings when you met Mickey Rooney for the first time?"

"*My feelings*?" She looked at me as if I had asked her to reopen an old wound.

"Can you remember what he said, what you said?" I said speculatively.

She turned the question over in her mind for a minute or so, sipped her wine. "You know, it's very odd, trying to remember how you felt about anything as a kid. I've read so many versions of my life when I first went to Hollywood. The bastards never get it quite right," she said.

"Well, now's the time to put the record straight," I said.

She looked amused. "I can remember that first meeting with

Mick very clearly—probably because he was wearing a bowl of fruit on his head. At least that's what it looked like. He was playing this Carmen Miranda character—do you remember Carmen Miranda? You probably don't. She had a brief fame in the forties. She was a Brazilian dancer, a hot little number while she lasted. Mickey was playing her, complete with false eyelashes, false boobs, his mouth smothered with lipstick.

"It was my first day in Hollywood. I was being hauled around the sets to be photographed with the stars. He came over to me and said, 'Hi, I'm Mickey Rooney.' He did a little soft-shoe shuffle kind of dance, and bowed to me. God, I was embarrassed. I don't think I said a word. I might have said 'Hello' or something. I was overwhelmed. His Andy Hardy pictures made the studio millions and cost peanuts. So did his Mickey and Judy [Garland] pictures. I wanted to ask for his autograph but I could barely open my mouth."

Years later, she said, the psychoanalyst her second husband, Artie Shaw, made her go to, to try to find the cause of her drinking—"a fifty-minute session, six days a week on the couch, I felt like a character in a *New Yorker* cartoon"—had a theory about why she could hardly speak when she first met Rooney. "It might have been a bunch of bullshit, but it kind of made sense, too. Shall I tell you about the shrink? I know you hate me jumping around."

"If we can stay with the Mickey story for the moment," I said.

"You don't like it when I wander, do you? But I'm more relaxed when I can say things directly from my thoughts," she said.

"One thing we don't have right now, Ava, is time. The clock's running and it's important that we have at least half a dozen chapters for Ed to show Richard Snyder as soon as possible. It'll be quicker and easier for me if we concentrate on one subject—"

"And it's easier for me when I can say things as they come into my head," she said angrily. "Why the hell shouldn't I tell you what comes into my head? You should be pleased, at least you know I'm not holding anything back. That's how I did it with the shrink and it seemed to work fine for her."

"The shrink and the Artie Shaw story can wait, Ava," I said bluntly. I hadn't meant it to sound aggressive, or like an ultimatum, but it did. I knew we were on the edge of another argument. She knew it, too. She looked at me steadily for a long moment, in silence. I imagined she was making up her mind whether she wanted to continue with the book or not. Then she said quietly: "Let's get on with it, honey. Where the fuck was I?"

I felt duly reprimanded for interrupting her flow. "The publicity man was taking you around the sets. He'd introduced you to Mickey Rooney," I said.

"He said, 'Mickey, this is Ava Gardner, one of our new contract players.' Mick did another quick soft-shoe shuffle and bowed even more elaborately, like a courtier or something. The people on the set were laughing like mad at him. He loved an audience, of course. He was always at his best when he was in the spotlight. I just wanted the ground to open and swallow me up."

She fell silent for another long moment. Then she said, "I remember asking him one evening, shortly after we were married, what he thought of me that first time we met. We had a kind of truth game we used to play in bed. We'd spend a lot of time in the sack in the early days, *a lot* of time: talking, laughing, making love. We were still getting to know each other really. Mick was only a couple of years older than me, but he'd been playing the vaudeville circuits since he was a kid. That was some education. He had all the street smarts in the world when I met him. I must have seemed so fucking awkward, so fucking gauche. Anyway, I asked him what went through his mind when he saw me on the set that day. He said did I really want to know?

"Of course, I said, although I didn't expect he would tell me the truth. New husbands seldom tell the truth to their new brides—at least none of my three ever did! And especially Mickey!

"He said, 'Okay, when Milt Weiss said you were a new contract player, I figured you were a new piece of pussy for one of the executives. The prettiest ones were usually spoken for before they even stepped off the train. I didn't give a damn. I wanted to fuck you the moment I saw you.'"

Ava smiled. "Mick was always the romantic," she said. "I guess he meant it as a compliment but I was shocked. I was still capable of being shocked in those days."

She lit a cigarette, inhaled deeply, and let the smoke drift out slowly through her mouth and nostrils. It was a seductive piece of business. Men had fallen in love with her because of that performance. I had seen her do it a dozen times. It took me a while to realize that she never finished a cigarette once the performance was over. She used it to play for time, to avoid an issue, often to change the subject. As I watched her crush out another barely smoked cigarette, I asked why she didn't give up smoking altogether.

"I used to smoke Winstons. They had the highest content of nicotine and tar around. A pack could keep the smile on Marlboro Man's face for a month. I was smoking *three* packs a day. I hardly had enough breath to get from my bed to the bathroom. I called John Huston and asked him how he stopped. He said, 'Honey, when I *had* to.' A few days later he died of emphysema. It's such a hideous disease. To think I only started smoking to make me look sophisticated—after I saw the gold cigarette case and gold lighter Lana Turner carried around all the time. The dumbest move I ever made."

"You once said that marrying Mickey Rooney was the dumbest thing you ever did," I said, getting her back to the subject of Rooney.

"Yeah, well Mickey . . . you have to remember, I was eighteen!

August 1941. I was still a virgin. That was a long time ago, honey. A lot of booze has flowed under the bridgework since then. The studio photographer took a bunch of pictures of us, with Mick mugging it up. The whole business took five minutes, tops. But that evening, he called me and asked me out to dinner.

"I still didn't know that he was the biggest wolf on the lot. He was catnip to the ladies. He knew it, too. The little sod was not above admiring himself in the mirror. All five-foot-two of him! The complete Hollywood playboy, he went through the ladies like a hot knife through fudge. He was incorrigible. He'd screw anything that moved. He had *a lot* of energy. He probably banged most of the starlets who appeared in his Andy Hardy films—Lana Turner among them. She called him *Andy Hard-on*. Can we say that—*Andy Hard-on?*"

"I don't see why not," I said. "It's a funny line."

She looked uncertain. "Let's think about it, honey. I'm not sure that you should use Lana's name . . . not until I'm pushing the clouds around anyway." She had used that line a few times now. I should have paid more attention to it.

She said, "Anyway, Mick called me that night and asked me out to dinner. I said no. I wasn't playing hard to get. I wasn't into that Southern Belle shit. I was just too shy. I said I was busy. That was a stupid thing to say. Who the hell was I busy with, fahcrissake? It had taken about six minutes flat to unpack my only suitcase and brush my teeth. I didn't know a goddamn soul in Hollywood, except my sister. And I'm *busy*?"

Rooney continued to call her; she continued to say no to his invitations. But he was funny and cajoling and persistent. "He could talk like all creation," she said. He would call her every day from his dressing room in the lunch hour, between calls to his bookmakers, and again late in the evening. On the phone, she lost some of her shyness with him; she laughed at his jokes, and enjoyed the gossip about the stars he shared with her. He was laying siege to her. She was flattered.

"Every conversation ended up with him asking me to have dinner with him. Finally I just ran out of excuses. I thought the hell with it, and said okay—but I have my sister Bappie staying with me, I told him!"

"'Fine, bring Sis along, too,' he said, bang-off. He was like Frank Sinatra in that way. He said he'd call Dave Chasen and pick us up at seven. The last thing I wanted was for him to see where we lived—in a goddamn walk-up on Wilcox Avenue!

"'We'll meet you at the restaurant,' I said desperately. He wouldn't hear of it. That wasn't his style. His chauffeur-driven limo arrived at exactly seven o'clock.

"The only other time I'd seen him he was wearing that Carmen Miranda shit on his face. I'd seen him on the screen a hundred times but that was in black-and-white. His looks in the flesh, without the Carmen Miranda makeup, came as a shock. He still wasn't what I'd call a *handsome may-an*, and his shortness surprised me, but there was definitely something appealing about him. He had thick, red-blond wavy hair, crinkly Irish green eyes, and a grin that was . . . well, it definitely wasn't innocent, honey, I can tell you that!"

Chasen's was run by Dave Chasen, an ex-vaudevillian, like Rooney. Along with Romanoff"s, the Brown Derby, and Perino's, it was *the* place to eat and be seen. And Rooney made sure that Ava was seen. He took her from table to table, introducing her to the celebrity diners. Ronald Colman, Cary Grant, James Stewart, and W. C. Fields were all regulars. But caught up in the whirlwind that was Mickey Rooney—"and after a glass or two of champagne, and I wasn't used to booze at all in those days, I was feeling no pain"—Ava couldn't remember who she met that night, except for Jimmy

Durante, who gave an impromptu performance of his classic number, "Inka Dinka Doo."

"We left Chasen's and went to the Cocoanut Grove, at the Ambassador Hotel, where Freddy Martin's band played, and then on to Ciro's. They became our favorite hangouts," she said.

That was the start of something.

12

Mickey Rooney made no secret of his obsession with Ava. He took her out every night: dinner at Romanoff's, dancing at the Grove one night; dinner at Chasen's, dancing at Ciro's or the Trocadero the next. He took her to the races at Santa Anita and to watch him play golf at the Lakeside Golf Club. "He acted, he sang, he danced. He told jokes, did impersonations—Cary Grant, Jimmy Cagney, Lionel Barrymore, he did them all. He'd have even turned somersaults if I'd asked him to," Ava recalled.

Some idea of her apparent coolness to Rooney's approach can be judged from the Pinteresque conversation on their first date at Chasen's, remembered by Rooney himself:

"Would you like to hear me impersonate Cary Grant?" I said.

"Would you like to impersonate Cary Grant?" Ava said.

"Sure," I said. "I do it great."

"Well, go ahead, if you want to," Ava said.

"It wasn't that I was immune to his charms. I was just so fucking overwhelmed by his energy. I couldn't think straight. I was so shy I could barely open my mouth, honey. Mick was manic, he was a complete hambone. He was always *on*—he was always on heat, too. At first, I didn't know whether he was trying to woo me or entertain me," Ava said. "It was flattering being with him, knowing that people were wondering who the hell I was. But it was goddamn exhausting, too. Mick was so famous. You have no idea how famous he was. Everybody loved him. Everybody wanted to be his friend. He'd introduce me—'This is my girlfriend. Isn't she pretty? She's gonna be a big star!' he'd say. Most times he'd forget to mention my name! 'And this must be the Girl with No Name,' said Frank Morgan [a popular MGM character actor; the Wizard himself in *The Wizard of Oz*] when Mick introduced me to him for about the third time one evening at Schwab's. He meant well though."

Under the name of Mickey McGuire, the Brooklyn-born son of vaudevillian comic Joe Yule Sr. and chorine Nell Carter, Rooney had appeared in dozens of two-reel comedies for a B picture unit before changing his name to Mickey Rooney. Rooney was soon cast as Puck in *A Midsummer Night's Dream,* and in 1934 MGM gave him a contract. His performance was acclaimed by the critics and fans alike. "Rooney's Puck is truly inhuman," critic David Thomson later wrote in the *New Biographical Dictionary of Film*, "one of cinema's most arresting pieces of magic."

But Rooney really hit the jackpot in 1937 with *A Family Affair*, the first of his Andy Hardy family series. By the time Ava arrived at MGM in the summer of 1941, he was the hottest property the studio had, turning out several Andy Hardy movies a year plus the equally cheap and profitable "Hey, let's do the show right here" musicals with Judy Garland. And movies with Spencer Tracy—*Captains Courageous* and *Boys Town* (1937, 1938)—further enhanced his popularity.

On screen, in the Andy Hardy series, he had endeared himself to audiences, especially American ones, with his sassy, boy-next-door persona and embodiment of family values, which earned him a special Academy Award for "bringing to the screen the spirit of youth." Mayer watched over his protégé's screen image like a hawk. When he noticed at a preview that Rooney had failed to remove his hat when he entered a room, he made the director shoot the scene again. In one classic Andy Hardy scene, written by Mayer himself—and reflecting the mogul's own sentimental affection for the American family—Rooney falls to his knees and, clasping his hands together, prays for his sick mother: "Dear God, please don't let my mom die, because she's the best mom in the world. Thank you, God." ("Let me see you beat that for a prayer," Mayer said triumphantly when Rooney finished the scene.)

Off screen, Rooney remained more than a handful for those who were assigned to take care of his needs. He wanted a direct telephone line to his bookmakers on the set. He got it. He expected a copy of the *Racing Form* delivered with his first cup of coffee on the set each morning. It was there.

"Poor baby, Mick was hooked on the horses," Ava said. "That's one vice I've never had. Installing that phone on the set for him was fatal. I was surprised the studio would do it, but I guess they'd do anything for him as long as he was making money for them. His pictures were cheap and made millions for the studio. Those Andy Hardy pictures paid for MGM's great movies, *Ninotchka*, *Camille*, *Two-Faced Woman*, all those other Garbo movies that were a bust at the box office. Mickey's movies kept the studio running."

They also more than satisfied Mayer's greed, and the old showman was always willing to overlook his star's extravagant whims. When his minders warned Mayer that on weekends Rooney often drank insatiably, Mayer ignored them. "He would say I was a good little fella and pat me on the head—he made about ten million dollars a pat at the box office," Rooney said, when all the money was gone and his liver was shot.

Whatever Rooney did off screen, it was important that his Andy Hardy image remained unsullied. "If you let Andy get too crazy about girls you'll lose your audience," was Mayer's view. It was all right for Andy to be smitten by some passing beauty—played by a series of MGM starlets, including Lana Turner, Donna Reed, Kathryn Grayson, and Esther Williams—so long as in the final reel he'd wind up with plain Ann Rutherford, his reliably chaste, faithful, and patient girlfriend.

His pursuit of Ava had a familiar ring to it. "He was like an eager puppy dog. He followed me everywhere. When he realized I didn't have a car and had to travel to the studio on public transport, he insisted on picking me up every morning at Wilcox Avenue and bringing me back every evening—in time for me to powder my nose ready for the evening round of dinner and dancing. He was a pretty good dancer, by the way."

"Wasn't it tiring for you, Ava?" I asked.

"I must have enjoyed it. I always accepted," she said.

The only thing she didn't accept were his proposals of marriage, which he made at the end of every evening.

"Please marry me, Ava," he would say.

"No," she would answer.

"Please, please marry me, Ava."

"You're too young," she would tell him.

"I'm twenty-one, fahcrissake!"

"Well, I'm eighteen and I'm definitely too young to marry anyone," she said. He really put the works on her, but she always played it straight with him, she said.

"He vowed he'd keep asking me until I said yes. Now that was *tiring*. He even went to work on Bappie. That was a smart move because Bappie was all for it. She loved the idea of being Mickey Rooney's sister-in-law. She thought I was crazy to keep turning him down. The truth is, I suppose, I was having too much fun being wooed by him. I didn't want it to stop."

The news that they were an item soon spread around the studio.

Starlets who had previously enjoyed Rooney's attention—many of whom had grown to count on it—took his neglect to heart. Eventually, Les Peterson, Rooney's personal publicist and minder, as well as his friend, decided that it was time to warn L. B. Mayer of the seriousness of his star's interest in Ava. Mayer—who had to have Ava pointed out to him, some five weeks after she joined MGM—asked how serious.

"He wants to marry her, Mr. Mayer," Peterson told him.

"Tell him he can't," said Mayer. "He belongs to MGM. Tell him a married Andy Hardy would break the hearts of all those little girlies out there who want him for themselves. Who knows what that would cost—him, me, the studio?"

"I've already told him, L.B. I've told him that at his age he should still be playing the field, and having fun. He won't listen," said Peterson.

"Is he slipping her the business?"

"He swears he's not, L.B."

"Why doesn't he fuck her? He fucks all the others."

"He says she's holding out like no dame he's ever known, L.B."

"She ain't the fucking Virgin Mary," Mayer said.

"He says it's giving him terrible headaches," Peterson said.

"He should just boff her and get her out of my fucking hair."

"This was before he wanted to become a Catholic," said Ava, who loved to tell the story of Mayer's meeting with the hapless publicist. "One of his daughters, I don't know whether it was Irene or the other one, Edith Goetz, talked him out of it. She said people would laugh in his face—a short, fat, famous Russian Jew—if he converted to Catholicism. Well, in Hollywood they definitely would have.

"I liked Les, and I think he liked me. He was devoted to Mickey, of course. But he knew which side his bread was buttered. And who can blame him? Mayer was the boss of bosses. He was the king.

They all owed their careers to him. Afterward, after Mick and I were hitched, I asked Les whether there was *anything* Mayer liked about me?

"Les had to think about that. 'Well, he once told me you obviously had cunt power,' he said.

"I said, 'Am I supposed to be flattered by that, Les?'

"He said, 'Well, that's just about the highest compliment L.B. can pay a girl, honey.'"

Nevertheless, the idea that his most profitable star—the hero of the lucrative Andy Hardy franchise, who made more money for him than all his other stars put together, and who had been voted three years in a row the most popular star in the universe—had fallen in love with a hillbilly starlet was intolerable.

"I swear to God, I had no idea of the fuss I was creating. I had no idea that Mayer—uncle L.B. as Mickey called him—had ordered Mick to stop seeing me. He'd actually forbidden it! That shows you the power Mayer wielded in those days. And it shows the power—and the guts—Mickey had to stand up to him the way he did. I still hadn't met the man! I didn't know that he considered me the devil incarnate. I didn't know that he thought I was going to eat his fucking meal ticket.

"I had to hand it to Mick. While all this was going on, he hadn't said a word about it to me. He must have been under enormous stress, poor darling. I still hadn't agreed to marry him but he was laying his whole career on the line in the hope that I'd eventually say yes. The man must have been fucking insane. Believe me, when L. B. Mayer leaned on you, you knew you were being leaned on. He would use charm, threats, floods of tears to get what he wanted. He could destroy careers. God, he was a piece of work. He was manipulative, cunning, and profoundly sentimental. He treated his stars as if they were his own children. He could wrap them around his finger—especially Mickey. L.B. was the best actor on the lot.

He could turn on the tears like a faucet. He and Mickey were the best criers on the lot. I'd have paid good money to be a fly on the wall at those meetings."

In spite of Mayer's efforts to keep the relationship quiet, the gossip columnists—Louella Parsons, who would become Ava's bête noire, Jimmie Fidler, Sidney Skolsky, Hedda Hopper—eventually got on to the story. "They always mentioned that I was a North Carolina beauty and much taller than Mickey. Their bulb pressers always managed to get pictures that made me look as if I towered over Mickey—which, of course, I did. Mick never seemed to mind, but it embarrassed the hell out of me. The way those press people kept on about it made me feel like a freak. I offered not to wear my high-heeled shoes when we were together but Mick wouldn't hear of it.

"I was spending a lot of time in the picture gallery doing 'leg art' for Clarence Bull's people. At least that's where I was when I wasn't having voice lessons to get rid of my hopeless accent. Mickey didn't want me to lose it. He said he was just beginning to understand what the fuck I was talking about! Anyway, Clarence Bull was the man who did those great portraits of Garbo. He shot all the studio's important stars—Kate Hepburn, Harlow, Grace [Kelly], Lana Turner. *Lassie!* He didn't bother with me until much later, after I'd divorced Artie Shaw but before I married Frank. But I was getting a lot of space in the papers and magazines with that cheesecake stuff.

"Mama must have collected every one of those clippings. Bappie found them in her bedroom after she died. She was my biggest fan. She was my only fan—well, her and Mickey Rooney. She was thrilled when she read that I was dating Mick. She must have known that already, of course—Bappie and I wrote her every week—but reading it in the newspapers made it real for her. It was news to her when she read in a local rag that I'd soon be appearing in a new MGM picture at the local Raleigh movie house. It was news to me, too. I still hadn't made a single movie at that point."

From August to November 1941, Ava managed to keep Rooney at bay and on heat. "I was having a ball. It was a fast life but we were both kids, we could handle it. One night we'd had a nightcap at Don the Beachcomber, which was often our last stop off before Mick took me back to Wilcox Avenue. The Beachcomber had become a favorite spot of mine. They served the best zombies in California. They tasted so good and seemed so innocuous. Have you ever had a zombie?"

I said I didn't think so.

"Oh, you'd remember if you had: Bacardi, dark rum, light rum, pineapple juice, lime juice, apricot brandy, orange juice, a sprig of mint, and a cherry. Only I always told them to hold the mint and the cherry!"

"Very sensible," I said.

She smiled. "I might have been floating a little bit, but I definitely wasn't drunk. I swear I still hadn't ever tied one on in my life at that stage. No matter what time I'd gotten to bed I always woke fresh as a daisy. I definitely knew what I was saying that night when Mick again asked me to marry him.

"'Okay, Mick,' I said.

"'I asked you to marry me,' he said. He sounded stunned.

"'I know you did, and I said okay—but not until I'm nineteen,' I said.

"I think I was a bit stunned myself. Maybe I'd heard what a rough time L.B. was giving him over me. Maybe I felt guilty about that. I really can't remember. I just remember thinking: why the hell not? Mama was saying marry him, Bappie was saying *Do it, do it! He's a nice guy! What's keeping you?*

"So I said okay. But I still had this thing about being a virgin on the day I was married—and nineteen years old. I don't know why

I wanted to wait until I was nineteen, perhaps because Mama was nineteen when she married Daddy, and it always seemed like it was the right thing to do."

It had been a good session and we both knew it.

"I must try a zombie next time I'm passing Don the Beachcomber," I said.

"But you must get them to hold the mint and the cherry," she said. "That's the secret of a good zombie."

13

When I showed Ava the revised first chapters of her memoir, more than twenty thousand words, she read them at a single sitting in complete silence. I sat in an armchair opposite her, sipping a glass of wine, watching her facial expressions, trying to judge her reaction to the pages. I knew there would be passages that she wouldn't like and things she would want changed; some she would definitely cut.

She was a slow reader. She wore a gray track suit, her legs tucked beneath her. Some pages she went back to and read again. Once she read a whole chapter twice. Her expression never changed. Based on our interviews, her asides and ad-libs, the gossip and thoughts we had exchanged in our middle-of-the-night telephone conversations when her defenses were down, the copy was funny and frank, a God-honest read. She was candid about herself and others. I had ignored her request to tone down her profanities, which she said made her sound like a "fishwife." Her expletives had a kind of eloquence of their own and I'd let them fly.

I knew I had betrayed her confidences and repeated many of her funny but strictly off-the-record remarks. It was a deliberate risk I had taken to make the book as honest and edgy as she was herself. I knew I had gone too far in places, but this, I told myself, was to be my bargaining chip—when push came to shove, I'd be prepared to forsake a certain amount of vulgarity to keep one indiscreet revelation. It would be an interesting game to play.

But the torrent of invective I expected her to unleash any moment at the liberties I had taken never came. She continued to read on in absolute silence, the rustle of the read pages falling to the floor the only sound in the room.

Her sustained concentration eventually began to unnerve me. The idea of bargaining chips went out the window. I began to think of what I would say when her anger finally erupted—what lines would I fight for? which would I sacrifice? And if she fired me as her ghost, what would be my parting shot then? Several excellent exit bon mots went through my mind. "Fuck you, Ava!" was my favorite.

She finished reading the revised chapters. The discarded pages were scattered around her, on the sofa, across the floor. She removed her glasses, and began cleaning the lenses with a Kleenex. I was now sure she was preparing to give me a severe scolding before she let me go.

"It's good, honey," she finally said.

The sense of relief—and surprise—went through me like a shot of adrenaline. I couldn't believe that she hadn't objected to a single four-letter word, nor complained about the amount of material I had lifted from our private conversations and her off-the-record stories.

"I'm pleased you like it," I said.

"I didn't say I *liked* it, honey," she said. "It's too fucking close for comfort, honey." After a pause, she added: "But I'm sure the publishers will love it."

"It needs polishing," I said out of sheer relief. She had read it as carefully as I had seen her read anything and I couldn't believe she had accepted it without a fight. She sipped her glass of wine that had remained untouched by her side. "You okay with the language?" I said.

"Shouldn't I be?"

"I've used a few words you asked me not to use," I said.

"So I noticed," she said dryly.

My first response was to laugh. "And you're happy with all that?" I said. I knew I was pressing my luck but I didn't want her to have second thoughts after we delivered the copy to the publishers. "If you have any doubts, it's best you tell me now," I said.

"I think it's got to be all or nothing, don't you, honey?" she said.

"I'm sure that's right, Ava," I said.

"What the hell. The publishers are going to love it," she said again after a thoughtful silence.

I still had to be certain. "You don't want to discuss it with Spoli, or with Paul Mills?" I said. I regretted it immediately.

She turned the question over in her mind. "Do you think I should?" She looked at me steadily.

I said I'd rather she didn't. I knew what they'd say, and so did she.

"They're wise old birds," she said. "Especially Spoli."

"They'd still be second-guessers," I said. We'd had this discussion before, I reminded her, and I really didn't want to get into it again. "They have already made their views plain, Ava." I knew that the more people who become involved in a manuscript, especially when they're friends, well-meaning friends, with their own prejudices and ideas about the story line, the more muddled it can become. But if she wanted a second opinion, it was up to her, I said.

"It wouldn't bother you?" she said.

"Apart from the fact it'll add months to the schedule? No, it doesn't bother me," I said.

"Balls," she said.

"I don't want to write anything that would hurt you, Ava."

"Then you'd prefer me not to show it to them?" she persisted.

We were going around in circles. I said, "It's your decision, Ava."

She poured herself a second glass of wine, then another for me. "I trust you," she said after another thoughtful silence. She sounded unusually hesitant and I didn't comment. "Anyway, I agree, too much discretion would bore the pants off people, right?" she said eventually.

I lifted my glass in a toast. "I'll drink to that," I said.

"What happens now, honey?" she said. She put a cigarette in her mouth but didn't light it.

"I don't want to show anything to Dick Snyder until we have another couple of chapters in the bag. Now I know you're okay with what we've done, we should be able to move ahead much faster," I said.

She removed the cigarette from her lips and crumbled it in an ashtray. "Just remember, I'm not getting any fucking younger, honey," she said.

ALTHOUGH IT CONTINUED TO be impossible to get her to express her thoughts in any coherent order, we settled into a successful, if occasionally tetchy, working relationship. I would spend a session digging into a period of her life, sometimes into a particular incident I thought was interesting; the following session, preferably the next evening, we would discuss the reasons for her behavior and why she had reacted in a particular way. I'd then write a first draft for her to read and see if there was anything we could add.

For example, a few months after her marriage to Rooney, Peter Lawford, another young MGM contract player—who became a somewhat mischief-making confidant—told Ava about the little black book of girls' telephone numbers Mickey still kept and continued to use. She hadn't wanted to expand on this in our interviews; in the draft, I had her conclude tamely: "I was pretty angry when I found out!"

"*Pretty angry? Are you kidding me?* I was fucking furious, honey. Goddamn fucking furious, baby. What young bride wouldn't have been? *I was spitting blood.* If we're going to use that story, let's use all of it, honey," she said.

That night, she said, she had gone through Rooney's pockets while he slept and found the little black book. "Most of the names were starlets and bit players. I knew some of them. They were the regular studio pushovers—Bappie says back home they were called sharecroppers. Others were the kids I told you about, the ones who had to put out at the end of the month when the rental was due. Anyway, I set fire to his fucking little book. But I always used it against him whenever we had a fight: *What about Lana, was she a good lay? I never fucked Lana*, he'd insist. *Well, her name was in the fucking book*, I'd say. *And so was my fucking bookie's, sweetheart, and I never fucked him either*, he'd say."

A week had passed since she told me about the night Mickey again asked her to marry him and she had at last said yes. I suggested we pick it up from there.

"Once he'd recovered—and realized that my acceptance didn't mean I was going to make out with him that night—Mick was all business. We'd announce our engagement on Christmas Eve at a birthday bash for me at Romanoff's, he said. Then there was this odd sort of silence. I wanted to hear violins play but there was just this awful silence.

"'Is there something wrong, honey?' I asked.

"He said, 'There's a problem, sweetheart.'

"He sounded so fucking serious. I thought he might be having second thoughts about the marriage thing. 'What's the problem?' I said.

"'Who are we going to break the news to first—Ma or Uncle L.B.?' he said.

"I was just thankful he didn't throw in old Louella [Parsons], too. Anyway, we tossed a coin, and Ma won. I had a feeling she always would!"

Ava's first meeting with her formidable future mother-in-law was one of her favorite stories. "I would replay it in my head whenever Mick did something so outrageous I wanted to kill him. I only had to think of that meeting to make me laugh, and all was forgiven. You had to forgive any boy who had a mother like Mick's Ma," she said.

"I was nervous and very shy. Ma was sitting cross-legged on the sofa with the *Racing Form* across her lap, a bottle of bourbon by her side, and a big glassful in her hand. Did you ever see the comic strip Maggie and Jiggs?"

I said I hadn't. It was an American strip.

"Well, Ma was a dead ringer for Maggie, even the tight, little curls were the same—like carroty Ping-Pong balls. The scene was bizarre. It's something I'll never forget: Ma sitting in this big, beautiful house Mickey had bought her in the [San Fernando] Valley, sipping her whiskey, and studying the horses. She had divorced Joe Yule; she was married to Fred Pankey, a cashier at the studio.

"Mick said, 'Ma, I want you to meet Ava. We're going to get married.'

"She looked at me for a second or two, her expression didn't change. She was as calm as custard. 'Well,' she said, these were her first words to me: 'I guess he hasn't been in your pants yet, has he?'"

This was always the starting point to Ava's story about her future mother-in-law. She loved telling it. "God Almighty, what a meeting that was. I have never been so embarrassed in my life. Today I would think it was one of the funniest opening remarks I'd ever heard, but then I just wanted to curl up and die."

On the way back from the Valley that evening, Mick asked Ava what she thought of Ma.

"She certainly knows her son," Ava said, who rather liked her once she had gotten over her embarrassment and the shock of meeting a woman who could cuss better and more often than she did.

"That was the easy part," Rooney told her. "Wait till you meet Uncle L.B."

THE PLAN WAS TO announce their engagement at a party at Romanoff's on Christmas Eve. But after Pearl Harbor, on December 7, 1941, Rooney jumped the gun and gave the story to Hedda Hopper. "It was a slap in the face for Mayer. He'd gone down on his knees and begged Mickey not to marry me. The story of Mick's defiance was the talk of the town. Not many people stood up to L.B. and lived to tell the tale."

Ava still hadn't met Mayer but a few days before her nineteenth birthday, Rooney told her that Uncle L.B. wanted to see them both in his office the following morning.

"I didn't want to go. Mick said Uncle L.B. wanted to give us his blessing. I doubted that. He wouldn't touch Mickey, of course, not right away, but men like that have long memories. I felt much more vulnerable. Old Uncle L.B. could make me disappear in the middle of the next scene, if he wanted to!"

Ava and Rooney arrived at Mayer's office together at eight o'clock the following morning. Mayer summoned Rooney in first. "While Mickey was talking to Mayer, I sat in the outer office with Ida Koverman. She'd been Mayer's secretary forever. If L.B. dropped dead tomorrow, she could have run the whole show," Ava said.

Koverman had been Herbert Hoover's secretary before he became president. It was through Koverman—a widow rarely known to smile, it was said—that Mayer became interested in politics and began making big, fat donations to the Republican Party. "It was

Mayer who made me realize that I could never be a Republican. He would call you up if you voted the wrong way, or went to the wrong rally. God knows how he knew but he always did. Later, I became a great Henry Wallace fan when he ran for president against Harry Truman on an independent ticket [for the Progressive Party]. Jesus, did I get a lecture for that! Mayer's idea of a Red was any liberal; anybody who was not an out-and-out Republican was a dangerous pinko.

"Anyway, there I was, sitting in Ida Koverman's office, scared half to death, waiting to meet Uncle L.B., wondering what the hell was keeping Mickey so long. Ida was giving me the silent treatment. I remember her first words to me were, 'You know, young lady, a leopard doesn't change its spots.' Between that and his Ma saying 'so he hasn't been in your pants yet,' I should have been warned. I should have walked out of there right then. In fact, I was just about to do just that when Ida said, 'You can go in now, young lady.'"

Mayer's office, paneled in buttery leather, was no larger than a small ballroom. A furled American flag stood behind his desk; on the wall photographs—from his favorite racehorses to the Duke and Duchess of Windsor—testified to the range and grandeur of his friends and interests. Mickey sat across the room beside a table containing a family Bible, the Hollywood trade papers, a silver statuette of the Republican elephant, and photographs of his wife, Margaret, and their two daughters, Edith and Irene.

Mickey introduced her as "My future wife, Uncle L.B."

"I'm delighted to meet you, young lady," Mayer said.

"He was perfectly polite. I could see why some people said he had plenty of charm when he wanted to use it, although he did remain seated behind his enormous desk. I didn't think that was very polite. He was not an attractive-looking man, which wasn't his fault, but he made me uncomfortable the way he looked at me through his small, round, gold glasses. I'm sure he wouldn't have objected if I'd genuflected to him," she said.

Fifty-six years old, Louis B. Mayer was the highest salaried man in the United States, and as proud of that fact as he was of the studio that bore his name. Below average height, he had a mottled-pink face, a thin, hard mouth, and a large head of thinning white hair. But neither his expensive suits nor the rose-colored polish on his manicured fingernails could detract from the power of his body.

He lectured them about the state of the country, the problems of the movie business, the genius of his London shoemaker. Told them how much he loved Clark Gable and respected Spencer Tracy and always trusted his own judgment. "I put your boy here in a couple of pictures [*Captains Courageous, Boys Town*] with Tracy and made your boy a star," he said to Ava meaningfully. "He explained why the chopped liver at the Beverly Hills Derby was better than the chopped liver at the Vine Street Derby," she said.

"He was very sure of himself, and could be very funny, too. I don't know whether he meant to be, but he was." *My whole life is making movie stars,* she mimicked his liturgical cadence. *All the billboards in the world don't make a movie star. Only Louis B. Mayer can make a somebody outta a nobody.* "Well, *you* couldn't argue with that," she said.

I laughed. "Is that how he spoke?" I said.

"I think he had voice lessons later," she said. "Anyway, he was very polite to me. Very paternal, although he could be a bastard if he didn't take to you, or got a grudge against you. Even when charm was coming out of his ears, you knew you wouldn't want to get on the wrong side of him. That's why Mick was so brave to stand up to him the way he did over me. I'm sitting here talking to you now because Mickey Rooney had the nerve to tell Louis B. Mayer he was going to marry me and if he didn't like it to go fuck himself. Frank Sinatra had the same rage in him, the same defiance. Artie Shaw was capable of it, too, but not so much. I've always found that attractive in a man," she said.

"Did Mayer tell you why he sent for you and Mickey?" I said. "Did he give you his blessing?"

"Eventually he got around to it, I guess. I don't actually remember a blessing. He gave us the whole business about marriage being sacred, about not running away and getting a divorce at the first sign of trouble. He had a list of all the solid Hollywood marriages he knew of—Eddie G. Robinson, Paul Muni, a whole list of them. We should copy their examples, he said. Well, he was getting religion at that time," she said.

14

The day after her meeting with Mayer, Ava was summoned to Howard Strickling's office. The publicity chief was one of the good guys at the studio, she said. "He was the man who taught me never to sue no matter what lies the scandal sheets wrote about me—and I never did. He said that magazines like *Confidential* wanted you to sue because the publicity would boost their sales, and they had no money to pay you damages anyway. When one rag reported that Clark Gable had been slammed in the pokey for drunk driving, Howard flatly denied it. Clark might occasionally sip a small glass of wine with his dinner, he said, but he would never dream of driving afterward. Clark—a *small* glass of wine! *And the press believed him!* Howard was a very persuasive man. He got most of us out of jams at one time or another," she said.

Strickling was waiting for her with the studio's general manager, Eddie Mannix. Ava had never met Mannix before but she knew that he was close to Mayer. "Mickey said he did Mayer's 'dirty work' for him, and Frank later told me that he had Irish Mafia connections in New Jersey. Whether that was true or not, I don't know."

But in all likelihood, Sinatra was right. Mannix had been a

ticket scalper at the Palisades Amusement Park in New Jersey when Joe and Nick Schenck had taken him on as their bodyguard. When they sold the Palisades in the 1930s to concentrate on their movie interests, they took Mannix with them to keep an eye on the studio activities on the West Coast. By the 1940s he had become a trusted Mayer man.

Ava still had no idea why Mannix had sent for her. "I thought he was going to get on my ass about something. I don't know—too many late nights, keeping Mick up dancing till the early hours. Howard hadn't given me a clue what it was about, he didn't say much at all, but I felt more comfortable with him there. Then Mannix began discussing the wedding. Until that moment, I hadn't given it all that much thought. I don't think Mick and I had discussed the actual wedding at all, not the ceremony, not in any practical terms anyway. It seemed strange to be sitting there with this old Irishman, this complete stranger, discussing my wedding. He had a face like a raw potato in shades, that's how I still remember him."

She laughed; then said, "But he was always sweet to me, despite the fact that he was about to piss on me—and that was only because Louis Mayer had ordered him to. It was nothing personal. That was his job, to carry out Mayer's orders," she said.

"Ava, are you making this up?" I said warily.

"Mayer had gone down on his knees and begged Mickey not to marry me. I was not Uncle L.B.'s flavor of the month."

I was still puzzled. "Why would Mayer order Mannix to piss on you, Ava?"

"Do you want to hear the fucking story or not, honey?"

"Of course I do," I said.

Mannix, she said, told her that the studio had worked out Mickey's shooting schedule on his new Andy Hardy picture and the perfect date for their nuptials would be January 10, 1942. "I had no idea he wanted to discuss our wedding plans—he didn't look like a fucking wedding planner to me, nor to anyone else, I imagine—but suddenly I got this crazy fucking notion that MGM was going to take care of everything: a reception at the Beverly Hills Hotel, or the Beverly Wilshire, a star-studded guest list, one of the studio's top designers to create my bridal gown. I was carried away. After all, Mick was MGM's biggest star, he was one of the most successful movie stars in the world. Of course his own studio would want to put on a show for his fans! I just got carried away, honey. I don't blame Eddie Mannix. I let my imagination run away with me."

"I know what's coming, Ava," I said.

"I was a kid. I was nineteen years old. I didn't see it coming at all, honey," she said.

"Mannix was there to do Mayer's dirty work," I said.

"He was there to piss on my parade, honey," she said.

There would be no white wedding, no glamorous guest list, just a hole-and-corner ceremony someplace as far away from Beverly Hills as possible. Mannix told her that this was to avert Mickey's fans turning her big day into a circus—"into a 'fucking donnybrook' were his exact words, I've never forgotten them," she said.

But Ava knew that in spite of Mayer's earlier lecture about the importance and sanctity of marriage, he was not prepared to break the hearts of millions of adolescent girls and risk destroying the fan base of the studio's most valuable asset.

THE WEDDING TOOK PLACE on the morning of January 10, 1942, in a tiny Protestant church in a village called Ballard in the Santa Ynez Mountains, California. Ava wore a smart navy blue suit and a corsage of orchids. The wedding party consisted of Ava and Mickey, Bappie, Mickey's father, Joe Yule, Ma, and Mickey's stepfather. Rooney's personal publicist and minder, Les Peterson, also attended with a studio photographer.

"I think Larry Tarr was there, too—Bappie's husband, the guy who took the picture of me that started it all. By this time, their marriage was on the skids; Bappie had had a little fling with the manager of the Plaza, where we stayed when we first arrived in Hollywood. Anyway, Larry might have been at the wedding. I can't remember. It was not a memorable occasion, honey," she said.

After the ceremony, the guests drove straight back to Ma's place in the Valley in one car—"Larry must have been at the wedding because there was a tremendous drunken brawl at Ma's place that night and my sister said Larry was in the thick of it, as usual," Ava remembered in a later interview at Ennismore Gardens—and the bride and groom, and Les Peterson, took off for the Del Monte Hotel on the Monterey Peninsula in Rooney's Lincoln Continental, a gift from Henry Ford.

"I liked Les. He was a young guy, but already quite bald. It wasn't his fault he was tagging along on our honeymoon. But I was pleased he was there that first night. I invited him to our suite for a glass of Cristal. I still wasn't much of a drinker at that time but I had a glass of champagne, and another glass of champagne. Les kept trying to excuse himself and I kept hanging on to him. Oh, one more glass. Talk about first night nerves. We were going through the Roederer's Cristal like it was tap water. I was scared out of my fucking wits. I didn't want Les to leave us. I would have felt a whole lot more relaxed if Mick and I had got it on weeks before. But I was so determined to be a virgin on my wedding night, I'd barely let him give me a belly rub.

"All week, I had been saying to Bappie, *What am I going to do? What am I going to do?* She'd say: *Relax, you're going to do fine, honey. Nature will take its course. Just open wide!* That was funny but it did nothing to gentle me down. She finally bought me a sexy negligee. She sent me off with that—and a douche bag. 'That's all a girl needs on her wedding night, honey,' she said, and as usual she was right."

Everything *was* fine. It was a perfect wedding night, except she was terribly shy, she said. "But I caught on quickly. Very quickly. I enjoyed the whole thing thoroughly. Mickey was tender, actually he was sweet. He couldn't have been a better first lover for a lady. He'd been around quite a bit, of course—and marriage didn't stop him for very long either."

The following morning, Ava woke up with "the teensiest hangover"—and the start of her menstrual period. "I was soaked. All the excitement and everything had brought it on two weeks early. I couldn't get out of bed because I realized what had happened. Mick had already gotten up and wanted me to go with him to play golf. I was too embarrassed to tell him what had happened. I told him that I had a splitting headache. I knew he'd understand that," she said.

So while Rooney spent the day on the golf course, Ava—too shy to ask the hotel staff to take care of the situation—occupied herself washing the blood off the sheets and from her bridal negligee. "There was so much blood. I never saw so much blood. Well, not until GCS [George C. Scott] beat the bejesus out of me in Rome," she said.

I WAS WORKING LATE into the night on the first draft of her honeymoon chapter and having doubts about whether I should use her George C. Scott line at that point, or keep it for later. It was simply a matter of construction. Scott had not yet made an appearance in the book and I was wondering if I could use the line more effectively when I came to write about her torrid affair with him in Rome in 1964—she played Sarah to Scott's Abraham in John Huston's *The Bible*—when their drinking often became dangerously uncontrollable and he regularly beat her up.

I was still turning the question over in my mind when Ava called.

"Hi, honey," she said. "What's happening?"

It was a funny question to ask at two o'clock in the morning, but I didn't want to get into a discussion about a small technical detail that could be easily fixed in the editing.

I told her I had been working on the story of her honeymoon.

"Which one is that, honey? I had three," she said.

"Your first one—the one with Mickey Rooney," I said.

"How I lost my virginity. What do you think of that stuff?"

I told her that I thought the whole episode, from the wedding ceremony in Ballard to the wedding night, was touching and funny.

"You don't think a little too much detail, honey—the blood on the sheets, and all that stuff?" she said. There was a dangerous hesitation in her voice. "Maybe I've been a little too graphic?" she said.

"It's perfect, Ava," I told her firmly. "It's very honest. I'm sure a lot of young women will identify with that situation. I don't think we should change a word of it."

"Bloodstains are hard to get out of bedsheets," she said. There was still hesitation in her voice.

"It's perfect," I said again.

"You don't think it makes Mickey sound too fucking . . . well, too fucking insensitive? For not noticing I'd been bleeding—for going off to play golf for the day?"

"Maybe he *had* noticed, and was being discreet," I said.

"You think so, honey? You really think that's possible?"

"I think it's definitely a possibility. After all, he was a young guy," I said. I knew I had to choose my words carefully. "I think you should just leave it as it is, and let people make up their own minds."

"Maybe," she said. "Anyway, I want to read it first," she said unnecessarily, for that was already our arrangement.

She would see it as soon as I'd finished it, I said. "I promise you, Mickey comes out of it fine," I assured her.

"I hope so. I don't want to hurt him. Poor darling, he ain't got a fucking cent. He's been raked over the coals for millions by those goddamn wives he kept getting married to after me. What is it they say? The fucking you get for the fucking you got?"

It made me laugh, as she meant it to. She continued to speak kindly of Rooney, and amusingly of his passion for golf. "I had to learn to play golf quickly otherwise I'd never see the boy," she said. "I became very good at it, too. It became the best game I played and the one I liked least."

I was pleased she had dropped the negative discussion about the blood on the sheets. "What other games did Mickey play?" I asked.

"He played the horses. He was at the track a lot. He played a lot of gin rummy, usually with Les. He continued to be a fanatical golfer but whenever he got in a slump, he'd break our clubs," she said. "He had a real Irish temper. He took up tennis—which I adored. I was still playing it when I had my stroke."

It was almost 3 A.M. "You must be tired," I said.

"I'm fine, but I'm keeping you up," she said in her special tone of sympathy. "You'd better get some sleep."

"You, too, Ava," I said.

"Good night, honey."

Three minutes later she called me back.

"Did I wake you?"

"I was about to brush my teeth."

"I'm still not sure whether we should use that stuff about scrubbing the bloodstains out of the sheets while Mick was out on the golf course," she said.

"Okay," I said.

"Is that okay, we won't use it? Or okay—okay what?"

"It's okay, we'll talk about it tomorrow," I said, keeping it as light as possible.

"But you do understand my concern, don't you, baby?" she said.

"Not really, Ava," I said. I knew that was a mistake the moment I said it.

"I think people will find it distasteful," she said.

"I don't see why they should," I said. "It's frank but it's not distasteful."

"It's unnecessary," she said.

"I think it's honest."

"We're not going to have a fight are we, baby?" she said.

"I hope not. I've already explained why I think it's so good, Ava."

"I have a head like a fucking sieve these days. Tell me again," she said.

"First of all, and most important, a lot of women and young girls are going to understand that situation," I said. "If it hasn't happened to them, it's happened to someone they know. It will strike a chord with a lot of women."

There was also a directness about it that was pure Ava Gardner and that was why I was determined not to lose it, although I didn't tell her that. After I had finished explaining it to her, there was silence on the line. I tried to remember how many times she had called me "baby"; more than twice was not a good sign.

The silence continued. I said: "Ava, it's gone three. We're both tired. Why don't we discuss it tomorrow?"

"I'm not tired. I'm going to be awake all fucking night worrying about it," she said.

"Okay, I'll put it in the draft, we'll sleep on it. You can always remove it at the editing stage, if you still don't like it. It's your book," I said.

"Then why put it in at all, for fuck sake?" she said. Her voice had hardened.

"You might have a change of heart," I said.

"I'm serious," she said.

"I know you are, Ava. But I'd hate to lose it, and things get forgotten if they're not in the first draft," I said. I knew it wasn't a convincing argument, it might not even have been true, but I didn't want to give her an inch. She wasn't a woman you should ever give an inch to. Anyway, I wanted her to know how determined I was to keep it in. I wanted her to understand how good and important her observation was.

"It's unnecessary, honey," she said softly, and put the phone down.

At least we were back on "honey" terms. I typed up the conversation, cleaned my teeth, and decided to finish the draft of the honeymoon material before I turned in.

15

How much longer is this fucking book going to take, baby?" Ava demanded as soon as I entered the apartment. It was 12:30 P.M., too early in the day to expect her to be at her most winning, but I wasn't expecting her to be quite so disagreeable either.

"The delay doesn't seem to concern you anywhere near as much as it concerns me. For you, there will always be another book. For me, this is it. This is my one shot, baby. I'm not asking for a literary masterpiece, fahcrissake. If I'd wanted a literary fucking masterpiece, I could have asked Robert Graves to write it for me," she said, referring to the late English poet and novelist, a devoted admirer whom she equally adored. "I just want a book that'll pay the fucking mortgage *now,* baby, not next year. Time's not on my side, you know that, fahcrissake. You're causing me a lot of fucking grief. You and I have a problem, baby."

I knew that she was becoming anxious about the time I was taking to finish the chapters to submit to Dick Snyder, and I shouldn't have been surprised by the frustration and anger in her voice, but I was. I hadn't regarded the pages I left with her the previous evening as in any way final but I thought at least they would have reassured her.

Her anger was paralyzing. And when she's in that kind of mood, Dirk Bogarde had warned me, and so had Peter Viertel, you just had to duck and weave and keep your distance. "Jesus, she can be tough on her friends," Viertel had said with feeling, concluding a story about her displeasure at a scene he had written for her in *The Sun Also Rises*. "Just remember, she believes that writers only respond to pressure," he'd said wryly.

Forewarned, I didn't argue with her. When she was in that frame of mind, there was nothing I could say that would not be wrong. I didn't even remind her that I had written several chapters she had loved, drafted a few more, which I was sure she was going to like, and was continuing to interview her two or three times a week. I'd also been moonlighting on my novel *Theodora* but, heeding Ed Victor's advice, I hadn't told her about that at all.

Fortunately, I hadn't planned to do any work with Ava that day. I had simply dropped by to hear what she thought of the new draft pages, and to give her a copy of the final volume of historian Martin Gilbert's official biography of Sir Winston Churchill. She had met the English statesman aboard Aristotle Onassis's yacht in the south of France in the 1950s; along with FDR, he was a hero of hers. Gilbert had footnoted *Ari,* my biography of the Greek tycoon, and I'd hoped that this tenuous link might elicit some odd detail that would unlock a memory Ava could be unconsciously holding back. It was a ploy I'd successfully used before in interviews, and, indeed, it would later remind her of a boozy evening she'd spent with Churchill aboard Onassis's yacht in Monte Carlo. ("W.C. had had his share of vino and was feeling no pain, I was downing ouzo," she recalled.)

But right now, reeling and dazed at her outburst, I couldn't think of a thing to say. I just wanted to get out of the apartment as soon as I could.

This portrait of Ava taken by her brother-in-law Larry Tarr led to a screen test with MGM. When Ava left for Los Angeles, her mother told her, "Enjoy yourself, my darling baby. You are going to be a movie star."

2

Ava with her beloved older sister Beatrice, known as "Bappie." Bappie accompanied Ava to Hollywood and chaperoned her on her first date with future husband Mickey Rooney.

Nineteen-year-old Ava with her new husband, Mickey Rooney. "He went through the ladies like a hot knife through fudge," said Ava. Lana Turner nicknamed him "Andy Hard-on."

3

4

The newlyweds with Ava's mother, Mary Elizabeth "Molly" Gardner, in the Gardner home in North Carolina. Ava's mother had been diagnosed with cancer and had been too ill to attend their wedding. On that visit Rooney put on a terrific show for Ava's mother. "Nothing had ever touched me as deeply as Mickey's performance for Mama that day."

5

Lana Turner was Ava's idol. Lana had had an affair with Mickey Rooney and had married Artie Shaw. "First Mick, then Artie . . . she beat me to both of them. And to Frank, too," Ava said. "Even so, I liked her."

Left: Howard Hughes "was in my life, on and off, for more than twenty years, but I never loved him," said Ava. "*Till death us do part* would have been a whole lot sooner than later if we had tied the knot."

Below: Ava married star bandleader Artie Shaw in 1945. She admired his intellect, but he bullied her emotionally: "He was always putting me down. I was afraid of his *mind*. He was a dominating sonofabitch."

7

8

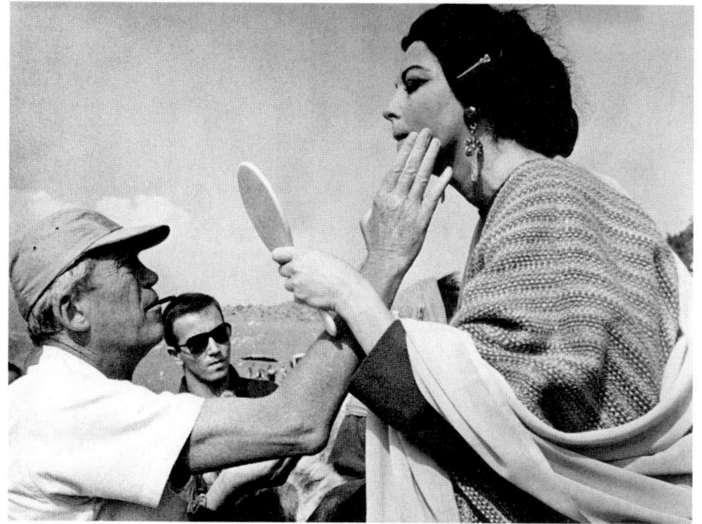

John Huston working with Ava on *The Bible*. Huston once said that it was seeing Ava's open-mouth kiss with George Raft in *Whistle Stop* that persuaded him to cast her in *The Killers*. Although she resisted his advances, she remained close to him throughout his life: "He knew me better than anyone alive, better than I knew myself."

9

Ava and Clark Gable in *Mogambo*. "He was my hero when I was a kid. He was still my hero when we made our first movie together and until the day he died."

Above: John Ford directed Ava in *Mogambo*—he was crusty and a hard-drinker, but he and Ava had a strictly professional, if feisty, relationship.

Right: Ava with Frank Sinatra, husband number three. The first time they met, Ava claims Sinatra said, "If I had seen you first, honey, I'd have married you myself."

12

"The trouble was Frank and I were too much alike. Bappie said I was Frank in drag. . . . [But] you don't pay much attention to what other people tell you when a guy's good in the feathers."

13

Humphrey Bogart, Ava's costar in *The Barefoot Contessa*. Their working relationship was not a happy one. "Bogie hated learning lines," Ava said. "He knew every trick in the book to fuck up a scene and get a retake if he felt a scene wasn't going his way. . . . I just didn't like him very much as a man—and he had no respect for me at all."

14

Ava became involved with George C. Scott in 1964, when she played Sarah to his Abraham in John Huston's *The Bible*. "When GCS was loaded, he was terrifying," Ava said. "He'd beat the shit out of me and have no idea next morning what he'd done."

15

Ava in her apartment in London Though debilitated by a stroke and having replaced her glamorous outfits with a track suit that became her uniform, she never lost her wicked wit. "You can sum up my life in a sentence, honey," she told Peter Evans. "She made movies, she made out, and she made a fucking mess of her life. But she never made jam."

She hadn't stood up, and I kissed her forehead. "Let's talk later," I said.

She was too angry with me even to tell me to fuck off.

THAT EVENING, READING THROUGH the transcripts of the interviews I needed for the next chapter, I was surprised and reassured to see how much ground we had covered. Pinned to the top sheet was a heavily underscored note reminding me of her reply when I questioned something she'd said that contradicted the reference books: "It's my fucking life, hon. I'll remember it the way I want to remember it."

Reading the line again made me laugh as much as it did the first time she said it when we'd been arguing over the infallibility of memory versus the reliability of research. Then she'd stuck to her guns as only Ava could when she was in the wrong.

It was now eleven o'clock. She still hadn't returned the call I made earlier in the evening. I had no idea whether she wanted me to continue with the book or not. I wouldn't have put money on it either way. I didn't want to call her again that evening but neither did I want to give up hope. It would be a disappointment if she decided to give me the bullet, but if she did . . . well, I'd be devastated and embarrassed; it would hurt my professional pride. On the other hand, I wouldn't have missed the experience for the world.

She was infuriating, bawdy, frank, and unreasonable. She was also kind, affectionate, trusting, and often touching.

And I adored her.

Meanwhile, using a reporter's guile to write around the gaps in the interviews, and keeping as many of her epithets as I could, I would try to finish a draft of the chapter that night and show it to her the next day.

I still hoped that they wouldn't be the last pages I'd get a chance to show her.

Slowly, I began to type:

Mick and I were crazy in love, even though we were still almost strangers to each other when we married on January 10, 1942. We'd seen each other practically every day since I arrived in Hollywood with Bappie the previous summer. But most of that time had been spent in nightclubs and at the Santa Anita racetrack. We had never had a serious conversation about anything. We had never made love. That was no way to get to know a person well—certainly not well enough to marry them.

I was nineteen. What the fuck did I know?

The war had been going for a month. Nothing had worsened; that is to say it hadn't yet touched us, except that Mr. Mayer said that he wanted Mick to go out on the road selling war bonds to show his patriotism—and, oh, by the way, he said, as if it were something that had just popped into his head, Mick could also do a little promotional work for the latest Andy Hardy movie!

Uncle L.B. never missed a trick.

But the trip didn't start out well. We were driving up to San Francisco when we heard the news that Carole Lombard, Clark Gable's wife, had been killed in a plane crash over Las Vegas. That was when we knew there was a war on. She was on her way back from her own war bond tour, and Mickey was devastated. So was I, although I was never close to her, I was more of a fan than a friend. Mick, of course, was a great friend of both of them, and Clark was beyond grief.

A few years later, when we made *The Hucksters* together, and became close, Clark took his wallet out of his back pocket and showed me the last cable Carole had sent him on that tour. It was in a cellophane wrap. It said, *HEY PAPPY, YOU BETTER GET IN THIS MAN'S ARMY.* He joined the air force soon after that, even though he was in his forties. He was my hero when I was a kid. He was still my hero when we made our first movie together, and until the day he died.

Anyway, we left Mick's Lincoln Continental in San Francisco. God, he loved that car; there was a gold plate on the dash saying that it was a personal gift from Henry Ford to Mickey Rooney, which I always thought was a bit chintzy. Ford later gave Clark a similar car. But Mickey was proud of the fact that he got his first. Anyway, as I said, we left Mick's in San Francisco for the studio to pick up and take back to the studio while we took off on a whistle-stop tour selling war bonds and Mickey's new movie. Chicago, Boston, Fort Bragg in North Carolina, Washington, God knows where else.

But wherever we went, thousands of screaming bobby-soxers were there to mob him. I swear to you, they were every bit as wild as Frank's fans when he was at the top. It was phenomenal. Mick called them his San Quentin quail club. But the enthusiasm, the hysteria of those kids made me understand why Mayer was so fucking desperate to keep our marriage off the front pages.

Les Peterson, who was still with us, never introduced me as Mickey Rooney's wife, which pissed me off. I knew he was only doing what Mayer had told him to do—as Eddie Mannix was only doing what Mayer told him to do when he put the skids under my dreams of a white wedding. That was another thing that pissed me off: everybody obeyed Louis B. Mayer.

Les said all I had to do was sit on the arm of Mick's chair at the press conferences and keep looking at him like a fan, like I was one of the bloody bobby-soxers—oh, and I had to make sure the reporters got a good look at my pins! He was incorrigible. "I'm only doing my job, honey," he'd say whenever I put up a squawk.

But I was enjoying myself, so was Mickey. We were two young kids having a whale of a time. We never for a minute forgot that it was our honeymoon! We were discovering new things about each other all the time—as I said, there was plenty of scope for that! Like he was athletic in the sack, and I was pretty verbal, and we were both *very, very* loud!

It was a hoot, and we made sure there was always time for a quickie. I was seeing and doing things I never thought I would do and see in my life.

In Boston we had dinner at the mayor's house. It was a very formal affair, with silverware out to here on this side and out to there on that side. I was on my best behavior but terrified about using the wrong knife and fork.

There again you see, if I'd been drinking in those days, the shyness wouldn't have been so bad, and I wouldn't have gotten into such a panic. At least I'd learned not to wipe my knife and fork on the napkin! I swear to Christ, that's what I did at the first smart dinner party Mickey took me to in Hollywood!

He said to me afterward, "You made a little faux pas at dinner, sweetheart." I was too dumb even to know what a faux pas was. But I learned pretty fast.

From Fort Bragg we took a little side trip to Raleigh to visit Mama. I hadn't seen her since Bappie and I took off for Hollywood the previous August. She had been too ill to go to our wedding. She was bedridden, and we all knew it was cancer by that time. My sister Inez and her husband had set her up in a little den next to the front room. This was the first time she had met Mickey, and she'd gotten herself dressed up to the nines. He made such a fuss of her. He was marvelous. My whole family turned out for him: my brother, all my sisters, nieces, and nephews. And Lord, when Mick had an audience was he good. He did his impersonations, he sang, he danced. He clowned. He was the complete movie star and Mama loved her movie stars! He made her the center of attention. It was probably the last truly great day of her life, although she survived for another year. I've never been able to express my gratitude for the things that touch me deeply and nothing had ever touched me as deeply as Mickey's performance for Mama that day. He treated her like a queen.

Driving up to Washington that evening—we had been invited to President Roosevelt's sixtieth birthday party at the White House—I tried to tell Mick how much his show for Mama had meant to me. I couldn't do it. I couldn't get the words out. Finally, I just said, "I'm so pleased I married you, Mickey Rooney."

He said, "Of course you are, sweetheart. Who wouldn't be?"

He made a joke of everything, but I meant it. I don't often blub, but I wept twice that weekend: once for Mama, because of her joy; and once for Daddy, because I missed him so. He would have been so proud to see me at the White House, having dinner with his hero, FDR. We watched the president give one of his famous Fireside radio broadcasts and all I could think was, Daddy would have loved this, he would have been so proud of me.

I was still working when the phone rang. It was 2 A.M. I knew it would be Ava.

"Why are you still up at this hour?" I said, picking up immediately.

"I can't sleep, honey."

"What's troubling you?"

"I have such a fucking headache. It's not even a hangover either."

I said I was sorry to hear that.

"What are you doing up, hon?" she said.

"Working on your book," I said nobly. Encouraged by a "honey" and a "hon" on the trot, I wondered whether she would say sorry for having accused me of dragging my feet. "I work better at night," I said.

"How far have you gotten?" she said.

I wasn't going to get an apology. But neither, apparently, did she plan to fire me on the spot.

"I'm wrapping up the story of your honeymoon, you and Mick visiting your mother in Raleigh," I told her.

"Have you written about going to the White House for Roosevelt's sixtieth birthday?"

"Yes."

"Well, you've covered the highlights of that marriage, honey," she said philosophically.

I knew she was deadly serious, but I laughed anyway.

"It went downhill so fucking fast from there." She laughed, too. Nobody could laugh the way she did. But the disintegration of her first marriage always seemed to fascinate her, as if she still couldn't figure out why it had gone sour so quickly. "If the sex hadn't been so good, it wouldn't have lasted as long as it lasted. It's a pity nobody believes in simple lust anymore," she said.

I started making notes. Although I suspected that she had said it before, or something very much like it, I wanted to make sure I remembered it. I would certainly use it. After a longish silence, she said wearily: "Oh Peter, I'm so depressed. I've made so many fucking mistakes in my life, honey."

"Christ, we all make mistakes, Ava."

"Do you love me?" she said. "The *truth*."

"Of course I do."

"It doesn't matter . . . as long as you're still my friend."

"I'm still your friend."

"I wake up at night thinking of all the fuckups I've made. I wish I could turn them into funny stories. The way Dorothy Parker used to. Maybe you can do that for me? Make me sound witty and not so fucking dumb every time I open my mouth?"

"You're not at all dumb. You make me laugh."

"I may have to marry you," she said.

"It's a pity nobody believes in simple lust anymore," I repeated her line, but she didn't seem to recognize it. She didn't seem to find it funny, anyway.

"How's your head?" I asked. We had been talking for about an hour.

"I've taken a tablet."

I heard her yawn. "You should try to get back to sleep," I said.

"I will. A drink might help. But I can't be bothered to get out of bed."

"You shouldn't drink, not if you've taken a tablet," I said.

"Okay," she said.

"Promise?"

"Yeah. Good night, hon," she said quietly and put down the receiver.

I made a few more notes, and went to bed. The next morning I typed up the notes of our conversation and went back to her story.

It's a shame that it didn't work out with Mick. The idea of being married had always appealed to me, and I was hopelessly in love with him by this time. We lived in a tiny apartment on Wilshire and Palm Drive in Westwood that we'd rented from Red Skelton. One bedroom, living room, kitchen, and a tiny dining room. (There's a big high-rise there now.) We were out all the time, all the time. Oh God, Mickey and I were out practically every night of our lives together. We danced, he drank a fair amount—I was catching on pretty fast. But Mick was working every day, too. He was carrying the weight of the studio on his shoulders. I don't know how he did it. We had a damn good goosefeather mattress, I suppose that helped the boy!

I wasn't working. I wasn't doing a fucking thing. I had no talent, I had no training. I went to classes—dance classes, which I loved. But the drama classes were a joke. I spent a lot of time doing photographs—which are rolling in all the time now—leg art. They'd say, "Who's got good legs and nice tits and isn't filming? Okay, Ava, you'll do; report to the stills gallery." I was always available for pinups. I was nineteen. It wasn't such a bad life, if you didn't have ambition. I slipped into it real easy.

For a couple of months anyway I had no doubt that Mick was going to be my mate for eternity. We were seen everywhere together, Hollywood's most devoted couple. Well, that's what I believed, anyway. We were madly in love. Well, we were screwing a lot.

A week or so after we got back from our honeymoon, I woke up in the middle of the night with the most godawful pain in my stomach. I was in agony. Mickey drove me to the Presbyterian Hospital. Like everybody in my family, I had a misplaced appendix, and they diagnosed a tubal pregnancy. Thank God, they had a wonderful surgeon there who realized, when they started to cut, that it wasn't a tubal pregnancy at all but an inflamed appendix.

In those days you stayed in the hospital for three weeks after even a minor operation; now they have you up and walking the next day. So I came home and the first night I found evidence that Mick had been screwing somebody in our bed. On the fucking goosefeather mattress! That ain't a very nice thing for a nineteen-year-old bride, quite pretty, too, to discover. I'd been away for three weeks and he'd already dragged somebody into our bed. I don't know who the hell it was but I knew somebody had been keeping my side of the bed warm.

I remember it had something to do with a douche bag—somebody had been using my douche bag. I had what they called a tipped infantile uterus and I always used a vinegar douche. Except one time with Mickey I experimented with a rubber. I didn't like it one little bit. No, no, no. But I never got pregnant, not until I was married to Frank anyway.

Anyway, I knew that someone had been using my stuff. I called Bappie. She said, don't you dare touch it! Get the little bastard to clean up his own fucking mess. He denied it, of course. He played the little innocent. Nobody could pile on the applesauce like Mickey. He was the best liar in the world—well, Frank Sinatra can tell a good story, too. He sawed off a few whoppers in his day, but I don't believe he was ever unfaithful to me. I'm leveling. I really believe that.

Anyway, Mickey tried to make up for that rotten douche bag business. In his fashion he did. He bought us a small house in Bel Air, which I helped to choose and decorate. It was my first taste of real film-star living. Metro renewed my contract, and gave me a small raise. I was getting small, walk-on parts but nothing to write home about. The first line I ever said on screen—I played a carhop girl in a drive-in—was "What will you have?" I did a lot of things like that. I played a hat-check girl, I did a lot of club scenes, I danced with a man in a ballroom scene. I've forgotten the name of that first film, except that it was also Fred Zinnemann's first [American feature-length] movie. He became one of the great Hollywood directors; he put Frank Sinatra right with *From Here to Eternity*. Frank wouldn't mess around with Zinnemann.

Mick also bought me the most beautiful diamond ring, a real iceberg—and asked for it back the following week to pay off his bookies. Talk about feast and famine, honey . . . although not many people knew about the famine side of that marriage. In true Hollywood style, they only saw the feast.

Actually, I didn't mind the ring going back, well not too much, anyway—diamonds are an acquired taste and at nineteen I still hadn't acquired it. Anyway, diamonds look tacky on a woman before she's forty. But Mick promised he'd get me another one, twice as big. A diamond as big as the Ritz, he promised. He never did, but he always believed that he had a sure thing for tomorrow at Santa Anita, or a dead cert at the Del Mar track the day after. I'd like to say that sort of thing was a rare occurrence, but it wasn't. His relationship with his bookies was built on eternal optimism. That's why he's so broke now, the poor darling. All those wives took him for a bundle but no more than the bookies did. He had a kind of cartoon resilience.

But once I knew he was still fooling around, even though he continued to deny it, I should have checked out right there. Even though I knew the girls he was screwing didn't mean a thing to him, that's what I should have done. He was just a lecherous sod who loved getting his rocks off. Everybody was fucking everybody in those days. Maybe it was the war! Lana Turner, who had become a good friend of mine, knew how distraught I was. She said a fuck meant nothing to men like Mickey. I should just brush it aside, she said.

I couldn't do that, I told her.

"Well, if you're not going to leave him, you must do something to let the little bastard know how you feel," Lana said.

That night we had dinner at Chasen's. Afterward, Mickey insisted on buying drinks for the whole bar. I knew that once he bought for the bar, he'd have to stay around until the bar bought drinks for him. It was a machismo thing. I left him to it and took a cab home.

When he came in at God knows what hour, I was fast asleep, or pretending to be—having ripped up every sofa and overstuffed armchair, every cushion and all the drapes in the house. It was overkill but I knew the marriage wasn't going to last anyway. We were playing injury time with benefits—for both of us! We both liked screwing too much to give that up cold turkey. That's what complicated it, I suppose.

But I must say, it's a lonely business fucking someone you no longer love. Especially a husband.

• • •

I stopped typing. And read that line again:

It's a lonely business fucking someone you no longer love. Especially a husband.

Tough, funny, vulgar, cynical, it was a classic Ava Gardner line.

It rolled off the tongue. I didn't want to lose it.

The problem was I couldn't reconcile it with something she had told me earlier—that she was "even more in love with all three of my husbands the day I left them than the day we married."

I knew that sometimes she lied to me, of course. She was an actress and that's what actresses do. Sometimes they say things for effect, sometimes to avoid a situation they don't want to talk about, or simply because they've forgotten what they told you the first time around.

I was still trying to figure out which quote to go with—it made no difference to me; if there was a contradiction, I always used the quote that was most interesting—when I remembered another thing she'd said:

"It's my fucking life. I'll remember it the way I want to remember it."

It still made me laugh.

16

It had been a couple of days since Ava's irrational outburst when I dropped off a copy of the new Winston Churchill biography at her apartment. She had been expecting me to deliver an already overdue draft chapter of her own book. I saw the look of disappointment in her face when I handed her the Churchill volume instead. She thanked me with a rather distant smile. "How much longer is my fucking book going to be, baby?" she said. I asked her to be patient for a few more days. But her remark still rankled.

I knew that the delay was as much my fault as hers. I had let her get away with murder as an interviewee. She never stuck to an idea or story line. She talked in vignettes, snapshots, and digressive asides. She interrupted herself to tell dirty jokes. She was all over the place; she had no regard for continuity at all. Sometimes it was deliberate evasion. Sometimes she was plainly bored: "Jesus, Pete, I had no idea how fucking tiring this remembering back game was going to be!" And there were matters about which she was just naturally close-lipped.

It was fascinating stuff, as well as frustrating, but it was fun. And it all took time.

Shortly before I left for a lunch with Ed Victor, I wrote a note to her accepting the blame for the delay. It wasn't entirely accurate or wholly truthful, but it would pass as an apology, and maybe she would see the need to increase the pace rather than just bitch about it.

Dear Ava,

I understand your frustration and disappointment at our progress on the book. You are right to be angry and I am wrong not to have explained the reason for the delay before. Since your material is so rich and wonderful, and we want to secure a deal as quickly as possible, a couple of weeks ago I decided to try to eliminate the first draft and go straight for the jugular! Unfortunately this approach, which I thought would speed things up, has not only slowed me down, but also failed to convey the sense of immediacy, the spontaneity and bite of our late-night conversations, when you are at your best. I shall now return to our original routine of letting you see a chapter for your thoughts before I begin a final polish. I hope this will put us back on track—as well as taking us closer to the book we both want.

Hope you had a better night.

Much love,
Peter

PS: I'm enclosing the draft of the chapter continuing the breakup of your marriage to Mickey. I hope you agree it really moves the story forward apace. I look forward to your comments. PE.

• • •

Despite the stress our marriage was under, Mick and I continued to go out practically every night. If we decided to have an evening at home, the house became mysteriously filled with strangers—his press people and yes-men, the hangers-on, in fact, Mickey's usual entourage. I saw through those people. I saw through Hollywood. A naive, little country girl that I was, I saw through the phoniness, and all the crap.

No wonder, when I think of that marriage now, I think of nightclubs: the Palladium, Ciro's; the Cocoanut Grove, where we danced to Tommy Dorsey's band. My God, those names bring back memories. The Cocoanut Grove was my favorite club, even though Mick often abandoned me while he sat in on drums with the Dorsey band. The music was great, and Mickey was a terrific drummer, but left alone at the table for hours on end I felt like a B girl, as we called the hookers who worked the bars in those days.

Guys didn't trouble me much, most of them knew I was Mickey's wife, but that's where I learned to drink, I mean to drink seriously—not just the Beachcomber's zombies, although they were damn lethal, too, but real grown-up girls' drinks. All the clubs were hot on underage drinking but Mick would slip me dry martinis in coffee cups. The furtiveness of it gave the whole thing a kind of Prohibition glamour. I loved it. Sipping a dry martini out of a coffee cup seemed as glamorous as hell to me. It made me feel sophisticated but I was just another starlet, a kid seeking approval.

That doesn't mean I let Mick off the hook. I brought up his cheating all the time. I couldn't help myself. We fought constantly. "I've had it with you, you little shit," I'd scream at him. He'd look all hurt and innocent—a real Andy Hardy look. Boy, he was some actor. He'd say that no one could love me more than he did. No one could be more faithful than he was. How could I ever doubt him? My allegations were ridiculous, he insisted. Not once did he admit to two-timing me. Neither did he ever say he was sorry.

I might still have settled for an apology and a promise not to cheat on me again. Even an empty promise would have been better than his lies. I wasn't stupid and I resented him treating me as if I was. His lies were a kind of sadism toward me, as if I didn't matter.

Nevertheless, when he was feeling flush, or had made a big score at the track, he would try to placate me with nice pieces of jewelry. I remember a beautiful pair of diamond drop earrings. But quite a few of those peace offerings had to go back when the bookies came knocking, and those that stuck didn't stay around for long either. Jesus, I was careless with my good pieces in those days.

Anyway, in spite of the humiliation of knowing Mickey was cheating on me, I still wanted him to want me. I wanted him to want me all the time. I was just pissed off with his screwing around. In the end, I started throwing in a few curves of my own.

For instance, after we'd made love—and we never stopped doing that, we never got bored with each other in bed, that's for sure—I'd say things to him that I knew would hurt him. I'd taunt him about his height. I'd tell him I was tired of living with a midget. I'd say I'd kill him if he knocked me up. That was cruel, I know, but I couldn't help myself.

I know that it hurt him because he told other people what I'd said. He told Peter Lawford, for instance, who repeated it to me. It was always a mistake to tell Peter Lawford anything. I liked him but he was a terrible gossip. He said that Mick was in tears when he told him how I ridiculed him about his height.

I didn't care. I was pleased I'd hurt him. His unfaithfulness was tearing me apart. I had visions of him having sex with other women. I'd go into towering rages trying to figure out who they were. I'd go through all his leading ladies: Gloria DeHaven, Ann Rutherford, Judy [Garland], of course Lana [Turner]. I was pretty certain he'd had Lana. I was out of my mind with jealousy. Wasn't I beautiful enough for him? Wasn't I sexy enough? What were the others doing that I wasn't doing—or was doing wrong? I was nineteen! I was always willing to learn, for God's sake.

He told Peter Lawford how demanding I was in the feathers. How I would say to him, "Let's fuck, Mick! *Now!*" I don't know whether I ever said that. I'm not denying I said it. The gist of it was true. I was insatiable at that age. I just didn't like the idea of him bragging to his mates—to another *actor,* fahcrissake—about what went on in our bedroom.

Lawford was a new contract player at the studio, a good-looking English kid, about my age. He was as ambitious as hell. He looked like a guy who did hand stands on the beach, which wasn't my type at all. He worshiped Mickey. He'd made two movies with him, *A Yank at Eton* and *Lord Jeff,* and was always hanging around. He often sat with me at the Grove, keeping me amused, when Mick was sitting in with the Dorsey band. He was there the night I finally made up my mind to leave Mick.

Mickey had been drinking throughout the evening and was as high as I'd seen him. I don't remember how many of us were there. The usual crowd, six or eight of us, I guess. Peter Lawford; Sid Miller, the songwriter—he and Mickey were close. A whole bunch of his regular sidekicks were there. Mick was showing off, the center of attention as usual. I was just sitting there looking beautiful as usual. We'd had a big argument over something before we came out, and he was completely ignoring me.

I knew that he'd been spoiling for a fight all evening. Finally, he took out this little book full of girls' numbers. Too drunk to give a damn, and the guys egging him on, he started reading off their names and saying what they were good at in bed—*in front of me*!

That was it! I left. I tried to make a dignified exit. I don't know how many coffee cups of martinis I'd had but I couldn't have been too steady on my feet. Fortunately, Peter Lawford was keeping an eye on me. He followed me out. He told me later he was terrified that I was going to fall ass over tip down the staircase that led to the Ambassador lobby. He said he thought I was going to break my neck.

Peter took me home that night and I poured out my heart to him. "I know that something's going on," I said, "and I know it's been going on for some time. I don't think it's ever stopped. I'm leaving him, Peter. When he sobers up tell him goodbye for me."

I didn't know it then but there was a lot of Iago in Peter. If there was any lingering doubt in my mind about that marriage, Peter ended it right there. He told me, "There is a girl Mick's seeing. She's about fifteen. Mickey has to be careful. Her older sister is her go-between. She fixes meetings for him at the Lakeside Golf Course. It's been going on for quite a while."

I kicked Mickey out the same night. Or I did when he got home, whatever time that was! He moved out to his Ma's place in the Valley. I wouldn't take his calls. I was driving him crazy. One night he tried to kick my door down. When Louis Mayer heard about that, all hell broke loose. Eddie Mannix was ordered to patch things up between us.

Everybody was scared of Mannix. I wouldn't have liked to cross him, but he always treated me with respect. He promised to try to get me some decent parts if I promised to behave. The usual route for an MGM contract player on the way up was to put her in an Andy Hardy movie: Donna Reed, Esther Williams, Lana Turner, Kathryn Grayson, they all followed that road. Not me. Uncle L.B. wouldn't hear of it. Not even Mickey could persuade him to give me a break. I knew I was being punished.

Anyway, Eddie Mannix got me a role in *Ghosts on the Loose*, a Bela Lugosi picture with the Dead End Kids. It was a cheap loan-out to Monogram, an awful little Poverty Row studio—I think the whole picture took about ten days to shoot, and no retakes, *ever*! But I got my first billing on that picture, so it's still kind of special to me.

Eventually I allowed Mick back in the house. Well, on and off I did. After all, we were still married and the sex was legal—and still pretty good, thank God. There was no point in giving that up just because we were semidetached, I told Bappie.

"You're learning, kid," she said.

I loved Bappie's attitude to life. I learned a lot from her. She was a good drinker, too. Although she was never a morning drinker, like me—she said it spoiled her afternoon drinking! She lived in New York during Prohibition. She had a little flirt with R. J. Reynolds, the Winston cigarette heir. They went to all the high-class speakeasies. She was a happy drunk, too. She wasn't compelled to get into mischief the way I was when I had a load on.

When I told her I was going to divorce Mickey, she was dead against it. She was also very practical. "Put some money in your purse first, honey," she said.

It was good advice and of course I didn't take it.

I knew that dumping Mickey was a risk. Career-wise, it could have been the end of me. Pretty starlets were ten a penny at Metro, and anywhere else in Hollywood. The turnover was frightening. If I stopped being Mrs. Rooney, they wouldn't think twice about letting me go. But I really had no choice. Mickey was never going to change his ways. He was always going to be fooling around with some pretty new thing, and that wasn't my idea of marriage.

Right up to the courtroom door, Bappie was pleading with me not to do it. I was filing for a formal separation, which was the first step to "splitting up the act," as Mickey called it. That was on January 15, 1943—exactly one year and five days after we were hitched in Ballard. But it seemed a lot longer than that. It seemed like a fucking lifetime.

Mickey wasn't happy—and neither was Louis Mayer, who set his attack dog Eddie Mannix onto me. Eddie liked me but I knew he had a job to do. He said, "You know, Ava, you'll be finished at this studio if you try to take Mickey to the cleaners. Mr. Mayer owns this town. If you do anything to hurt Mickey's career, you'll never work in Hollywood again."

I said I knew that.

Eddie was sympathetic. He said, "It was never going to work out with Mick, you know. He is never going to be a one-woman man, kid."

I felt my temper rising. "Why the fuck didn't you tell me that before?" I said.

"You didn't ask," he said mildly, but he was obviously startled by my language. So was I. Most people were afraid to say boo to him. "You got a mouth on you, kid. I give you that," he said, and started to laugh.

I was lucky he didn't fire me on the spot.

When he stopped laughing, he said: "Now listen to me, young lady. I'm going to give you some good advice. Mr. Mayer isn't going to mind you telling it to the judge. He just doesn't want you telling him more than you have to."

I didn't understand what he was talking about. I truly didn't. I was barely twenty years old. I could look smart and sophisticated as hell in those gallery pictures they took of me all the time. The truth was, I didn't know beans when the bag was open.

He obviously saw my confusion.

"Mr. Mayer doesn't want you to sue for adultery, kid," Eddie spelled it out for me. He handled me like a baby. "Mr. Mayer doesn't want Mickey's name dragged through the courts along with a bunch of dames you reckon he might have shafted. He doesn't want some shyster lawyer claiming Mickey beat you up, or did this, that, and the other," he said.

The penny dropped. "I'm not going to name anybody," I said. "I'll sue the little sod for incompatibility."

Actually, it was an idea I'd been discussing with Bappie, who'd been having her own marital problems with Larry Tarr. He was just as unfaithful as Mickey. Actually, so was Bappie, to be honest! But apart from that, they got on well together. Anyway, sue for incompatibility, Bappie said, that way nobody gets hurt.

"Incompatibility, you'd settle for that? Mr. Mayer would really appreciate that," Eddie said. "I think the least said the soonest mended, don't you?"

It was such a childish thing to say, the kind of rubbish you say to kids, I wanted to laugh. But the way he said it was so chilling, I thought better of it.

"Incompatibility then? That's what you'll go for? Can I give Mr. Mayer your word on that?" he said.

"Sure," I said casually, but I really meant it. I knew that if I had sued Mick for adultery, and named some of the girls he'd been fucking, it would have blown his wholesome Andy Hardy image right out of the water. It could have destroyed his career stone dead. I truly didn't want to hurt him. I knew that citing "incompatibility" was the cleanest and fastest route out of the marriage.

Eddie said, "You're not as dumb as you look, kid."

He asked me what I was going to do after the divorce. The question surprised me. I knew the final decree would take at least six months or maybe even longer to come through and I hadn't planned that far ahead.

I said, "If the studio renews my contract, I'd like to try to make a go of acting."

"I think you should," he said.

A couple of weeks later, the studio renewed my contract and increased my salary.

It put my mind at rest.

I put the copy and my note into an envelope and biked it over to Ennismore Gardens. Then I went to the Caprice for lunch with Ed Victor.

17

We spoke at least once a week on the telephone, but I hadn't seen Ed Victor since we met with Snyder at Ava's apartment a couple of months earlier. The Caprice, on Arlington Street, a hundred yards down from the Ritz, was one of Ed's favorite London restaurants. A territorial man, he was already there when I arrived, seated at his regular table with a discreet view of the whole room. I suspected that he liked the restaurant because not only was the food good, and he knew many of its famous clients by their first names, but it also possessed an atmosphere of wealth and privilege in which it was possible to talk megabuck deals at one's ease.

He was in no hurry to ask about Ava. We chatted amiably for twenty minutes; we had many mutual friends, and there was no shortage of amusing gossip and trade talk to exchange. We eventually studied the menu. We both ordered fish with a chilled Pouilly-Fuissé.

"How is Ava behaving?" he finally asked.

"Good days and bad days," I told him.

"How good are the good days?" he said.

"Good enough to make me stop worrying about the bad days," I said.

"And *Theodora*?" he asked. "How is that coming along?"

"It's not. I've decided to put it on ice for the time being."

"Is there a problem?"

"Ava's too demanding," I said. His suggestion that I continue to work on *Theodora* during the day and Ava at night had not been very practical, I told him.

"Well, it was worth a try," he said philosophically. But his smile gave the game away: he had never expected me to be able to work on both books at the same time anyway.

"I'll be able to understand Theodora better when I can give her my full attention," I said casually.

"Why is that?" he asked quietly with sudden curiosity in his voice.

"I'm discovering a lot from Ava about movie actresses of a certain age," I said as inconsequentially as I could. The question had surprised me and it was the best I could come up with.

"Such as?" he persisted.

"Oh, you know. Their vanities, and insecurities. The self-protective fibs they all tell. The delusions they have about themselves. Some touches I'd like to give to Theodora," I said. I didn't want to get into a discussion about Ava at that point. I didn't want to tell him her doubts about the book's frankness. I definitely knew it would be a mistake to mention her disquiet at seeing her ribald language repeated so accurately on the page. Her dialogue was one of the book's strengths. I didn't want to put doubts in his mind; I didn't want to spoil his lunch. Anyway, I was convinced that these were problems I could handle, or more likely she'd simply forget all about them, the way she dealt with most of her problems.

"Do you like her?" Ed suddenly asked, watching my face closely.

I said I did, very much. "She's smart. She's funny. She can be difficult, though."

"In what way?"

"She's like Onassis. She doesn't respond to question-and-answer interviews. She's a lady who likes to lead," I said.

He nodded thoughtfully. After a moment, he asked, "Is she going to deliver all that she promised?"

"I'm sure she will, Ed," I said.

"No second thoughts?" he said. He was a perceptive bastard. But that was what made him such a brilliant agent.

"Was it just the Louis Roederer Cristal talking? Is that what you're asking me?" I avoided a straight answer.

"The thought had crossed my mind," he said, and laughed. "Is she still drinking?"

"Of course, but she can handle it. It doesn't seem to have affected her memory. You won't be disappointed," I said with assurance, although a conversation I'd had with Ava a few nights earlier did bother me.

"I STILL DON'T KNOW whether I'm doing the right thing going ahead with this lousy goddamn book, honey," she'd said. Her voice was raspy. It was one of her early hours of the morning conversations. "Frank's not going to be happy when he finds out that I'm writing a fucking book," she said.

They were still close, and I was surprised that she hadn't told him. They talked all the time on the phone, although she hadn't seen him for at least five years. "We live in different worlds, honey. We get along best when we're apart," she said.

"Are you going to tell him about the book?" I knew that it was a stupid question the moment I asked it.

"I'll have to choose my moment. I don't want to do it on the phone. He'll find out sooner or later. I'll have to choose my moment," she said again. "I don't want him to hear about it from someone else."

When they were first married, she said, they had agreed that neither of them would ever write their memoirs.

"That was a long time ago, Ava," I reminded her.

"Nineteen fifty-one," she said. "November 7—a Wednesday," she added with ironical precision.

"The whole fucking world's press was on our necks. Reporters loved making a scandal out of our lives, and Frank's behavior never helped. He hated the press. He loathed reporters with a passion. They were all sonsofbitches. I don't know how they did it but those creeps always knew where to find us, and how to get a rise out of Frank."

Sinatra was obviously on her mind. I got up and went to my study, and started making notes.

"Boy, they were good at that, those hacks," she went on with that curiously fierce and at the same time oddly amused way she had of recalling the bad times with Sinatra. "He hated being called Frankie; they called him Frankie. Except in Mexico. In Mexico, they went one better: they called him Mr. Gardner. You can guess what he thought of that! When he was flying high, he'd been a cocky bastard. That was his nature. It was part of his charm. Now they were killing him for it."

"Reporters have long memories," I said.

"As well as long knives," she said.

"Once, Frank was on a comeback tour in Europe. I was making a movie in England. *Knights of the Round Table*, a piece of medieval malarkey. Robert Taylor was Lancelot; he did all the fighting. I was Guinevere, all I had to do was sit around and look pretty. I was good at that. But I got fed up with it after a while. I flew off to Italy to catch a few of Frank's gigs. I had to have been in love with him to sit through those performances. Let's say he was not at his best. He was playing to half-empty houses. The Italian press felt he was patronizing them.

"One evening they must have paid the guy who worked the spot to turn it on me in the middle of one of Frank's numbers. The audience started chanting: *Ava, Ava, Ava*. It was embarrassing for me and humiliating as hell for Frank. I got up and walked out. So did Frank.

"They quieted down once I'd left. Frank went back on and finished his act, which I thought was brave of him. When he got back to the hotel that evening he blamed me for the disturbance. We had another fight, of course. The next day I flew back to England to face the music for taking the run-out.

"It didn't matter a damn, of course. The studio didn't even know I'd gone. It gave more hokey dueling time for Bob and Mel Ferrer. But I had to be punished for going AWOL, and another year was added to my contract. That way they could keep you under contract for a hundred fucking years if they wanted to."

She paused. "Are you making notes of this, honey?" she said.

"Maybe I should," I said hesitantly. I didn't want her to know I always made notes of her three o'clock in the morning calls, or when she didn't realize she was saying anything useful or indiscreet. I never told her that, of course. I didn't want to inhibit her. "You should keep a diary, Ava," I said.

"I don't have to, honey. I'm talking about my life. Some things you never forget."

After a pause, I said: "Anyway, you were telling me about Frank."

"It was all about Frank in those days. I once won a bet with Bappie that she couldn't find a single picture of Frank in which he wasn't snarling at a photographer. It was a nightmare time. Our affair. The collapse of his marriage to Nancy. His kids begging him to come home. He was going through a terrible time. We both were. It was hell, but it was worse for Frank. Nancy was taking him for practically every penny he had.

"She played hardball, but I couldn't blame her. I've never blamed her. She'd been a good wife. She was the mother of his children. She had every right to fight for him, for their marriage. She'd stuck by Frank through thick and thin. That's something I should say in the book, by the way.

"I stayed right out of it. But she must have hated my guts. She wouldn't withdraw her objections to his Nevada divorce until he paid off his back alimony. He owed about forty thousand dollars. She wanted a further payment when she got a California divorce. She threatened to take over Frank's Palm Springs place unless he paid up. That was about the only asset the poor darling had left.

"As I said, his voice had gone. The bobby-soxers had moved on. His career had nosedived. Mine was on the up, thank Christ. The studio was starting to pay me decent money at last. I got a hundred and forty grand for *Show Boat,* even though the bastards finally dubbed my voice for the musical numbers. It was still less than they got for loaning me out, but I wasn't complaining, and it kept us afloat—in more ways than one! We were both drinking far too much. Jesus, we were really knocking it back, and fighting all the time. Jesus, did we fight—and make up!

"Anyway, that's the time we made this stupid pact never to write our memoirs. 'Those news bums love memoirs,' Frank said. 'You give them a pot to piss in and they'll pour it over your head the first chance they get.'

"Some of the papers offered damned good money for Frank to tell our story. A tabloid, the *New York Daily Mirror* I think it was, or it might have been one of the syndicates, I forget now, but they offered more than he got for *Meet Danny Wilson,* a crappy little movie he'd just made with Shelley Winters. He needed the money badly, but he told them to get lost. He had principles, I'll give him that."

"It's been forty years, Ava. Frank's not going to hold you to it after all this time, is he?" I said.

"He's never written *his* memoirs," she said.

"Maybe he's never had to," I reminded her of her present difficulties.

"You're not listening to me, baby. Frank was flat broke when we tied the knot. The poor darling was on his ass. His voice had gone. His records weren't selling. His movie contract had been dropped. His confidence was shot.

"I don't know where those stories came from that the Mafia was taking care of him. They should have been. But the fucking so-called Family was nowhere to be seen when he needed them. It really ticks me when I read how generous the Mob was when he was on the skids. But I was the one paying the rent when he couldn't get arrested. I was the one making the pot boil, baby. It was *me*!"

It was wonderful copy. I was sorry when she said she was tired and put the phone down. I think she was crying.

ED WAITED UNTIL THE end of our lunch and had signaled for the check before he told me his news.

"Have you read Kitty Kelley's biography of Frank Sinatra?"

"Not yet," I told him.

"You must read it. It's full of interesting stuff about Ava."

"I will," I promised.

After a long silence, he said: "You don't know the story Ava tells about the size of Frank's penis?"

"No," I said.

"He's very blessed."

"I must read it."

"You must. I'm astonished you haven't read it. It's an Ava classic. She's very graphic."

"I'll read it tonight," I said.

"Dick Snyder says he wants you to ask her about it."

"Dick wants me to ask Ava about the size of Frank Sinatra's cock?" I repeated dully.

"He's very keen that we use it in the book."

"How the hell can I put a question like that to her, Ed?"

"You'll think of something," he said. "You're the writer."

18

There were five messages on my answerphone when I got home. Three of them were from Ava. The first one said, "Got the new chapter. Let's talk, honey. Call me." The second one, timed one hour later, said, "Where the hell are you? Call me, fahcrissake." The final message, at 5:15 P.M., sounded more conciliatory: "It's Ava. Call me when you get in, please. I don't understand your note. Jesus Christ, when have I bawled you out about *anything*, honey?"

"How much longer is this fucking book going to take, baby?" did cross my mind, but I let it go. I was still worried about Dick Snyder's request that I ask her to repeat the story about the size of Frank Sinatra's cock. Without appearing puerile or overly inquisitive, there seemed to be no polite way of bringing up the subject. It was a three-pipe problem all right.

Ava was still irate when she called again just before six. "I've been trying to get you all afternoon," she said crossly. "Where the hell have you been, baby?"

"I had lunch with Ed. He says hi."

"It was a goddamn long lunch. I'm surprised you can find the time."

It was clearly not the moment to ask her about the size of Frank Sinatra's dick. It still seemed to me bad form to ask anytime. "Have you read the copy I sent you?" I said pleasantly. I didn't want to get into an argument about how long I took for lunch, but I saw the funny side of her irritation. Anyway, she changed the subject.

"Do I really swear that much?" This was the third time she had questioned me about the accuracy of the dialogue I wrote for her. She seemed genuinely puzzled. "I don't swear that much, do I?"

"I'm afraid you do, Ava."

"Maybe I swear a little when I'm angry," she said. I knew she couldn't really believe that, and her solemn tone made me laugh.

"Why are you laughing?" she asked.

"Ava, I've quoted you verbatim."

"You make me sound like a goddamn tramp," she said petulantly.

"Last time you said I made you sound like a fishwife," I said, and laughed to let her know I wanted to keep it friendly.

There was a puzzled silence in which I knew she was making up her mind whether to be angry or amused. "We've had this conversation before, haven't we?" she finally said with a laugh I had not expected. It was her husky, smoker's laugh. It was disarming and sexy.

"Once or twice," I said.

"Well, it won't do, honey. It won't do at all. I want you to clean up the obscenities for the book. We don't need that shit at all."

"I think it would be a mistake, Ava," I said.

"Why do you think that?" she asked sharply.

It was the kind of question Peter Viertel had warned me about. When they were making *The Sun Also Rises,* in which she played Hemingway's Lady Brett Ashley, he told me: "I'd show her the script, she'd ask something innocuous like, 'Would Lady Brett say that line?' or 'Does Lady Brett need to say anything here? Jake [Barnes, the narrator and hero of *The Sun Also Rises,* played by

Tyrone Power] will understand from her *look* what she's thinking. There will be no need to spell it out.'

"And suddenly she's embroiled you in an almighty argument about the script, or about the book you're trying to write for her. You can't reason with her because she never approaches anything intellectually. She is the most intuitive woman I know. About roles, about men, about anything—her decisions are made totally without any reasoning at all."

She gets away with it, he'd said, because she expects men to fall in love with her. And usually they do, he'd added.

"It makes us awfully vulnerable to her whims. She turns men around like no other woman I know. The problem is, she prefers strong lovers—but wants her writers and directors to be weak as piss. That's a pity because she is so much better with men who stand up to her. Guys like John Huston. He doesn't put up with her nonsense—and neither should you, by the way!"

Viertel stopped and looked at me solemnly for a long moment, as if deciding whether I was up to the task of taking her on. "Anyway, that's the way to play the game, but it's easier said than done," he'd said, and burst into laughter. "Don't let it worry you, not many of us can handle Ava. Not when she turns those green eyes on us."

I could feel her green eyes on me now. Nevertheless, I was determined to make my point. "Ava, I really don't think we should mess with your dialogue. I love it the way it is. It would be a mistake to try to gentrify it."

"Well, I think it's fucking vulgar, I won't have it, honey," she said again.

"It's uninhibited, but that's you, Ava," I tried again.

"It's crass, honey. All those fucking cuss words are undignified."

"Without a few cuss words, it just wouldn't be the same. It wouldn't sound like you, Ava," I said.

"An occasional cuss word might be fine, honey. But this stuff is full of fucking cuss words. Anyway, I hate foul-mouthed women."

I managed not to laugh. There was a long silence on the line.

"Am I still going to see you this evening?" she eventually said, abandoning the argument, convinced she'd had the last word.

"I hope so. That was the plan, wasn't it?" I said tentatively.

"We have to get on with it. We've wasted enough fucking time on this book. Say hi to Ed for me, by the way. I like him," she said and put down the receiver.

I ARRIVED AT HER apartment at 7:30. The wine had already been opened and left to breathe on the coffee table beside a couple of glasses. It was a bottle of Berry Brothers' Good Ordinary Claret, the wine I had introduced her to a few weeks earlier. I saw it as a peace offering. "Where do you want to begin, baby?" she said, all business. "We've really got to move our asses. We've got to finish this goddamn book. Where did we get to? Where shall we start?"

"Why not pick it up with you waiting for your decree absolute from Mickey," I told her. I switched on the Sony VORs, a tape for her, one for me.

"Do you have to use those bloody things? They inhibit me. I start thinking twice about everything I say. Can't you just take notes? If I say anything interesting you can just jot it down, can't you?"

Perhaps it was a kind of reprisal for not being at her beck and call that afternoon, or for not wanting to clean up her language. But I was not bothered. "I'm okay taking notes," I said easily. "In some ways I prefer it."

"*Really?*" She sounded surprised. She had no idea that I made notes of nearly all our telephone conversations. "But isn't a tape easier for you?" she said. I didn't know whether she was being awkward or unduly solicitous of my time.

I said, "Transcribing a tape takes twice the work, but it does have its advantages."

"What advantages are they?" she said.

"Well, for starters, next time you question the number of swear words you use, I'll just play you the tape and we can count them," I said.

She smiled sweetly. I think she was genuinely amused. "Okay, I'm waiting for my decree absolute," she said as she filled my glass thoughtfully, "but still screwing the ass off Mickey—"

"I didn't write that," I said.

"And you're not going to use it either," she said.

"That's a shame," I said. "I thought that is what you said."

"I said I was sex mad—at least with Mickey I was." The idea seemed to amuse her.

"So it's a matter of semantics: I can't say you were screwing the ass off Mickey but I can say you were sex mad?" I said seriously, pretending to make a note of the distinction.

"Mick was still the only man I knew in a biblical sense," she said, ignoring my feeble joke. "I never cheated on any of my husbands. Until I got that legal piece of paper in my hand, I wanted to remain faithful to Mickey. What bloody sentimental things kids are."

"Well, I think it would be a shame to lose it. It's a titillating fact, but it's your call."

"What's a titillating fact, honey?"

"That you and Mickey continued sleeping together while waiting for your divorce to come through. But it's your call," I said again to show how reasonable I was being.

"That's right," she said flatly. "It is my call."

"But you did say you wanted an honest book. To admit you continued sleeping with Mickey . . . that's honest, isn't it? I would love to use it, of course I would," I said again. "I think it's important, but no matter."

"Why is it important?"

"Well, maybe not important per se, but it's a lovely insight," I said.

"How is it an insight? Insight into what, fahcrissake?"

"It tells us a lot about you at that age."

"Don't be so fucking obscure, Peter. What the fuck does it tell us?" she said, no longer hiding her impatience.

"That you and Mick were still good friends, still close, in spite of the divorce," I said, but I knew that was pussyfooting around the point I really wanted to make. "It tells us that you were a young woman who liked sex *a lot*," I added bluntly.

She was never careful about hiding her disapproval when I said anything she considered to be out of line and I didn't know how she would react to my bluntness. I was surprised when she said mildly: "You could say that, honey."

"So it's all right to say that you and Mickey continued to make love while you were waiting for your divorce to come through? You wouldn't mind if we said that?" I was pushing my luck. "It was a long time ago, nobody's going to complain. It's not a hanging offense, for God's sake."

She thought about it for a moment without smiling. "We'll see, honey. Let me think about it," she said, and changed the subject. "Anyway, I was determined to keep my nose clean, when Howard Hughes arrived on the scene."

"I thought Artie Shaw came next?" I said. The more I could keep her on some kind of track the easier it would be for me.

"Artie was my next husband. Howard Hughes was the next man in my life. He was the first thing to come around after Mick. He came around about five minutes after I filed for divorce, as a matter of fact."

"Did you know him?" I said.

"I knew *of* him, of course. He was one of the most famous men in America. But I'd never met him."

"He called you out of the blue?"

"Yes and no," she said.

"What does that mean, Ava?" Pinning her down could often be a struggle.

"Nothing was ever an accident with Howard," she said. "He had people meeting every plane, train, and bus that arrived in Los Angeles with a pretty girl on board. He had to be the first to grab the new girl in town. It was a matter of pride for him. When he read the story of my divorce in the papers—it was all over the papers, on the radio; Mickey's name made it headlines, not mine—Howard decided I was the new girl on the loose."

"Okay."

"On the phone I thought he'd said his name was 'Howard Hawks.' That was another thing about Howard Hughes: he *mumbled* a lot. But Howard Hawks was famous, too. He was one of the most important directors in Hollywood. He had directed one of my favorite movies, *Bringing Up Baby*. It was a wacky screwball comedy with Kate Hepburn and Cary Grant. I thought he must have me in mind for a new picture.

"I was thrilled. Mannix had renewed my contract for another year, and given me a small pay raise to encourage me, but there was no such thing as security at MGM. At least if you were me there wasn't! Louis Mayer could still drop me in a heartbeat for going ahead with the divorce. Nobody thought I would. Not even Bappie. Anyway, Howard Hawks's invitation was wonderful. Who needed Mickey Rooney when you had Howard Hawks knocking on your door?

"Anyway, the night he was supposed to take me out, Johnny Meyer turned up instead. I opened the door and this fat, bald guy was standing there, grinning from ear to ear. He said, 'Miss Gardner, Howard has been called away on urgent business. Like Miss Otis, he sends his regrets—and asks will I do?' Well, I just burst out laughing. It was such a funny line."

Johnny Meyer was her first date since she split with Mickey. "The photographers were all over us like a rash. They all wanted to get a picture of the new guy in my life. It was just fun in those days. The snappers *wanted* you to look pretty. Today they can't wait to get you with a finger in your nose, up your ass. They've hit the jackpot if they get you looking looped. In the old days, if they got a bad photo of you coming out of a nightclub they'd tear it up. Hymie Fink was a little Jewish guy who had the biggest nose I've ever seen in my whole life. He had little squinty eyes and big thick glasses; it was a face you could never forget—but he was a dear. I loved him. He did all the nightclub pictures and would burn the negatives rather than use a bad one. That's why the magazines were filled with beautiful, glamorous women in those days.

"Oh, another thing about Johnny Meyer, he had nice hands. He polished his fingernails with a pale varnish. Not many guys did that in those days. Today, people would think he was my 'walker.' But he wasn't a fag. He wasn't a bit faggoty. In fact, I think he had quite a few wives in his time.

"Anyway, he took me to dinner at Chasen's. Johnny took me to plenty of dinners after that, as a matter of fact; Howard got called away a lot on business! At least that was his excuse, and Johnny was his regular stand-in. I didn't mind, Johnny was always fun. That first night, he let me do twenty minutes on how thrilled I was to be asked out by Howard Hawks before he told me I had the wrong Howard.

"My date was Howard *Hughes,* not Hawks, he said. They both made movies but Hughes also owned TWA, the airline. That seemed to mean a lot more to Johnny than it did to me at the time.

He said Howard was loaded, and also as deaf as a post, only he didn't want people to know that. If Howard grinned at me like an idiot, I'd know he hadn't heard a word I'd said. Best advice about Howard anybody ever gave me," she said.

"Johnny wasn't the handsomest man in town, he was no Clark Gable, but he wore nice suits, he always smelled good. The opposite of his boss. Howard Hughes never cared much about what he wore, or what he looked like. Maybe on our first dates he did—or sometimes when he had to be presentable he would make an effort—but he went downhill pretty fast after that. He was never really aware of his personal hygiene even then, and I'm told it got worse. He definitely got crazier, that's for sure."

That evening, Johnny plied her with flattery and questions about her life: where was she born, what did her parents do? Questions about her brothers and sisters, and what she wanted out of life. "I liked being the center of attention. I was flattered. I didn't feel he was coming on to me. I didn't know he was just checking me out for Howard. Checking out girls for Howard Hughes was one of Johnny's regular chores.

"Anyway, I must have passed the test because next day Howard Hughes called and apologized for standing me up. He was very charming. He must have been because I invited him around for a drink—I had a little place on Franklin Avenue. That was where I still occasionally entertained Mickey after we split.

"With hindsight, I should never have gotten involved with Howard. He could be damn nice but he was seventeen years older than I was. He was a low-key guy sexually. He was a real slow-burner romantically. Well, after Mick he was. Mick and I were still kids. You have to remember, I was eighteen when I met Mick, nineteen when I married him, and twenty when we split. With us, everything was fun and games—and fast. It was always Party Time.

"Howard could sometimes be heavy-going, except when he

talked about planes. His passion was flying—he was always trying to break some airspeed record or other—and women, of course. He was passionate about them. He always liked to have a few on the go at the same time. He had them stashed all over town. Lana Turner told me he was once engaged to her and Linda Darnell at the same time. She thought it was hilarious, but I couldn't have put up with that shit.

"He was filthy rich, of course. He inherited a fortune from his Daddy. Daddy owned the Hughes Tool Company in Houston. When Daddy died, Howard got the lot, the whole kit and caboodle. I think he was twenty, twenty-one when his father passed. 'That's when I realized that women found me attractive,' he once said to me. I still haven't figured out whether he was that naive about women! I don't think he was being funny.

"Anyway, he always had plenty of women to console him. Lana, she did a good job for a while; she really expected to marry him. Ida Lupino, Ginger Rogers. Jean Peters—he married her. Kate Hepburn. Linda Darnell. Oh my God, he had so many women. Jean Harlow, Jane Russell. They were all beauties, too. Kate Hepburn wasn't a great beauty but I'm told she could turn guys on. Kate's what now? She must be at least eighty?"

"About that," I said. "Apart from Howard's wealth, was he attractive?" I didn't want to be sidetracked.

She thought about that for a while before answering.

"He was a skinny guy, not bad-looking, tall, well over six feet, maybe six-foot-four. He reminded me a lot of Daddy," she said slowly. "He had a kind of remoteness about him like Daddy had, and that's always attractive in a man. He was partially deaf, of course. That may have accounted for the longueurs in his conversation, and probably explained his shyness, too. Anyway, he never talked much. He was no raconteur; I called him the Quiet Texan.

"I'm talking about a time before he became that crazy basket case holed up in a Las Vegas hotel surrounded by fucking Mormons, and as mad as a hatter. I never knew *that* Howard Hughes, thank Christ. *That* Howard made me sad. I'm pleased I never met him.

"When I first knew him, he'd made *Hell's Angels*, a helluva picture about pilots in World War I. It was the blockbuster of its day. I bet it still stands up. He was a pilot himself; he had an obsession with flying; he was what they'd now call an 'action hero.' He was badly injured showing the stuntmen on *Hell's Angels* how it should be done. I think quite a few pilots died on that picture, too. He was a demanding sonofabitch. But he had plenty of guts, you have to give him that.

"A couple of months after we started stepping out together, he was in a serious plane crash in Nevada. I'd flown to Las Vegas with him and some of his people. He was going to pick up an amphibious aircraft he'd designed to put it through its water trials. He dropped me off in Las Vegas and went on to Lake Mead, where the plane crashed, killing a couple of the engineers on board.

"Howard was badly injured. He called me from the hospital to tell me what had happened. 'I want you to know I just killed a couple of my guys,' he said. 'But don't worry, kid, I'm going to be okay.'

"I read that he grew a mustache while recovering from the burns—he said the burns on his face made shaving too painful. That was probably the truth of it, but he told me he grew it because I was a fan of Clark Gable, and Clark had a 'stache! I'm sure that was a load of applesauce, but it did make me laugh, and old Howard didn't do that too often."

She stopped and smiled at me. "What else can I tell you?"

"I don't know? What else can you tell me?" I said. It had been a good session and she was looking tired. I didn't want to push her. I was happy to wrap it up for the night.

"We shared the same birthday: December 24. We were both

Christmas Eve Capricorns," she said. "Apart from that, we didn't have much in common. I was a good dancer, he was bloody awful. I don't know why he always insisted on dancing with me. I dreaded it. In fact, apart from Mick, who wasn't bad but a bit lacking in the height department, none of my husbands was any good on the dance floor. Frank and Artie both had two left feet.

"What else? He was born rich. I wasn't. He was a WASP. I definitely was not. He was a racist. You know *I'm* not. When I told him that my closest childhood friend, Virginia, was black, he didn't call me for about six weeks. I think he was sulking! He could be a sulky bastard. I didn't give a damn. Fuck him! He wouldn't employ blacks in his aircraft plants? Fuck him! Fuck all bigots."

She lifted her glass in a toast to scorning bigots.

"To hell with all bigots," I said, and raised my glass.

"Is any of this stuff usable?" she said, suddenly serious again.

"Of course it is. You mustn't have any doubts. I'll hardly need to touch it." It was not the first time she had questioned the value of her story, or how she was telling it.

"I ramble too much," she said. She checked the wine. It was nearly all gone; she poured a little into her glass, then the rest into mine. "I'm all over the place."

"I can pull it together. That's my job. It's good stuff," I told her again. "I promise you, it's all there."

"The amazing thing is, Howard was in my life, on and off, for more than twenty years but I never loved him. I don't think he ever really loved me, although he was a dogged sonofabitch. He wanted me to marry him so much. He was driving me crazy. I thought, Shit, I'll marry the man and be done with it. I mean it was not a bad move marrying Howard Hughes, the richest man on the planet. I was still waiting for my California divorce from Mickey to come through. That was going to take a year, I reckoned.

"Howard didn't want to wait that long. He wanted me to go to

Nevada to get a divorce. I went up to see Louis Mayer—I was still a good little MGM starlet—and told him I wanted a quickie divorce. It was no skin off his nose. But he was still in his Catholic phase and gave me another stern lecture on marriage being sacrosanct. 'Wait the year, show some respect to Mickey!' he said.

"Anyway, we never did tie the knot. He stayed loyal and generous. He was always keen. But I eventually drifted out of the marriage zone, I guess.

"It's a pity—we might have had such a damned good time together," she said, paraphrasing Lady Brett with a smile.

It was late. She was tired, and I had to go.

"It's time for bed," I said.

"Oh, I wish it were, honey," she said.

19

The size of Frank Sinatra's penis had been on my mind for weeks. I don't know why it was bothering me so much, but it was. It went back to an incident several years earlier in Kenya during the shooting of *Mogambo.* John Ford, the crusty, hard-drinking director with whom Ava had an erratic and feisty but strictly professional relationship, had asked her to explain to a visiting English diplomat what she saw in Sinatra—"that one-hundred-twenty-pound runt you're married to," as Ford referred to her husband.

"Well, there is only ten pounds of Frank," she said, refusing to rise to the bait, "but there's one hundred and ten pounds of cock."

It was one of the many outrageous anecdotes told about Ava, and whether it was true or apocryphal, it was now part of her legend.

Snyder was keen to get her to repeat the story to me, so that we could include it in the book in her own words. I certainly wanted to use it. It was a classic Ava Gardner story, and I happened to believe it was true. Spoli Mills had assured me it was, so had Dirk Bogarde. My problem was that there seemed to be no easy way to bring the subject up without sounding coarse or inappropriately inquisitive.

• • •

It was a Sunday evening and I was about to call Ava to discuss the material we would need for the next chapter when, at eight o'clock, the phone rang.

"Hi, honey."

"Ava, hi," I said, surprised by her call at that hour.

"What are you up to?" she said.

I'm thinking about how I can ask you about the size of Frank Sinatra's cock, would have been the honest answer. But I ducked it.

"I was just about to call you," I said.

"I'm going to try to get an early night, honey," she said. "I'm beat to the chops. I didn't get a wink of sleep last night."

"Go to bed *now*!" I said sternly. "We'll talk tomorrow."

"There was a time when I *never* wanted to go to bed. Not to rest anyway," she said.

I said I believed her and laughed.

"I had stamina in those days. I could dance all night, go straight to the studio at six. After a nap in Hair and Makeup and a glass of champagne, I'd be ready for my close-up at nine, thank you Mr. DeMille. I don't know how I did it. I sure couldn't do it now. The makeup man would say, Oh boy you went to bed early last night, didn't you? I puffed up with sleep; I never puffed up with alcohol. But I was never late, I always knew my lines. I'd learn them on the way in. But I figured that was all I had to offer: to be on time and know the words. Because once I got there, I wasn't much of an actress! But sweet Jesus, I loved those days!"

"They must have been fun," I said, although I had my doubts. "You should sleep well tonight."

"It's got to be better than last night, honey."

"Why didn't you call me?" I said. She sounded low, and I really meant it.

"What good would it have done, honey? I'd have just kept you awake, too. It's bad enough I can't sleep," she said. "Anyway, I need you fit and well and writing."

"Insomnia's not contagious. You should have called me," I said.

"The small hours are a bitch. Thoughts get stuck in your head and go round and round. They haunt you all fucking night."

"What kind of thoughts, Ava? Tell me about your ghosts," I said cheerfully to encourage her.

"God, you're a prying bastard. You sound like a fucking shrink. I know practically nothing about you—and you want to know everything about me."

"That's my job."

"Asking about my ghosts?"

"The things that keep you awake at night," I said.

"I don't know, honey. It's usually shit that goes straight out of my head the next morning. Thank God."

"You can't think of a single thing that keeps you awake at nights? Nothing stays with you, nothing sticks? I can't believe that, Ava," I said.

After a silence, she said: "All kinds of fucking things keep me awake at nights: thoughts about dying, how much it hurts to breathe, thoughts about why I don't have any sexual energy anymore. And this fucking book keeps me awake at nights, too. Sometimes I wish I hadn't started it."

"Writing a book is damn hard work, Ava. But just think of the money," I said.

"I should have thought of that last night," she said, and laughed. The laugh became a cough, as it increasingly did at this time. I heard her take a drink. "I don't know why I'm laughing, honey, but I like the way that sounds."

"Just think of the money," I said again. It would be a disaster if she backed out now. The book was beginning to have a definite shape in my head. I was even beginning to enjoy working with her.

It was fun discovering little things she wanted to hide, and finding ways of slipping them into the copy, hoping she wouldn't notice. Sometimes she did, sometimes she didn't. It was a game we played. I'm sure she knew that as well as I did.

Several moments passed, her coughing stopped. She said reflectively: "You are right about the ghosts. Last night I couldn't get the picture of Daddy dying out of my head. I kept thinking how bloody lonely he must have been in that hospital ward in Newport News, waiting for me to visit each day when I got home from school. Fifty years ago and it was as clear in my mind as if it happened yesterday. The way his eyes lit up when he saw me come into the ward. The way he said, 'You make this place feel like I'm home, Daughter.' I guess that was the first time I realized he was dying."

"How old was he then, Ava?"

"Fifty-nine. Younger than I am now, fahcrissake. He must have known he'd never make it to sixty."

"That's no age."

"He was born in 1878."

"It must have been a hard life," I said.

"He was just waiting for it to end. He was burnt out. Life had burnt him out. He knew he was dying."

"You really think so?"

"When he said I made him feel like he was home, the way he looked at me. He knew all right. He wanted to reassure me he was going to be fine. He was telling me he was ready to go, and I mustn't worry. He was very good at telling you things, making things clear, without spelling them out.

"I remember telling him I wanted to be a good daughter. I wanted him to be proud of me. He said, 'You've done fine, Daughter.' I don't think they were his last words, but they're the last words I remember."

"We must use that in the book," I said, already making a note of it.

"Don't you *dare*! Don't even *think* about it!"

The vehemence in her voice surprised me. "Why not?"

"Because I don't want you to that's why not, honey. Jesus Christ! That's just between the two of us," she said.

It was a poignant moment and I didn't want to lose it. It was the kind of detail that gives a memoir substance and authenticity.

"But this is wonderful material, Ava. It's the kind of stuff that makes a book a page-turner. I can see it as a number one bestseller now."

"I don't want you to mention it, okay? Push it, I promise I won't ever trust you again."

"But it tells us so much about your closeness to your father. It's a wonderful insight into your relationship with him. It hits exactly the right tone. It explains the kind of remarkable man he was."

"I don't need you to tell me what a remarkable man Daddy was," she said.

"But people don't know that, Ava. It's the kind of detail that will distinguish your book from the cut-and-paste jobs that most movie stars settle for in their memoirs. I think you should talk about the sleepless nights, the things that keep you awake," I said.

"My ghosts?"

"We all have them."

"Most women are close to their fathers. I think of my mother, too, I was close to her, but Daddy's the one I see in my dreams."

"That's exactly what I'm saying, Ava. It's such an intimate detail. The clarity of that memory after fifty years, isn't that worth mentioning? I think it's extraordinary."

"I wish I hadn't mentioned it," she said, but there was hesitancy in her voice.

"Don't you think it would give a kind of closure to your childhood? I think it would," I said.

After a silence, she said: "It's mawkish."

"Not in this context," I said.

"In any fucking context, honey. It's schmaltzy."

"A little sentimental maybe," I said, giving a little tactical ground. "There's nothing wrong with that. Let me write it up. You can see how it reads. You might like it better on the page. Let's think about it?"

"I don't want a sentimental book. I hate sentimental books," she said. "Daddy was never sentimental. Neither was Mama. They both dealt with what life threw at them and moved on. Let's move on, honey."

"Nothing is too sentimental if it reveals genuine feelings. Not if it's true," I said.

"Let it lay, baby." There was a sudden abruptness in her tone, a dogged finality. "Jesus, you want to louse up my image? Forget it," she said.

I decided not to ask what she thought her image was. Later I would use the incident, write it up, and see what she said then. Perhaps next time around she wouldn't feel so strongly about it; she might not even comment on it at all. It had happened before. I kept forgetting how important it was to write around her moods.

"Ed Victor told me a lovely story about his dad," I said. I didn't want to end the discussion about her father on such a negative note. "The night before Ed was to meet you for the first time, he called his dad in the States. His dad was about to have an operation for colon cancer. Ed knew he was a fan of yours and told him that you were a new client of his. He said he was going to have dinner with you the next day. He knew it would cheer him up.

"His dad said, 'You're having dinner with *Ava Gardner*?'

"'Tomorrow,' Ed said, knowing it would impress him.

"His dad thought about that for a moment, and said, 'Well, just be careful, son!'

"'Why should I be careful, Dad?' Ed said, puzzled.

"'She's a very beautiful woman, son. She might try to seduce you.'"

Ed's story made her laugh, as I knew it would.

"Ed's dad sounds like a very nice old boy," she said. "I hope the operation was a success?"

"He never woke up from it. He was in a coma for about a month and then passed away."

"Oh my God, that's so sad. He obviously loved his son very much," she said. I could see she was moved by the story.

I said, "Ava, that's it for this evening. You really sound exhausted. I think you should take a few days off. I have plenty of material I can be working on. I'll wrap up your divorce from Mickey, and I have plenty of material on Howard Hughes I can use."

"How long is that going to take, honey?"

"Maybe four or five days," I told her optimistically. "Let's say a week?" Surprisingly, she didn't argue. "We're getting there. I might even be able to cover some of the Artie Shaw years," I said.

"The Artie Shaw *year*, honey," she corrected me with droll precision. "We married in '45, October 17. He dumped me one week after our first anniversary. The bastard broke my heart."

I didn't say anything. I didn't want to encourage her. It was getting late. I wanted her to go to bed.

"Jacob Ben-Yitzhak Arshawsky," she mused. "Don't you love that name? His mother called him Arthur. *Arthur!* That has no music in it at all. His mother was always a problem. His parents split when he was a kid. His mother, Sarah, was Austrian. She was a Jewish albatross around his neck all her life. She was crazier than a quilt. He could barely stand to be in the same room with her.

"He had issues with his father, too. He had issues with most people but he really disliked his father. He was a Russian. But it was his mother who drove Artie into the arms of the shrinks, although Lana [Turner]—a couple of wives before me, she was wifey number three; I was number five, there have been eight of us altogether, so far—didn't help.

"He'd just come out of the navy when he met Lana. He'd served in the Pacific. He was deaf in his left ear from when he was bombed at Guadalcanal. He'd had a nervous breakdown when he was discharged. I think Lana did, too. They were two messed-up people. Lana was eighteen. The classic MGM starlet. Artie had an IQ of—I don't know what it was. It was right up there. The intellect isn't connected to the pelvis, he told me once when I asked what had attracted him to her.

"Mickey reckoned he made her pregnant when she was seventeen. Before he knew me. He probably did, although Lana always denied it. She had to, of course. She was in an Andy Hardy film with him. He said she had great knockers. First Mick, then Artie . . . she beat me to both of them. And to Frank, too. Even so, I liked her. We became good friends. She's a couple of years older than me. I thought she was so sophisticated. I started smoking because of her. I told you that story, didn't I?"

"The slim gold cigarette case and lighter," I said to let her know I remembered the story. It was late, she was tired, and I really didn't want to encourage her. I again suggested she turn in. She said she would, as soon as she finished her nightcap.

"What are you drinking?"

"A little glass of red," she said. "It'll help me sleep."

"Okay," I said.

"Artie was difficult, he was complex, but I was stuck on him. I was crazy about him. I had it hard. He was smart as an apple. He always knew what I was going to say next. To tell the truth, I was always a little afraid of him. Not physically. Not the way I was scared of GCS [George C. Scott]. When GCS was loaded, he was terrifying—he'd beat the shit out of me and have no idea next morning what he'd done. I'd be lying next to him, black-and-blue and bleeding, and he couldn't remember a thing. He just had no recollection at all.

"Artie was another kind of bully. He was always putting me down. I was afraid of *his mind.* He was a dominating sonofabitch. I don't know which was worse: GCS's physical violence or Artie's mind games. He used to put me down so much I lost complete confidence in myself. When I went into analysis—that was something else he made me do—I insisted on taking an IQ test because I was at the point where I thought there was something seriously wrong with my mind. He had me thoroughly convinced that I was completely stupid.

"The analyst advised me not to take the IQ. I guess she feared the worst! But I took it anyway. Well, it turned out very well indeed. I didn't have an enormous IQ but I did have rather a high one. I had a good head but I didn't use it enough. I didn't like studying. It was the same at school. I'm not a bookish person. Artie got through a book at least every two nights.

"This is nice wine, by the way," she said.

"Finish it and go to bed," I said.

"Am I boring you?"

"Not at all, but you said you were tired," I said. "I'm only thinking of you."

"I owe Artie plenty. He made me get an education. We must say that in the book. Give the guy credit where credit's due. I enrolled in the University of California because of him. I more or less didn't work for a whole year because of him. I was always happy to quit work. I never liked acting anyway. I took correspondence courses. I was doing very well. My God, I was doing well. B-pluses."

"What year was that, Ava?"

"Forty-five. I also started hitting the bottle when I was with Artie. I drank with Mick, but that was kids' stuff. Those rum drinks that seemed so innocuous, and tasted so good. With Artie I'd get properly drunk. I got drunk because I was so insecure. I was completely out of my depth. Artie was very well read. He was completely self-taught. He was an auto-something—what's that word?"

"Autodidact?"

"An *autodidact,*" she said slowly, as if determined to remember it. "He always had his nose in a book. I had to get an education to keep up with him. He was mixing with a bunch of pseudointellectuals. I thought they were the real thing at the time. Most of them were Reds. I went to all those political meetings with him. I got seriously into socialism. Some of the books are still on my shelves. We'd go to the Russian consulate. We'd sit down to dinner and the vodka bottles would appear, and the caviar. We'd drink the vodka down the hatch. In one gulp, you know? That's when I got a taste for the hard stuff."

She paused. "People won't think I'm settling old scores, will they?"

"Some might. But it's honest," I said.

"Oh, it's honest, baby."

"This is Hollywood history," I said.

"That puts me in context, honey," she said.

I wondered if I had said something to offend her and didn't laugh.

"Artie was very conscious of being a Jew, you know," she said. "He once told me a story that showed how vulnerable he was. I don't know whether he was married to Jerome Kern's daughter at the time, or who, because he married everybody, but he was at a posh Hollywood dinner party when they started talking about Jews. It turned out that they were all anti-Semitic. He said he sat there in silence for a while—apparently nobody knew he was a Jew—then he joined in with their snide remarks about Jews. He said he'd never forgive himself for his cowardice.

"I felt such sadness for him when he told me that story. All my protective instincts came out. I really felt his pain. It made me love him even more. I was still mad about him at that time. I decided I wanted his baby. But he was very wise. He was protecting me—and I'm sure he was thinking of himself, too—he said this is not the time to have a child.

"I don't think in my heart I genuinely wanted a baby at all. I don't think I really did. I just thought: I'm going back to school, I'm getting an education, I'm being the good wife, to make it perfect I'll have a child. Maybe I was playing a part, who the hell knows?

"What the fuck, a few months later, he ditched me and married Kathleen Winsor, the woman who wrote *Forever Amber*—a fucking potboiler, he'd called it. He snatched it out of my hands and tore it to shreds when he caught me reading it. It was part of my self-improvement program. What did I know?

"Later I lost respect for him completely. He did a dreadful thing. He was called up before the Un-American Activities Committee in Washington and ratted on his friends. You just don't do that. There was a writer who was very, very far left, but a wonderful man, Hy Kraft. He wrote *Stormy Weather*, the all-black Twentieth Century-Fox musical which starred my friend Lena Horne. Hy was Artie's best man at our wedding. That's how close they were. It didn't stop Artie giving up Hy's name to the Un-American Committee. Can you believe that? His own best man! I still to this day don't understand how he could have done that. He suddenly became a super American patriot: *I love America, I love the flag, I love this country.* I think he was full of shit."

She continued to talk in a reminiscent tone maybe for another twenty minutes, almost as if I wasn't there.

"'Begin the Beguine,' 'Frenesi,' 'Stardust.' Remember those? 'I've Got a Crush on You.' You couldn't turn on the radio without hearing an Artie Shaw number being played. He was pulling down sixty thou a week in those days. That must be practically a million in today's money. The money was pouring in. But that didn't stop him watching the kopecks. He probably still has the first one-spot he ever made. If only his thrift had been contagious, believe me, I wouldn't be talking to you now, baby! I didn't take a penny from him, by the way. Not a fucking sou. I even paid for my own divorce.

"On the other hand, although he could be pretty rude about individuals, Artie didn't have a prejudiced bone in his body. He was the first white bandleader to employ black musicians. Billie Holiday, Roy Eldridge, the trumpeter—they called him Little Jazz, I loved Little Jazz. Before the war, I used to listen to him and Artie on the radio—with Coleman Hawkins, and Teddy Wilson on the piano.

"I went on the road with some of those guys for a while. That was the best time I had with Artie, touring with his band before we married. Louis Mayer wasn't happy about it. Although we'd been divorced a couple of years, my name was still linked to Mickey's, at least in the public's mind, and the studio was putting pressure on me to break off the romance with Artie, or at least make it legal. Uncle Louis was still on his high moral horse about actors 'living in sin.'

"My affair with Artie was hardly discreet, it was no hole-and-corner thing that's for sure. I'd moved into his place in Beverly Hills the minute he asked me, which was about five minutes after we'd met. MGM was pissed off with me. At least they weren't offering me much in the way of movies, although they didn't can me either. I knew that was supposed to be a punishment. Boy, did they get that wrong!

"I did one film in '45, a loan-out: *Whistle Stop,* with George Raft. MGM got five thousand dollars for me that time. I didn't mind. I liked George. He was coming to the end of his career, and mine still hadn't got started, but we dated a few times. He was a wonderful dancer—for his age! He must have been in his late forties at that time but he still had a good figure. I had to slap him down a few times to keep him in line. He still thought of himself as a lady-killer, a bit of a Casanova; apart from that he was okay. We had some laughs together. I told you, I first met him with Mickey when we used to go to the Friday night fights in L.A. He was going steady with Betty Grable in those days. They were a hot item for a while.

"*Whistle Stop* was my first leading role. I was very nervous, and I wasn't very good. I still didn't know my ass from my elbow acting-wise. But there was one scene that got me noticed. I kissed George with my mouth open! It was a mistake, I shouldn't have done it. It was forbidden by the Breen office, but it had the guys in the audience hanging on the ropes. ["With the dynamics of Gardner and Raft in it, *Whistle Stop* is certainly not a dull place," *Variety* noted.]

"Fortunately, it slipped by the Production Code people. They were very hot on what they regarded as lustful kissing in those days. But John Huston spotted it. He said it was the scene that got me the role in *The Killers*, my breakthrough movie as they call it today. It made me realize you didn't have to be an actress to sell tickets at the box office!

"I was still as happy as Larry traveling with the band, hanging out with Artie and his literary pals. Guys like Sid Perelman, Bill Saroyan, John O'Hara. They were all bright, funny, interesting guys.

"Artie said all I had to do was keep my mouth shut, sit at their feet, and absorb their wit and wisdom. I was happy to do that. I was comfortable with all those guys. But if I kicked off my shoes and curled my feet up on the couch, he'd go bananas. 'You're not in the fucking tobacco fields now,' he'd scream. He had a real phobia about me and tobacco fields.

"Ten days after he got his divorce from Betty Kern, we were married by the same judge who handed down his decree.

"For the first couple of months our marriage was fine, at least as far as I was concerned it was, although I was unhappy when he broke the band up. He said he didn't want his wife on the road with a bunch of musicians. He said it wasn't dignified. He was very hot on dignity. He once told me he couldn't respect a woman who made a living as a movie star—'movie acting has nothing at all to do with talent, it's all about key lights and cheekbones,' he said. I think he said that when I beat him at chess after he'd hired a Russian grand master to give me lessons. I guess I must have learned too well.

"I was already living in his house in Beverly Hills when we took the plunge. It was a beautiful big mock-Tudor place on Bedford Drive, full of books, records, pianos, harpsichords. I was twenty-two. I wasn't up to it. I was still a kid. I still identify with that little girl. The cook, the gardener, my maid were all black. They were like family to me. Living with Artie was like going home in that sense. He wrote the number 'Grabtown Grapple' for me on Bedford Drive.

"Contrast that with Howard Hughes, the racialists' racialist," she said. "Howard wouldn't piss on a black man to put him out if he was on fire. That's a fact, nothing I say can change it, and if I'm going to remember things as they really were, I have to face it. I told you about the doctors Howard flew to Mama's bedside when she was dying, didn't I?"

I said she had.

"Anything Ava wanted," she said, "Ava got. *Anything.*"

"You should have married *him*," I said.

"Marry Howard Hughes? Jesus Christ! Are you kidding me?"

"I'm kidding you," I said, backing off.

"Artie played the clarinet the way Frank sang. They both knew how to bend a note, stretch a phrase. They could do that stuff better than anyone alive. Frank once told me he used to practice by singing to Artie's music on the radio in Hoboken, although he said it was Tommy Dorsey who taught him about breath control. But Artie and Frank never played together, which is music's loss. They were at the top of their game at the same time."

"They were about the same age, weren't they?"

"Frank was five years younger. He was born in 1915." She yawned. "What time is it, honey?"

"Ava, it's time to go to bed. Tomorrow, I'll get on with the stuff I have on Mickey and Howard. With luck, I might even make a start on Artie. This is good stuff, by the way. It's been a wonderful session."

"I hope you can make sense of it. It's awfully muddled, honey. I must have covered the waterfront. You'll have to sort it out."

"That won't be a problem," I assured her.

"I won't see you for at least a week?" She sounded disappointed.

"A break will do you good," I said. "You really sound as if you need one."

"Are you losing interest?"

"You don't think that, do you?"

"You're getting bored with me! I'm fucking boring you!"

"Nothing could be further from the truth. That's a foolish thing to say."

"Christ, when even your biographer gets bored with you! What kind of fucking book is this going to be," she said.

"It's going to be a wonderful book, Ava."

"It had better be, baby. I've given it my best shot," she said with a final touch of her old acerbity, and replaced the receiver.

I rang her straight back.

"Good night, Ava. Sleep well," I said, and put down the phone.

And I still hadn't asked her about the size of Frank Sinatra's cock.

20

I'm sorry, honey. You said it'd be all right to call you."

"Ava, are you okay?" I said automatically. I'd been in a deep sleep. I checked the time. It was just after two o'clock, less than a couple of hours since we'd said good night. "Can't you sleep?"

She sighed unhappily. "I went off like a baby as soon as my head hit the pillow. I woke up gasping for a cigarette."

I reminded her of what the doctors had told her about her not smoking anymore.

"Fuck the doctors. They're all quacks anyway," she said. Her voice was so husky as to be barely audible. "I just can't sleep, honey. If we could talk for a while, it would help," she said.

I said of course we could, although I was surprised that she had anything new to talk about so soon after our marathon session earlier. What did she want to talk about? I tried to sound cheerful and encouraging but it wasn't easy.

"Don't be angry with me for waking you, honey."

"I'm not angry with you," I said.

"I had a panic attack," she said. "I woke in a cold sweat and a sense that—" She didn't finish the sentence. "I don't know, honey, I'm a fucking wreck."

"I think you should get a checkup. Let me book an appointment for you in the morning?" I said.

"What's the point?" She laughed bitterly. "I had checkups last time. I had checkups coming out of my ears. They didn't find a damn thing wrong with me. A couple of days later, bam! Strokes are as unpredictable as fucking earthquakes, honey. I was lucky I was already in hospital when they happened. I would have died if I hadn't been where I was." After a pause, she said: "Do you want to talk about that time?"

"Do you?" I said, hoping she didn't. I just wanted to go back to sleep.

"We haven't discussed it yet, and I can't sleep," she said. "Is it all right with you if we talk for a while?"

I switched on the tape that I now kept by my bed. "I'd better make some notes. What year are we talking about? Eighty-six?"

"Nineteen eighty-six. October 9," she said precisely.

"You were admitted to St. John's, Santa Monica, with double pneumonia," I said.

"A few days later, a couple of strokes were thrown in for fun," she said and did not stop talking for nearly an hour.

"They kept me in for three months. The irony is I'd kept fit all that year, swimming, playing a lot of tennis. I was sixty-four. I was in damn good shape for an old broad. I'd even been going to a hypnotist to help me give up smoking. It didn't do much good, but I was trying.

"It started with a cold that wouldn't go away. It wasn't unusual. Everyone in London had the same thing. For two or three days you'd feel pretty good again and suddenly, bang, forget it! This went on for three or four months. Being as strong and fit as I was, I didn't do anything about it. I wouldn't go to bed. I just put up with it. Then something happened that really worried me.

"One morning, I took a deep breath, and felt a terrible burning pain in my chest. I'd never felt anything like it before. It frightened the hell out of me. I was still smoking like a chimney although I knew all about emphysema. I'd seen old chums die of it—my friend Nunnally Johnson. He was a wonderful writer. I knew Huston was dying of it.

"I called my doctor, he called in a specialist. We did X-rays here in the flat, a bunch of breathing tests. The specialist said I had a heavy cold. I'd get over it, he said. I told him about my fear of emphysema. 'One thing is for sure, Miss Gardner, you'll never have emphysema. You have extremely strong lungs. There is nothing wrong with you. You have a nasty cold, that's all,' he said.

"Bullshit. I knew I was sick. I knew there was something wrong with me. The next day, I got on a plane and went home to my doctor in Los Angeles. I never have a temperature; that's one thing that runs in the family—low temperatures, even if we're dying. On the plane my temperature just soared. They cleared some seats in the back of the plane so I could lie down. They gave me oxygen, and called ahead for an ambulance to meet the plane. I was taken straight to St. John's.

"The next few days I was out of it. I had double pneumonia. My temperature kept rising. I think it got to one hundred and six. My brain was cooking. My arm was filled with needles and tubes of every antibiotic they could think of. They finally hit me with sixteen milligrams of cortisone. That may have saved my life, although I also think it could have caused the strokes. It's a fucking dangerous drug, I can tell you that.

"But it did the trick. My temperature started to come down. I was still having inhalations four or five times a day but the chest pains had eased. I was moved to a private room, with a little sitting room attached. I was sitting there after dinner one evening watching a Laurel and Hardy film with my nurse when I felt the tingling sensation I told you about. Like tiny pinpricks in the palm of my left hand, on the side of my face, down the side of my nose.

"The nurse must have had a suspicion of what it might be. She called the doctor. He gave me some tests: hold your hand out, close your eyes, touch your nose. My hand was weaving all over the place. It was going here, there, and all over the place. It just made me laugh.

"I went to sleep that night. No problem. I went out like a light. Maybe they gave me something, I don't know. The following morning, my whole left side was paralyzed: the leg, the arm, the side of my face, they had no feeling at all. I couldn't see out of my left eye. The strange thing was, although I realized immediately I'd had a stroke, I wasn't frightened. There was no *Oh my God, I'm paralyzed* moment. You'd think I'd have panicked, but I didn't. I was perfectly calm.

"Maybe if there is such a thing as a God, maybe He saves another part of your brain to protect you from the terrible shock to your system when something like that happens to you.

"I remember I did a lot of laughing in those early days. I told you how it also hit my bladder, which meant I had no control. I giggled and laughed and wet my pants a lot. I certainly had nothing to laugh about. I didn't realize how sick I was, or just how paralyzed I was.

"The seriousness of what had happened didn't hit me until later. I'd been concentrating on how to walk again; I had a marvelous Egyptian therapist who got some feeling back into my leg. He literally gave me the will to walk again. I had a wonderful young woman speech therapist who got my voice back. I think she shined up my Southern drawl a little, too. Although it was still nowhere near the way it was when I first went out to Hollywood—when Mr. Schenck sent my screen test to the coast without the soundtrack because he was afraid that my North Carolina accent was too thick for anyone to understand a damn word I said.

"The tragedy is my left arm. It still doesn't work. But because I use my right hand, and feed myself, I didn't realize how badly it was damaged. It didn't get as much early attention as my leg. I kept being told the arm was always the last thing to recover, and I wasn't to worry. The arm and the face usually repaired themselves without therapy, they said. It was a dreadful thing to say because they don't, honey. They just don't. This is it, this is as good as it gets. And the part of the brain that feels pain and hurt and anger that's still intact—just as that part that feels happiness is gone."

"I hope that's not true, Ava," I said.

"I can't help it. That's the way I feel, honey," she said.

After a silence, she said: "Anyway, enough of this." I sensed she was close to tears. "I'm ready for bed now. We'll talk tomorrow."

SHE CALLED THE FOLLOWING evening, just after nine.

"What I was saying yesterday about the stroke, and the part of my brain that still feels anger and hurt—I was never daunted by it, you know. I want you to say that in the book. You must make that clear. I don't want it to sound like one long sob story," she said.

"It won't, Ava," I said.

"I don't want to sound like old Mother Machree," she said. I had no idea who Mother Machree was but guessed she might have been one of her father's Irish sayings—or Mickey Rooney's. I said she had never sounded like Mother Machree to me.

"Good," she said with satisfaction.

"It's going to be an extraordinary book, Ava," I said reassuringly. "You will be proud of it."

She hesitated. "Do you want to hear something?"

"Okay," I said.

"I made some notes at the time. I fished them out this morning. Do you want to hear them?"

"Absolutely," I said.

"You must tell me if they're boring," she said. After a pause, she began to read slowly: "Nineteen eighty-six, before the stroke, was one of the best years of my life. I'd lived sixty-four years of great activity: work, play, and a bit of mental activity as well, but mostly physical. I loved sports and was good at almost all of them."

She stopped reading, and said thoughtfully: "Even as a little girl on a farm—and nobody knew about gymnastics and all that jazz—I won a blue ribbon doing very simple exercises. I lost the ribbon in my Daddy's cotton gin, or his sawmill, I forget which. I loved gymnastics. Had I had the training I might have been an Olympic star instead of a movie star and been a much happier human being. Another thing I loved was music. I used to go to Selma, North Carolina, near where we lived, to watch my sister Myra have piano lessons. She was never keen on the piano, but I was. It was a shame, Mama and Daddy couldn't afford lessons for me, too. At first I kept my disappointment to myself. But one day, I couldn't hide my frustration or jealousy any longer. I bit the keys off the teacher's piano. I had a terrible temper as a child."

"You bit the keys off the piano?" I said incredulously.

"I had strong teeth."

"That's very funny, Ava."

"It's true. You could see the tiny teeth marks in some of the keys. I wanted to dance, too. But again, Mama and Daddy couldn't afford the lessons. It's really terrible being poor as a child. But if you're going to be poor, be poor on a farm. I told you that before, didn't I?"

"I think so. But it's good to be reminded," I said.

"I played baseball with the boys and outran most of them and climbed higher trees and towers and God knows I have the scars to prove it. To get back to 1986," she said, and slowly resumed reading from her notes:

"It was a really healthy year. No booze, few cigarettes, I cut right down—actually I was still smoking like a fiend—but I had a very healthy diet. I was really getting myself together. I played tennis twice a week, swam every day, no matter the weather. I walked my little dog, Morgan, in the park for at least an hour a day."

She paused for a moment. "I must have lost six, seven, eight pounds," she said reflectively. "I was beginning to look good naked again. I decided to have some new dresses made by my darling friend, Franka . . . then came the fucking strokes," she said.

"That must have been devastating," I said.

"It was the last thing in the world I expected. I was so happy. Work was coming in. My name meant something on the marquees. Producers liked to use me for the name. I did a nice turn as an art patroness in *Priest of Love.* I was in William Faulkner's *The Long Hot Summer* with Jason Robards, and *Harem* with Omar Sharif. I'd played his mother, I'd played his wife. I said maybe next time I'll have a face lift and play your daughter. He said don't bother with the face lift! He is a nice man, a charming man, but he won't leave the gambling alone. What else? I had a run in *Knots Landing*, I played Agrippina in *A.D.* with James Mason. It was television and they weren't the biggest roles, but they were important parts, important character roles, and the money was good."

"You'd come a long way since the early days at MGM," I said.

"I was still afraid that people were going to catch on to me. But at least I was fucking fit. Those fucking strokes turned my life upside down. Didn't I cover most of this stuff last night?"

"No, this is new," I said.

"I don't want to sound sorry for myself," she said.

"You won't."

"I don't sound full of shit, do I? I don't want to sound full of self-pity."

"You are the gutsiest woman I know," I said.

"Franka's dresses are still hanging in the closet. They are beautiful but I still haven't been able to wear any of them. They probably don't fit me any longer. If I were the crying type, I would sit down and cry like hell. There they hang and here I sit," she said. "It's a bitch thinking back over your life, having to remember things you'd rather forget."

"I don't want you to forget a thing—not until we've finished the book," I said.

"I have a few more notes. Do you want to hear them?" She sounded hesitant.

"Of course I do. They have your voice in them," I said.

"It's my fucking voice, honey," she said dryly.

"Unmistakably," I said.

"These are the notes I wrote up before I thought of doing the book. I was very low. These were just for me, a kind of journal. It was probably my lowest point."

Hesitantly, she began to read: "Now it is 10:30 at night and I'm going to bed. After having various vitamins, and cider and honey, which is supposed to be good for the arthritis in my neck—which is a perfect drag. They told me that I would have to have an operation, but there is no real assurance that an operation will do the job. And certainly they can't operate until I stop smoking, which is about the only pleasure I have left in life.

"So I go to bed after an injection to stop my left side jumping and driving me crazy, which will last me five or six hours. Then what will I do? Go mad. Kill myself? I don't much care. [The swelling in] my arm will go down after a few moments in bed. But this is not something to give anyone hope or courage after a stroke.

"Being left in a semiparalyzed condition, with the threat of emphysema at any time if I continue smoking, scares the hell out of me. Even if I stop now, most of my lung power has gone. I've certainly lost all courage, something I always had, no matter what. I have no hope. No hope from my doctors and certainly none for myself.

"I wake reluctantly every day, thinking, Now what? Another day of pain and therapy—and, after one year and a half, no progress. Why bother? Why bother to get out of bed? I suppose I should be grateful for all the sixty-five years of health and fun and complete life. But I'm not. I'm bitter and I'm angry. And I wish to God I'd died. There is no joy and no happiness in the future. Shit. But that's the way I feel. I don't want to be half a person. I don't want to be."

She stopped reading. I could feel her despair. I didn't know what to say. I said nothing. After a long silence, she said: "It's such a bore, Pete. Life is a bore."

"When did you write that, Ava?"

"I don't know. It's undated. I guess when I thought I was going to kiss myself goodbye," she said.

"I'm pleased you didn't," I said.

"Sitting around, just waiting. If I were a great intellectual, I'd sit and read and study, but I'm not. I'm just a very ordinary woman. I don't want to paint. I don't want to write. I want to go out and play tennis, I want to swim. I'm purely a physical piece of machinery. Or I was."

"I think we should use it just the way it is," I said.

"Not until we take the 'poor little me' stuff out of it," she said in a tone I knew was nonnegotiable.

21

Ed Victor mentioned it casually over lunch: had I asked Ava about the size of Frank Sinatra's penis yet? He knew I hadn't, of course. I said it was a difficult subject to introduce into a conversation. "I can hardly say, 'Oh by the way, Ava, I heard that you told John Ford that Frank's penis is enormous. One hundred and ten pounds of it. Can we talk about that?'"

Ed gazed calmly at me while he mused over the problem. Finally he agreed there was no easy way to broach the subject. "But you'll think of something. You're the writer," he said. It was his usual solution to a problem when he couldn't think of an answer.

"Some help you are," I said.

"She's your friend." He grinned.

THE FOLLOWING EVENING, I slipped a copy of *His Way*, Kitty Kelley's biography of Sinatra—in which Kelley reported Ava's story of Frank's impressive phallus—into my bag. I still had no idea how I was going to bring the subject up; but I was sure it would be after a few drinks.

Ava was in a mellow mood when I arrived. An opened bottle

of red wine was on the table. A record of early Sinatra was playing softly.

"Is that the Dorsey band?" I said.

"He was great, wasn't he? Frank sent me a few of his early recordings when I had the stroke," she said.

"They must bring back a lot of memories," I said.

"For both of us, honey."

They had been divorced for more than thirty years but I stepped warily around the subject of Sinatra. She became defensive every time his name came up. She would treat the most well-meaning question about him as if it were the third degree. "What's this? A fucking witch hunt?" she once turned on me when I asked a question that could not have been more innocuous. After that, I had decided not to get into their marriage and the Sinatra years until I had the rest of the story wrapped up.

Nevertheless she seemed to be in a good mood.

"Was that the last time you and Frank talked? When you had the stroke?" I asked as casually as I could.

"No, we talk, honey. Not all the time, but two or three times a year. He always calls at Christmas. He never forgets my birthday," she said affably.

"He always calls on Christmas Eve?" I said.

"He's a sentimental man," she said in an amused voice.

"Do you ever call him?" I said.

"Never," she said.

"Never?" I said, trying to keep a sense of interrogation out of my voice.

"He's a married man, honey," she said, straight-faced. She continued to listen to the track, nodding her head gently to the music. "I love this number. [It was "Stardust."] I think Frank did some of his best work with Dorsey. They must have recorded it in the early forties. They didn't have the equipment and technology they have today. Frank would have done it in one take. If the vocalist or a musician hit a bum note they had to start the track all over again. Frank never sang this one again after he left the Dorsey band. I think it was a copyright problem with Tommy. But they got on very well."

She poured a glass of wine for me, and refreshed hers.

"Did you and Frank ever have a special song?" I asked offhandedly.

"You mean that we thought of as 'our song'?"

"That sort of thing," I said.

"Jesus, there could have been so many, honey. I can't pick out just one—not for the book anyway. It would be too fucking schmaltzy. Too fucking . . ." There was a kind of amused contempt in the unfinished sentence. "Frank would hate it if I said that," she said.

Her voice was still friendly. This was the first time she had talked with any ease about Sinatra and I felt the euphoria of being trusted. "Okay, can you remember the first words you exchanged when you first met Frank?" I went into interviewer mode.

"You sound like a fucking reporter."

"I am a fucking reporter, Ava. Indulge me."

She looked pensive, and sipped her drink. "I was with Mickey in the studio commissary. We had just gotten married. Frank came over to our table—Jesus, he was like a god in those days, if gods can be sexy. A cocky god, he reeked of sex—he said something banal, like: 'If I had seen you first, honey, I'd have married you myself.' I paid no attention to that. I knew he was married. He had a *kid,* fahcrissake! He was a terrible flirt. He couldn't help it. That was the first time we met.

"The next time was when we had that famous Metro group picture taken. We were all congregated on Stage 29, the studio's biggest stage, before a big lunch for the press and the theater owners of America. I was wedged in between Clark and Judy, which was pretty good company. All the Gs. Frank flirted with me then. We were leaving the studio in our cars; he overtook me, slowed to a crawl, I passed him, he passed me. That was Frank all over," she said. "He could even flirt in a car.

"Another time, I met him at a party in Palm Springs. I hadn't seen him for about a year. He was having a tough time. MGM had dropped his contract. He asked me what I was doing. I said, 'The usual. Making pictures. You?' He said, 'The usual. Getting my ass in a sling.'

"He was kissing the bottle at that time. We went for a drive in the desert and a little woo-poo. We really tied one on. We started shooting up a little town—Indio, I think it was; I don't know where the hell we were—with a couple of .38s Frank kept in the vanity compartment. We were both cockeyed. We shot out streetlights, store windows. God knows how we got away with it. I guess Frank knew somebody! Somebody with a badge. He usually did."

She had really opened up. It was so unexpected I didn't know what to say. "But you never had a song you thought of as 'our song'?" I said inanely.

"Practically every song he recorded has a memory for me," she said. "'I'm a Fool to Want You,' that's one that stands out. He wrote some of the lyrics himself."

She hummed the tune. "'I'm a fool to want you / To want a love that can't be true / A love that's there for others too,'" she murmured the lyrics. "They were very personal," she said. "He wrote it the year we married. It was a lousy year, wretched. Kicking our heels, waiting for his divorce from Nancy to come through, was hell. We were fighting all the time. Fighting and boozing. Breaking up, getting together again. It was madness.

"I dated other guys just to punish him. Frank was doing his share. He was seeing girls. I know he was seeing Marilyn Maxwell again. He'd been sweet on her for years. She was one of his regulars when he married Nancy. I wasn't surprised that she was still hanging around.

"I took off for Spain to make a movie [*Pandora and the Flying Dutchman*]. I had a fling with the bullfighter [Mario Cabré] who played my lover in the picture. My mistake was telling Frank about it. He was always banging on at me about guys he suspected I'd slept with. I'd slept with Mario once. He was a handsome devil. It was a one-night stand."

"A one-night stand?" I tried not to sound incredulous.

"For the book it was, honey." She didn't smile. "I was drunk. He was handsome. It was a terrible mistake, period," she said.

"You mean telling Frank about it?"

"Doing it—telling Frank about it wasn't too bright either. He followed me to Spain. He wanted to kill the poor bastard."

"He has a temper," I said.

"Bob Mitchum told me that he was afraid of only two things—and one of them was Frank Sinatra! I can't remember what the other thing was, it could have been spiders, but he said Frank was the only man he wouldn't ever want to cross.

"That was around the time I made a picture with Bob [*My Forbidden Past,* 1951]. I was dating him when my affair with Frank was starting to become serious. Bob was a tough guy. He had a bad-boy reputation. He'd been a hobo, a drifter, served time for marijuana possession. He did sixty days in the county slammer. He said it was like Palm Springs without the riffraff. He didn't give a shit about anything. I adored him. He was outrageous. On the set, in front of reporters, he'd call to his makeup man: 'Hey, bring me some of that good shit, man.' He didn't give a fuck.

"Out in the Valley working on location one day, he said, 'Sugar, have you ever tried this stuff?' He was smoking a joint. I said no, I never have. There was plenty of it around when I was with Artie but he wouldn't let me touch it. He said I got high enough on booze. Anyway, Bob said, 'I've got some great shit, really great. I want you to try it.' So we went into this old van where they carried all the equipment. I smoked a couple of sticks. Bob taught me how. You take a little air with it, deep, deep down and you hold it and hold it and hold it—no wonder they now say joints are much worse for you than ordinary cigarettes.

"Anyhow, I didn't feel a goddamn thing, nothing whatsoever. Bob was flying. He was fine and dandy. On the way home we stopped at a bar—dry martinis were the thing in those days—and once I'd had a martini, I felt as if I was sitting about two feet above the stool. Everything I reached for I reached a little off, a little to one side. It took the martini to bring on the feeling of the pot. Bob did his best to convert me to marijuana, I tried, but I never got into it. It never became a habit."

"What happened to Mitchum?"

"Our affair, you mean?"

"Yes."

"I was crazy about him. I know he was pretty gone on me, too. But the truth was—it still is—he was committed to his wife, Dorothy. She was a saint. She was devoted to him. I once proposed to him, kind of kidding on the square. He said, 'It's okay with me, baby. But you'll have to clear it with Dorothy first.'

"When I told him I was also seeing more of Frank, that's when he told me Frank was the only man he was afraid of. He said, 'Get into a fight with him and he won't stop until one of you is dead.' He didn't want to risk it being him, he said."

I could believe it. I'd had my own run-in with Sinatra, but I didn't want to tell her that.

"You must have been mad telling Frank about your fling with Mario. You knew how jealous he was. You must have known it would mean trouble," I said. "Why did you do it?"

"He kept on at me. I fell for the oldest con in the world. He said it didn't matter a damn if I'd slept with Mario or not, it was in the past. He just wanted me to be honest with him. He said if I told him the truth, it would all be forgotten. So I told him the truth and, of course, it was never forgotten. He brought it up every goddamn argument we had. Even when we weren't arguing, he'd bring it up. He never forgave me.

"You know, his eyes do the most incredible thing when he's angry. They turn *black*. I swear to God, they become as black as the ace of spades. It's frightening. It makes your blood creep the way he does that. He never forgave me," she said again.

"But he still married you," I said.

"November 7, 1951. A day that will live in infamy.

"Only days after his divorce from Nancy became final. It was too soon, but that was Frank all over," she said again. "He was always in such a fucking hurry. He insisted he had left Nancy years before: physically, emotionally, you name it. He said that except for the kids, she was out of his life. I believed him. Like I believed him when he said he'd forgive me for screwing Mario.

"Plenty of people told me I was mad to marry him. Lana Turner had had an affair with him after she divorced Artie. 'I've been there, honey,' she told me. 'Don't do it!' I should have listened to her. The girl had been around.

"The trouble was Frank and I were too much alike. Bappie said I was Frank in drag. There was a lot of truth in that. He was the only husband I had that Bappie didn't approve of straight off the bat. I'm not saying she disliked him. On the contrary, she thought he was great—but not for me. I should have listened to her."

"Why didn't you?" I said.

"He was good in the feathers. You don't pay much attention to what other people tell you when a guy's good in the feathers," she said.

"The fighting always began on the way to the bidet. Didn't you say that?"

She laughed. "It sounds like something I might have said. It sounds about right. Let's say I said it."

It was the perfect opening. "Didn't you also once joke that there was only ten pounds of Frank but there's one hundred and ten pounds of cock," I said.

She stopped laughing. *Abruptly*. "Who said that?"

"You apparently," I said.

She looked stunned. "I never said that. It's the most disgusting thing I've ever heard."

"On *Mogambo,* didn't you say it to a visiting British dignitary?"

"It's sick."

"John Ford apparently encouraged you," I said to jog her memory, and offer her a way out—and get me off the hook.

"It's vile," she said. "I would never say anything so disgusting. Ford would never have encouraged me to say such a thing."

"It's in Kitty Kelley's biography of Frank," I said.

"I've read that book. It's a piece of shit."

"Nevertheless, I think it's in there," I said.

"I'd remember it if she'd written something as disgusting as that. It's smut. It's sick. It's fucking obscene."

I had the Kelley book in my bag with the passage and her quote underlined but I decided not to embarrass Ava by confronting her with it. "I'll read it again. I'm sure that's where I saw it," I said.

"Don't bother. I'll ask Bappie. She's the family historian. She'll know if it's there. I'll call her. I'll ask her."

I looked at my watch. It was 8:15. It was after midday in California, and I suggested we call her at once.

"I'll call her later," she said.

"Okay," I said docilely, remembering how carefully I still had to tread around the subject of Sinatra. But to my surprise, she never mentioned the story again, except once. A few mornings later, in the early hours, she called me: "I've spoken to Bappie. She says that story you told me about what I'm supposed to have said about Frank's cock definitely isn't in Kitty Kelley's book. Bappie's read it again and it's not there."

"I could have sworn that's where I saw it," I said lamely.

"Well, it isn't. Forget about it. It's garbage anyway," she said.

I got the message.

22

Honey?" she said softly.

Before I understood the extent of her insomnia, I had encouraged her to call me anytime she couldn't sleep, and knew that I had only myself to blame whenever she phoned me in the middle of the night.

"Honey?" she said again, more urgently.

"Ava, good morning," I said. I tried to get my head together, and waited for her to tell me what was on her mind this time.

"Why do actresses always have this need to write their memoirs? If we want to be remembered we should keep our mouths shut. Orson got it right. He didn't just saw Rita in half," she said ambiguously.

I knew that Orson Welles had once sawed Rita Hayworth in half in his magic act, but I still couldn't follow Ava's logic. "How did Orson get it right, Ava?" I said.

"Didn't he say actors should never explain anything to anyone? Actors should keep their private lives private."

"He might have. I don't recall it," I said carefully.

"Wasn't it in *Citizen Kane*?"

"I don't think so, but I'll check," I said.

"I'm sure it was in *Citizen Kane*."

I let that go. I was tired. None of this was faintly interesting to me.

"Anyway, actresses should never put in writing anything that can bite them in the keister," she said.

That made me sit up. "You haven't changed your mind about the book, have you?" I was wide awake now, and worried.

"Why do you say that, honey?" she asked innocently. "That's not what I said. Have *you* changed your mind about the book? You must tell me if you have, honey. I won't mind."

I could tell she was amused, and I remembered it was the game she played with producers. "I like to make them think I'm indifferent about a role or a film they want me to do. That always gets them hot," she'd once told me.

"I haven't changed my mind," I said and changed the subject: "Can't you sleep?"

"I wanted a ciggie so badly. Old habits die hard."

"You didn't give in?"

"Frank says it's easy to give up smoking. He says he quits every day," she joked, ducking the question.

"That's very funny," I said. I wanted to get back to sleep. "Aren't you tired?"

"Frank smokes less than I ever did," she said, again ignoring my question. "He never smokes during the day. He never inhales anyway. Watch him next time he's on. He'll take two or three drags and stub it out.

"Smoking is part of his image. He does it with a lot of class. Although Bogart did it better. It was an art form with Bogie.

"But it killed the poor bastard in the end. He must have been smoking sixty a day when we made *The Barefoot Contessa.* He had a contract to promote one of the tobacco companies. He needed no encouragement. Chesterfields, I think it was. He said it was the best deal he ever signed. His dressing room was like a foggy day in London town every fucking day."

It was obvious that she wanted to talk. It was her way of getting through the night. Spoli Mills said Ava used to keep her awake at night and now that was my role. "You're the best thing that's happened to my night's sleep since temazepam," she said.

"If you want, we could talk about making *Barefoot Contessa.* We haven't covered that period yet." I gave in to the inevitable. "What was it like working with Bogart? Shall we talk about that?"

"He would often ruin our scenes together with his coughing fits. It wasn't the happiest movie I ever worked on," she said.

"Why was that?"

"Did you know him?"

"Bogart? No."

"He was a bastard," she said flatly.

"In what way?"

"In every way, honey. Mank [director Joseph L. Mankiewicz] liked to shoot long scenes, he was a dialogue man. Bogie hated learning lines. He knew every trick in the book to fuck up a scene and get a retake if he felt a scene wasn't going his way. Marius Goring [the English actor who played her lover, Alberto Bravano, a South American millionaire] was on to his games. He called him Humphrey Bogus."

"Why didn't Bogart like you?"

"Probably because he knew that it was my film, not his. He wasn't happy that I got the part. A lot of better actresses than me were up for it. Bogie didn't approve of me. He had no respect for me at all. He never tried to hide it."

"That never came over in the film."

"He was a good actor."

"So are you," I told her.

"He knew that I was being paid more than he was getting. That was another thing that pissed him. The money wasn't because I was such a great fucking talent, because I wasn't. But I was a box office name by that time. I'd just come off a run of big pictures: *Show Boat,* which made MGM a fucking fortune, *Pandora [and the Flying Dutchman*], *Snows of Kilimanjaro.* It doesn't get much better than that. Mankiewicz had to pay MGM a fortune to get me. My name on the billboards put bums on seats, as they say now."

"Do you know how much Mankiewicz paid for you?"

"I can tell you exactly how much, honey: two hundred grand plus ten percent of the gross over the first million." There was pride in her voice as well as anger.

"That was a lot of money."

"I didn't realize how hot I was. The two hundred grand–plus was the figure that stuck in Bogie's gullet. It pisses me, too, because the greedy bastards at MGM grabbed most of it. I was still under contract. The studio was making a fucking fortune out of me. I was their milch cow. I took home less than seventy grand for that picture. Bogie still pissed and moaned that I was getting more than he got, but he banked his usual hundred thou. It didn't make him any nicer.

"I told you, it wasn't the happiest film I ever worked on. I'd gone into it with such high hopes. Mankiewicz had gotten a wonderful performance out of Linda Darnell in *A Letter to Three Wives* a couple of years earlier, and another stunning performance from Anne Baxter in *All About Eve*. He'd gotten a reputation as a woman's director, although I don't think he was ever as good as George [Cukor, who directed her in *Bhowani Junction*]. George was gay; Joe wasn't. George understood actresses, Joe liked to screw 'em.

"I told Mankiewicz going in that I wasn't much of an actress. But I understood Maria Vargas [the contessa of the title]. She was a lot like me. That was an understatement! If he'd help me, I said,

I thought I could deliver a performance we could both live with. Well, something went wrong. I didn't get any help from him at all. He was a complete bust. I read somewhere that he knew it, too. He told a reporter he didn't think he was as much help to me as he would have liked. He got that right. The only good thing on that picture was Eddie O'Brien. He deserved his Oscar. I first met him on *The Killers*. He was a wonderful actor, and knew I was struggling. He would say little things, like: 'Don't be in a hurry to say that line. Wait a beat. It's a good line, it's important.' Eddie knew more about Maria Vargas than Mankiewicz did—and Mankiewicz created her!"

"But he based her on you, right?"

"Down to the soles of my feet, honey. Later he said she was based on Rita [Hayworth]. That was crap. There was too much shit in the script about my affair with Howard. Joe even included the scene in which I nearly whacked the bastard."

"*Whoa,* you nearly killed Howard Hughes?"

"I hit him with an ashtray. I think it was onyx. Anyway, it was heavy. I practically had him laid out on a slab. We fought all the time but I nearly put a lily in his hand that night."

The memory of it made her laugh until it became a cough. She said she'd tell me the story later. It was worth a whole chapter, she said. "It's funny now but Louis Mayer nearly had kittens when he heard about it. He was convinced I'd killed the guy."

"Tell me more about *The Barefoot Contessa,*" I said.

"It could have been called *Howard and Ava,* it was so fucking obvious. But Joe swore till he was blue in the face that it was based on Rita's life. Howard was a friend of his—most of those guys stuck together like shit—but he was on to him like a fucking tiger once he'd read the script. I didn't give Howard the script, by the way; Mankiewicz was convinced I did, but I know that Howard got it from Johnny Meyer, although Johnny denied it," she said.

Mankiewicz had used Meyer as the model for the publicity man Oscar Muldoon, whom Edmond O'Brien had played as a sweaty, sycophantic press agent, for which he won an Academy Award for best supporting actor.

"The film had wrapped and was ready to be shipped but Howard still demanded changes. It must have cost Mankiewicz a small fortune. The Hughes character, a Texas tycoon [played by Warren Stevens], became a Wall Street big shot. They had to dub pages of dialogue to remove the clues that pointed to Howard. I felt sorry for Joe. We had our differences but he always stood up for me when Bogie was being difficult.

"By this time Bogie was feeling his age. He looked burnt out, like Daddy at the end. I still admired the sonofabitch on the screen, I just didn't like him very much as a man—and he had no respect for me at all.

"He knew I was dating Luis Miguel Dominguín. It wasn't much of a secret. Frank had heard about it in New York. Luis Miguel was the most famous bullfighter in the world. Bogie was furious that I was giving Frank a hard time. He loved Frank like a brother. They started the Rat Pack together. 'I don't know why you want to two-time Frank with a goddamn fruit,' he'd needle me. 'I never had you down as a dame who'd go for a pantywaist.' Stuff like that. Luis Miguel was one of the bravest men I knew. He was definitely no fruit, I can tell you that. Bogie knew it, too. It was his way of winding me up. He was always trying to get my goat."

She paused thoughtfully. "What year was that?"

"You started shooting *Barefoot Contessa* at the beginning of '54," I said.

"My God," she said in a small voice. I heard her refresh her nightcap and wondered what she was drinking at three o'clock in the morning. She didn't sound drunk. "Frank and I had been married barely a couple of years. The marriage was obviously unraveling even then. Maybe I'm remembering some things wrong. It was a long time ago. I get mixed up, honey," she said. "That fucking stroke didn't help one little bit. You'll have to sort out the dates later."

She had told me that she had never cheated on any of her husbands. This couldn't have been true if she had started the affair with Luis Miguel Dominguín. But I let it pass. This was not the time to question things she had said in earlier conversations. As she often reminded me, it was her life and she'd remember it any way she wanted.

There was a long silence on the line.

"Ava?"

"Yeah, I'm here, honey," she said after a moment.

"I thought you had fallen asleep on me," I said.

"No," she said. "I'm just surprised the marriage lasted as long as it did. Although it was over long before it ended."

"It must have been a difficult time for you," I said sympathetically.

"It was a bad time for Frank. Poor darling, he was so insecure. He was broke. He didn't have a job. He was hanging on to his place in Palm Springs by the skin of his teeth. It was the last real asset he had. If he'd lost that, it would have been the end of the line for him. He had made a lot of enemies in his good years, before the bobby-soxers found somebody new to throw their panties at. Nobody wanted to be around him. There were no hangers-on. He didn't amuse them anymore. He couldn't lift a check. There was nobody but me. He had burned most of his bridges with the press. There was a catalogue of disasters: His voice had gone. MGM had let him go. His agent had let him go. So had CBS. On top of all that, the poor bastard suffered a hemorrhage of his vocal cords and couldn't talk, let alone sing, for about six weeks. That's when I saw through those people. I saw through Hollywood. Naive little country girl that I was, I saw through all the phoniness, all the crap.

I couldn't wait to get out of there. When I go back there today I realize just how right I was. It's just awful, it's still false, the yes-men and bullshitters are all still there."

"At least your career was on the up," I said.

"Thank God. *Time* magazine put me on the cover in 1951, just before we married. They called me Hollywood's most irresistible female, or some rubbish like that. A *Time* cover was a great accolade in those days. It was almost as sought after as an Oscar. We all wanted one—except Frank. *Time* was on his SOB list since they said he looked flea-bitten in some movie or other. He took that very personally. He could hold a grudge longer than anyone I know, even against friends. He turned against Sammy Davis for years after I did a Christmas spread with Sam for one of those big black magazines. They made up, on the surface they did, but Frank never really forgave him, he was always slapping him down. People thought he was kidding, but he wasn't."

"What was that about, Ava?" I said.

"Frank had just made a film with Shelley Winters [*Meet Danny Wilson*]. It wasn't very good. They sent out invitations to the premiere in New York. It wasn't a big do, I don't remember too many faces being there, but Sammy was sweet enough to come. He gave me a little pair of drop earrings, engraved AS [Ava Sinatra]. When he asked me to do a shoot with him for the Christmas cover of *Ebony* I think it was, I could hardly say no.

"He came round to the Hampshire House with his photographers. I dressed up in a pretty red dress, Sammy put on a Santa Claus suit and wore a hokey white beard. I spent all afternoon on a picture session with him, something I wouldn't normally do. Frank wasn't there, but my sister was, my maid Rene was there. I was on the wagon. I ordered Coca-Cola for everybody. When the session was finished they took some informal shots of Sammy and me—me on the sofa, Sammy sitting on the arm, looking happy, looking festive, that sort of thing. He put his arm around me in a friendly way.

"It must have been a couple of weeks later, Howard Hughes tipped me that *Confidential* magazine was planning to run a story claiming that Sammy and I had had an affair. They have pictures, he said. Frank hit the roof when I told him. 'Did you screw him?' he screamed. Of course I didn't, I said. Frank went through the whole there's-no-smoke-without-fire routine. How could he even think that? I said. Was he crazy? 'How the fuck does your boyfriend know all about it then?' he yelled. Howard was always 'my boyfriend.' Frank would never call him by his name. I said, 'I'll sue the fuckers, Frank. I'll sue their asses off.'

"'Yeah, do that,' he said.

"I was so naive. I thought it would be easy to kill the story. Whitey Hendry, who ran MGM's private police force, had a lot of muscle in that town. He could keep most of the studio's scandals under wraps. He said he'd get back to me. Instead I got a call from Howard Strickling, the head of studio publicity. I liked Howard. I had a lot of respect for him, everybody did. He'd been with the studio forever. He said, 'Ava, I don't want you to sue this rag. It's a piddling, jerkwater outfit. If you sue you'll get a small apology and no money—but they will get enormous publicity around the world. It'll hurt you, it will hurt the studio.'

"'You're not going to do anything about it?' I said.

"He said, 'Of course we are. We are going to ignore it.'"

I heard her sigh. "All my fucking ghosts," she said.

"We've got some good stuff, Ava. It's been our best session yet." I said, and meant it, although I knew that the narrative would need some fixing.

"You think so?"

"I know so. We probably have enough material for several chapters. The Bogart material is terrific."

"You think so?" she said again.

"We should always work through the night," I said.

"You, me, and my ghosts," she said.

"Good night, Ava," I said, but she had put the phone down and the line was already dead.

23

Burning the midnight oil, I finished the draft of the next couple of chapters in three days and couriered them over to her with a friendly, businesslike note:

Dear Ava,

I hope you've caught up on your sleep, and are feeling better. I am a great believer in the healing powers of sleep. Grab as much of it as you can, I say. One can never dream to excess!

*As promised, here are the drafts of the chapters we discussed. I think they work well, and move at a good pace. I've wrapped up your marriage to Mickey, continued to develop your relationship with Howard Hughes, and segued into your marriage to Artie Shaw (1945). It stops just short of your breakthrough movies (*Whistle Stop; The Killers*) in 1946.*

Since you talk about Hollywood and the 1940s better than anyone I know, I have used your own words and phrases wherever I can. The gossip, opinions, and asides are all yours, of course!

Anyway, these are first drafts; nothing is set in stone. After you have checked the facts, and corrected my inevitable errors and any misunderstandings, let me have your thoughts and suggestions, and I will get moving on the final polish.

xx Peter

This is what I wrote about the conclusion of Ava's first marriage:

It had been a civilized divorce as Hollywood divorces go. I'd taken Eddie Mannix's advice that things might not go well for me at MGM if I tried to take Mickey to the cleaners. Well, he had been a damn sight blunter than that; Eddie had a way of giving it to you straight, but with a smile on his face that always had a hint of sympathy in it—if you looked hard enough, that is, and did what he wanted!

Even so, I liked the old gangster. I know he liked me, too. Not in the way some of the front-office suits liked new starlets—as a regular supply of pussy. I'm sure he gave the bedroom eye to some of the other girls but he played it straight with me. Being married to Mickey gave me certain privileges on the lot—like not being hit on by lecherous producers.

Anyway, Eddie kept his promise to find me a decent role if I took Mick back after I kicked him out of the house the time I found a lady's hairpin in our bed, and discovered she'd been using my douche bag while I'd been in the hospital recovering from the operation on my inflamed appendix. Good old Eddie came up with the role in *Ghosts on the Loose*, for which I got my first screen credit. It was a nothing part in a rinky-dink movie but some things you don't forget.

I kept my side of the bargain, too. I hadn't demanded half of Mickey's dough and property ("Mickey's treasure," as Louis Mayer called it), as I was entitled to do under California law. I settled for $25,000, a car—it was the Lincoln Continental that Henry Ford had given to Mick, but with the silver gift plate discreetly removed from the dashboard. I also kept a few nice pieces of jewelry, and the mink jacket Mickey had given me for my nineteenth birthday—and hadn't taken back when he was in extremis with his bookies.

For those of you who like a touch of irony in their stories about movie stars, the dark blue suit I wore for the divorce hearing at the Los Angeles City Court was the one I got married in. I'd hardly had any wear out of it, and I was still a thrifty North Carolina gal at heart.

Thurmond Clarke was the judge—why the hell I should remember the name of the guy who divorced us but have forgotten the name of the preacher who joined us together I have no idea; Dr. May Romm would have had a field day with that one! She was the shrink Artie Shaw sent me to when he became concerned about my drinking. A fat lot of good that did me!

Anyway, I told the judge that Mickey didn't want a home life, he stayed out at nights with the boys, he wasn't attentive enough, da-de-da, de-da. I was careful what I said: nothing bad, nothing too damaging. Nothing the press could pounce on and make into a headline. I could feel Uncle Louis breathing down my neck, right?

The final decree came through on May 21, 1943. It couldn't have been a sadder day for me because it was the day my mother died. My tears were for her, of course, although a few were shed for the end of my marriage, too.

Mickey called me as soon as he got his copy of the legal paperwork—and before he'd heard my news about Mama. He said, "Thanks for going easy on me in court, babe. I really appreciate that. So does Uncle Louis!"

"That's okay, Mick," I said lamely. I wasn't expecting to be thanked. He sounded so humble. But neither was I prepared for what was coming next.

"Well, I hope it's what you really want, kid! It's not too late to change your mind, you know?" he said, reverting to his old bumptious, egotistical self. "I'll be more than happy to take you back, kid. No questions asked!"

Normally, that would have got my rag. He probably knew it, too. But I was feeling low, and just for a moment, a nanosecond, on hearing his cocky, confident voice, I wondered if it really was what I wanted. We had both behaved badly and said appalling things but perhaps that just showed how much we cared for each other. We knew each other so well, we both knew where to strike without leaving a mark.

Anyway, I didn't rise to the bait. I said, "I'll probably miss the good times, Mick. I might even miss your lousy jokes."

"So you'll come back?" he said.

"Are you fucking crazy?" I said.

"We can still make a go of it," he said. He was relentless.

"I don't think so, Mick," I said.

"We're still great in bed together, aren't we? Let's give it another try, baby. I promise you won't regret it."

"Don't hold your breath, Mick," I said firmly, although he had a point about how good the sex still was between us. We hadn't found a downside to it yet.

"Then how about a farewell fuck?" he said cheerfully.

"You've had all the fucking you're going to get from me, Rooney," I said. It was a nice try but I was determined not to let him laugh me into bed again.

"How about one for old times' sake?" he tried again. He knew my weak spots, and there was nothing subtle in his approach. "How about dinner tonight, seven o'clock, the Vine Street Derby?" he said.

"I have other plans, Mick," I told him. It was true, I was seeing Howard. Anyway, I knew Mick's game. The Derby was a short walk from the American Legion Stadium where we used to go to the Friday night fights with his Irish Mafia pals—Pat O'Brien, Spencer Tracy, the Paddywhack crowd, Mick called them. Betty Grable and George Raft, they were another couple of Friday night regulars. I knew he was playing the nostalgia card.

"Get it into your head, Mick, those days are over. We're finished. We blew it, honey," I said, but I felt like shit saying it. In spite of his bravado, I knew how deeply he would feel the brutal finality of those words.

"I should have taught you how to shoot." His voice was suddenly hoarse. "Then you could have shot me through the heart. It would have been far less painful," he said.

"For both of us," I told him.

I couldn't bring myself to tell him that I still loved him. I loved him even more than on the day we married. It sounds like a cliché when I say that now, but that was always the way it was with me and departing husbands: I just couldn't help myself. It was as if I had a compulsion to punish myself for walking out on them. Well, Artie Shaw walked out on me, actually. He didn't waste any time doing it either—that marriage had lasted just about a year when he called the cab on me—but I loved him just as much as I loved Mick and Frank at the end of those marriages.

"You were the perfect first husband, Mick Rooney," I told him.

I meant it as a joke but it made me sad saying it. I remembered all the good times we'd had together. They came back to me with a clarity that was overwhelming: the first night we'd danced at the Cocoanut Grove, the time he'd run *Captains Courageous* and *Boys Town* back-to-back for me at MGM's private screening room, after I told him I hadn't seen either of them; the evening we'd dined at the White House with President Roosevelt on his sixtieth birthday, and watched him give one of his famous radio broadcasts to the nation; the first day I took Mick home to meet Mama in Raleigh—she'd been too sick to come to our wedding—and the fuss Mick made of her. She had such a good time. It was probably the best time of her life. The whole family was there, and all the neighbors came by; word had gotten around that Mickey Rooney was visiting.

Mama had put on her glad rags, a green silk dress, with silver appliqué at the neck, which I knew Daddy had always loved her in. She had lost a bit of weight, I thought. That was the time Inez told me Mama had the big C.

Does she know? I said. I was shocked. "Of course she knows, honey, just as sure as anything in this world, but she doesn't want us obsessing over her. She's dying, but she refuses to let on, and neither must you," Inez said.

I didn't tell Mickey about Mama's condition, not right away, but he was marvelous anyway. He couldn't have been nicer, kinder, or more attentive. He might have been playing a command performance for the Queen of England. He sang to her—"Oh, You Beautiful Doll," which was one of her favorites, "Carolina in the Morning," "You Do Something to Me," he did a whole bunch of those numbers, "The Bells Are Ringing"—he clowned, he told her funny and mildly scandalous stories about her favorite movie stars: Judy Garland, Gable, Spencer Tracy. Mama had such a good time, the years just rolled away. She didn't seem to have a care in the world.

When we were getting ready to leave, she held me in her arms. "Ava child, you're a pretty woman now, and you've sure filled out nicely, but you'll always be my little girl," she said.

"I know that, Mama," I said.

"If only your Daddy was here to share this moment with me. He would have been so proud of you."

Remembering that moment, I began to cry. All those happy

days came flooding back to me. Imagining that I was weeping over the failure of our marriage—he was a conceited little sod but I suppose, at least partly, so was I—Mickey said: "Hey, what's with the sob stuff, honey? Don't let a little old divorce between friends spoil your day, sweetheart. It happens all the time in Tinsel Town. It means nothing."

When I told him that my Mom had died that morning, he broke into tears, too. He could cry at the drop of a hat. I told you that. He and Louis Mayer were the best criers on the MGM lot. But that was the first time I knew his tears were as genuine as mine.

The evening my divorce was made final, I had dinner with Howard Hughes. We had been seeing each other on a regular basis since he read in the newspapers that I had started divorce proceedings against Mickey. I didn't know it at the time, but Howard had a weakness for newly divorced women. He'd moved in on Kate Hepburn immediately after her divorce from Luddy Smith, he pursued Lana Turner straight after she split with Artie. I'm sure there were plenty of others. "Wet decks," Johnny Meyer called us, God knows why, although knowing Johnny, I'm sure it had some sexual, if not downright dirty, connotation.

Howard's appeal was the opposite of Mickey's. He was an older man and he was infinitely more serious and smarter and sophisticated than anyone else I'd dated up to then. He was richer, too, of course.

He was still seeing plenty of other women but that didn't stop him proposing to me all the fucking time. The fact that I had said yes to him once—the time he wanted me to get a quickie divorce from Mick in Nevada before my California one became legal and I succumbed to his flattery and said I would—only encouraged him. I told you, Louis Mayer talked me out of that, thank God. "It wouldn't be fair to Mick," he'd said. The hypocrisy of the man! Or maybe he was just sticking to the routine double standards of Hollywood in those days.

Anyway, that night, my first night back in circulation—at least officially—Howard took me to dinner at the Players, an exclusive private club on the Strip. I liked the Players. It was owned by his friend the movie director Preston Sturges. I never worked for Sturges but he ran a great club. Howard had taken it over—complete with its dance orchestra—just for the two of us. The events in Sturges's films often bordered on the surreal—he made *Sullivan's Travels,* a satire on Hollywood—and he must have loved the irony of his usually jam-packed club being exclusively possessed for the whole evening by two people.

By now, I was used to Howard's excesses, and this was not the first time he had persuaded Sturges to hang a "closed" sign on his restaurant when he didn't want to be disturbed or seen by other diners.

The first couple of times were amusing—although dining *a deux* in an empty restaurant can lack a bit of atmosphere, even if the service was great—probably because I knew that he wanted to seduce me with his wealth, and I was determined not to be impressed. That probably sounds blasé, but by this time there was no surprise, only a feeling of routine. It felt as if we were a couple of actors being served by other actors on a candlelit stage.

"Howard," I said, up front, "you really don't have to try to impress me. You know my answer is still going to be no."

He looked puzzled. "I haven't asked you the question yet," he said.

"Yes you have, several times. By the time we get to the lamb chops, you are going to ask me to marry you—again."

"How do you know that?" he said.

"You couldn't have made it more fucking obvious. Couldn't you have invited a few extras along to cheer the place up a bit—or at least look happy for us? Waiters' smiles are a poor fucking substitute for genuine happiness, Howard," I said.

He didn't like me swearing, or drinking too much. He didn't drink himself. He definitely didn't like me making fun of him. Both of which I enjoyed immensely. I often did it just to annoy him. I knew there was no way I was going to marry him. I don't know why I ever said I would the first time. Perhaps I just wanted to put distance between Mickey and me. At least it helped me to ease my way out of Mickey's bed.

Although Howard was crazy about me—this was before I realized that he was just plain crazy—we still hadn't slept together. I enjoyed the power I had over him. I enjoyed his frustration.

I knew that he had a reputation as a cocksman, but I always suspected that was a story Johnny Meyer had put around town for him. The powder-room scuttlebutt was that he was no great shakes in the sack—or he shtupped like a snake! Or he liked to make it with a couple of girls at the same time. Or he was a fag. You got all sides of the story in the powder room.

Anyway, I am not going to go into any details here, but I'll say this: he knew how to take his time with a lady. At least with this lady he did. He was a patient sonofabitch, the complete opposite of Mickey Rooney. In fact, Howard and I didn't get it on—I don't think he even tried to kiss me, apart from the mildest kiss-on-the-cheek good night—until after my final decree from Mick. I gave in to him—or my curiosity finally got the better of me—a couple of nights after our dinner at the Players, actually.

As a lover, I still only had Mickey to judge him by, of course, but let's say Howard Hughes was a pleasant surprise. He didn't have Mick's vivacity, his cheerfulness between the sheets—nor mine, to be honest. But Howard's timing was nearly always perfect. He taught me that making love didn't always have to be rushed. "Slow down, slow down, kid. We'll get there!" he'd say. He was like a fucking horse whisperer. We usually had a good time in the feathers.

Once, when I told him how satisfying he was in bed, he said: "That's because I don't drink, kid. Especially when I'm with a lady I intend to please." It took me a while to work that one out. That shows you how innocent I still was!

Although I never loved him the way I loved Mickey, nor the way I would love Artie, and Frank, he was a big part of my growing up and I loved him for that. We fought all the time, but I fought with all my men. It was my way of life, my way of loving, I suppose. But whatever it was, our intimacy never deepened. It never grew. We had no sense of complicity at all. We didn't even share a sense of humor. I could laugh with Mick, I could cry with Frank, but with Howard there was always this kind of . . . shortfall, I suppose you could call it. Something wasn't there. It wasn't just the age gap thing between us, because that wasn't really so bad, especially the longer it went on, but there was always something missing.

Bappie blamed it on me for taking his generosity for granted. He treated me like a princess . . . jewels, furs, suites at the best hotels. Limos and planes at my disposal. When Mama died and Bappie and I couldn't get a flight back to Raleigh for the funeral, Howard bumped a couple of four-star generals off the plane and gave us their seats. He said they were only flying desks in Washington anyway. Even so, in the war, bumping four-star generals off a flight was still something.

There were plenty of advantages in being wooed by the man who owned TWA—and, according to Johnny Meyer, had half of Washington, D.C., in his pocket. And Johnny should have known: his main business in those days was to make sure that the government didn't forget Howard's aircraft plants when they were handing out defense contracts. "I don't know where all the bodies are buried," Johnny liked to say. "But I do know where most of them are sleeping—and that's even better!"

Maybe I never appreciated all the things Howard did for me. Bappie said I was an ungrateful bitch the way I treated him. She had a soft spot for Howard. She always took his side when we argued. She thought I was insane not to want to marry him. But she said the same thing about Mick when I first stepped out with him. She was always a little starstruck.

She never saw Howard's faults—for example his jealousy. He was an insanely possessive man. He had a private detective watching me around the clock, 24/7, as they say now. His jealousy was petty and hilarious. He hated the Lincoln Continental Mickey had given me as part of our divorce settlement. I loved that car but Howard made me get rid of it. He bought me a Cadillac instead. When the Caddie needed its first service, he told me to take it to his aircraft workshop in Burbank. He said his mechanics would do a better job on it than the dealers. I thought that was nice because we'd just had a tremendous fight over something or other—I had actually blacked his eye. I wasn't expecting any favors from him until at least the swelling had gone down.

But when I picked up the Caddie, I'd only driven it a couple of miles when the engine fell out in the middle of Coldwater Canyon! That was Howard's idea of a practical joke. It was his money, so what the fuck.

He had a weird sense of humor, I must say, although I'm sure there was an element of revenge in it, too. It took me years to see the funny side of that prank.

I don't know why Howard stayed around so long. He stayed around a long time after it was clear that I was never going to marry him. I just couldn't shake him off. It was a strange relationship. I don't think he ever put his arms around me out of affection, or to comfort me. He'd only take me in his arms if he wanted sex—or to stop me from hitting him.

When I told him that Artie had asked me to marry him, he said: "Go ahead, kid, if that's what you want, but you'll regret it. It won't last five minutes. He doesn't love you—he just loves the idea of screwing you. Lana Turner didn't last five minutes, and neither will you, honey."

He was right about that. He had Artie pegged from the word go. Maybe he'd had him followed, I don't know. Anyway, in less than a year, Artie had tired of me and was sniffing around Kathleen Winsor.

If I had paid more attention to those Freudian manuals he was always laying on me, I might have smelled a rat. But I had no idea at all. A couple of months after our divorce, I fell apart when he married her. But it taught me a lesson. It taught me that hypocrisy isn't just the province of movie producers.

Anyway, let me finish the story about Howard Hughes. Bappie still thought I was mad for turning Howard down. She adored him. "Think of all that money, honey," she'd say wistfully.

She was now stepping out with Charlie Guest. Charlie started out as one of Howard's tennis cronies and ended up running his Beverly Hills property portfolio—which meant taking care of the houses in which Howard stashed his women, including Lana, of course, Ginger Rogers, me, Jane Russell, a whole bunch of us down the years. Charlie drank too much but he was a gold mine of information and gossip about Howard's girls.

Anyway, our relationship was volatile, let's put it that way. It was never as violent as my affair with GCS, that's for sure. But once Howard took a swipe at me and dislocated my jaw—that was the night I felled him with the fucking ashtray. I thought I'd killed the poor bastard. There was blood on the walls, on the furniture, real blood in the bloody Marys. I panicked. I think I phoned Mickey first. When I couldn't reach him, I called the studio. It was late, I don't know who the hell I talked to but I must have been hysterical and whoever it was they quickly got the message.

Someone contacted Ida Koverman. She was always the studio's first port of call in an emergency when they didn't want to disturb L.B.

Anyway, L.B. was disturbed. He sent his boys round to clean up the mess. They got me out of there so fucking fast my feet didn't touch the Orientals. I'm sure Mayer thought it was going to become a murder scene! I don't think he gave a damn about me, but he didn't want any scandal attached to his studio.

Fortunately, probably miraculously, Howard recovered—and again asked me to marry him.

But the mix was too volatile. Our chemistry was the stuff that causes hydrogen bombs to explode. Till death us do part would have been a whole lot sooner than later if we had tied the knot.

Howard was a control freak, and I was too independent to take his crap. He was out of his mind most of the time even then, and he got crazier through the years. He died in 1976, twelve years ago. But in a funny sort of way, I still miss him. I still think of him.

24

You've got to get rid of more of that language, honey. She still swears too fucking much," she said. Referring to herself theatrically in the third person threw me for a moment. "Why does she have to swear all the goddamn time? It makes her sound like a goddamn tramp."

"Ava, good morning," I said.

"I thought you were going to clean up her mouth," she said. Her voice was friendly enough but I caught the disapproval in her words.

"We can still do that, if that's what you want," I said guardedly. That was the last thing I wanted to do; without the epithets and profanities, her voice would lose its gritty individuality. Anyway, I relished the feistiness of her conversations. Without that, she wouldn't sound the same at all.

"I told you, it's a first draft. There are a few things I need to change. I just want you to check that I haven't made any factual mistakes." I was playing for time. "Anyway, why are you calling so early? We're not on studio time again, are we?"

"I might just as well be. I've been awake since four o'clock, waiting to call you. I was going to call at six. I thought that would be a little too early. Seven's okay, isn't it?"

"Seven's fine," I was grateful for her unusual thoughtfulness.

"I'm trying to cut down on the booze. What do you say to that?"

"That's good," I said.

"I'm not so sure about that, honey. Not drinking fucks up my head worse than a hangover sometimes. I can feel my mortality, baby."

"If you're not sleeping, it's no wonder you're exhausted."

"What I feel is more than exhaustion, honey. I am dying, Egypt, dying."

"Have you had breakfast?"

"Not yet."

"You'll feel better when you've had something to eat."

"Have you shown this stuff to Ed Victor yet?" she asked.

I had, of course, but her sudden change of tone made me wary. "Don't you want me to?" I vacillated.

"Let me think about it."

"What is there to think about, Ava? We're on the same side, aren't we? You must tell me if there is anything you're not happy with."

"No, it's fine." She sounded hesitant.

"But something's worrying you, I can tell," I said. If there was a problem it was better to get it out in the open and deal with it now.

"I'm not sure about some of the things we say about Mick and Howard, honey," she said slowly. "You've used an awful lot of personal stuff."

"Such as?"

"Like saying Mick and I continued to sleep together after our divorce."

"Well, you did, didn't you? That's what you said."

"I know. I just don't know if we should spell it out so plainly."

"Why not?" I said.

She changed the subject and her diffident manner gave way to something much harder. "The stuff about Howard, did I say that? I don't remember saying all that."

"You did, Ava. Maybe not word for word—I've used material from earlier notes but it's essentially what you said. I've kept the same feeling, the same line. That Howard taught you lovemaking didn't have to be rushed, how he talked to you like a horse whisperer," I said, grateful that I had discreetly omitted her remark that Mickey always woke up with an erection, and Howard never did. But I still had no idea of what the problem was, or its scale.

"The thing is, it could open up a can of worms," she said.

"I don't see how."

"I was also sleeping with Howard after I split with Mick."

"You mean you were sleeping with Mickey and Howard at the same time?"

"You don't have to be coy, honey," she said, and laughed. "I slept with them on and off for a while. Well, pretty much right up until I met Artie. It was only for sex. But we're not going to say that either, honey."

"Did Mickey and Howard know they were sharing you?" There was no point to the question except prurient curiosity, and I knew it was a mistake the moment I asked it.

"Jesus Christ, Peter!" she said angrily. "Does it matter?"

"I suppose not," I said sheepishly. "Anyway, we don't say that you were sleeping with both of them after your divorce from Mickey? We don't spell it out, do we?"

"And we're not going to," she said flatly.

"Then I don't see how it can open a can of worms. No one is going to know unless you tell them," I said.

"People have dirty minds, honey. Some smart-ass reporter is sure to put two and two together," she said. "It'll make me sound like a fucking *puta." Puta* was her favorite word for a slut. She despised *putas*.

"People aren't going to think that at all," I said.

"Bull-*shit*. You know exactly that's what they're going to think." I heard her take a deep breath. "Where we talk about what Mick and Howard were like in the feathers. Do we have to go into that?"

"You're complimentary about both of them," I said.

There was a silence on the line and I knew she was reading the copy again.

I had been scrupulous about quoting her exactly and her squeamishness surprised me. She had been inordinately discreet, even generous to both men. After quite a long silence, she said: "Yeah, I guess that's okay. I haven't said anything shitty about them, have I?"

"You've been sweet to them."

"But I thought it was just between us—not between you, me, and every Tom, Dick, and Harry who is going to buy the book."

"You want a bestseller, don't you?" I said.

"Telling how Howard measured up to Mick in bed—do we really have to use all that stuff, honey?"

"We don't *have* to but it's what you said, Ava," I reminded her again. "It sounds fine to me. Do you want me to lose it? We can do that but it would be a pity."

"I thought all that stuff was between us, honey," she repeated, avoiding my question.

"All *what* stuff? We're talking about maybe a dozen lines, probably less. Anyway, you knew the meter was running," I said. I hoped she remembered it was her phrase.

"I don't want a kiss-and-tell book," she said stubbornly. "I thought we agreed on that."

"But we want an honest book. This is honest. Emotionally it's honest to the bone. Only you could say these things the way you say them. Readers will love that."

"Fuck the readers."

I decided not to argue with her any further. "Fine, if that's what you want," I said. "Fuck the readers."

"You think?" she said, and laughed again.

"I told you what I think, Ava."

"I know."

I could hear the caution in her voice and tried again. "I truly don't see what the problem is, Ava. It's an exaggeration to say that you compare Mick and Howard as lovers. We are talking about no more than a few lines in the whole book. I don't think that makes it a kiss-and-tell book."

I heard her turn the pages of the chapters I'd sent her. "Am I right?" I said.

"It's ten lines," she conceded after a while.

"That's nothing. It's an aside," I said. "Blink and you'll miss it."

"You don't think it puts me in a bad light?"

"Why should it? It's honest. Women will certainly understand the truth of it."

"You don't think it makes me sound like a goddamn tramp?" she persisted.

"Ava, you are talking about something that happened more than forty years ago—you were *just a kid, a baby!* Your words, not mine. Moral attitudes have changed. There's been a whole sexual revolution since then. The whole world has turned."

"Tell me about it," she said bleakly.

I felt her resistance weakening. "Sexual mores have changed. Nobody is going to be hurt by it. Mickey isn't going to complain, is he?" I said. It was hard to believe that this apparently uninhibited woman whose sexual appetite at the height of her fame had been legendary, who had unashamedly taken matadors, big-game hunters, passing hunks, and leading men to her bed, whose romantic life had mirrored that of her most famous screen character—the lovely and amoral Lady Brett Ashley in Hemingway's *The Sun Also Rises*—was now fretting about minor indiscretions half a century before.

She said, exasperated, "Who the fuck knows what Mickey will say? He's got religion now."

"I didn't know that."

"He's got religion coming out of his fucking ears."

"I still think he's going to be flattered that you continued to want him physically even after you were divorced. No man's going to complain about that, especially forty years on."

"It makes me sound like a goddamn tramp," she said again, truculence in her voice. "It makes me sound as if I was there just for Mick to get his ashes hauled."

"That's ridiculous," I said, although it made me laugh.

"I don't want to have to watch every fucking word I say to you, Pete," she said.

"You don't," I said. It was too early in the morning to get into an argument about what was on and off the record. As far as I was concerned everything she said was grist for the mill, although I knew that when push came to shove we'd always do it her way.

I said, "Look, let's not get hung up on words. When we get to the end, we'll go back and look again at anything you're still not sure about. We'll rework anything you're not comfortable with."

"I think we should concentrate more on the career," she said. "Let's talk more about that, about the movies I made. I must have made over a hundred fucking movies if you count all the early quickies, the turkeys I did, when I was learning my trade."

"Sure," I said, happy to change the subject.

AROUND SEVEN THAT EVENING, we met at Ennismore Gardens. She wore a plain oatmeal sweater and a matronly plaid skirt that fell just below her knees. It wasn't the most flattering length for her marvelous legs—legs about which director George Cukor once remarked, "When she crosses the screen, you're bound to follow her." And he was gay. She poured the wine. "Who was the young man who delivered the pages yesterday?"

"My brother," I said.

"I thought he might be. He looks like you. What's his name?" Michael, I said. She questioned me about Mike, my family, my wife. "Are you faithful to your wife?" she asked, looking straight at me as she handed me my drink.

"None of your business," I said, surprised by the question.

"I don't see why not. You know everything about me. I know fuck-all about you."

"You checked me out didn't you?"

"Only professionally," she said.

"Who did you ask?"

"None of your business, kiddo." She gleefully repeated my own riposte. She knew I was aware of the people with whom she had checked me out: Dirk Bogarde, Peter Viertel, Deborah Kerr, Spoli and Paul Mills, and Bill Edwards, an MGM marketing executive—the same mutual friends I had questioned about her!

"I didn't know you had a brother but you know all about *my* brothers," she said with feigned petulance.

"I'm your ghost, I've got to know these things."

"A girl has a right to some privacy."

"That's not the way it works, Ava."

"Okay, what else can I tell you? I've told you everything, for fuck sake. You know about my sisters, my Mom and Dad, my ex-husbands, my lovers. You know about my first period, fahcrissake. You even know about my Grandpa in the crazy farm. I've never told anyone about Grandpa Gardner, fahcrissake," she said, but there was a hint of humor in her petulance.

"That's because the book is about you. Next time, you can write a book about me and ask the questions." It was a joke but she didn't laugh.

Even so, it was true what she said: she knew almost nothing about me. She had scarcely ever asked me anything more inquisitive than would I like a drink? Like many actors, especially those who have become legendary movie stars, she was almost without curiosity about other people. Did being at the center of a world where others are peripheral—planets circling the star—create, bit by bit, a dividing line between reality and make-believe? Between the person you pretend to be and who you really are? Can such a woman ever be sure which side of the divide she belongs on?

Like most actors, Ava told outrageous and exaggerated stories about herself and other actors in order to entertain and amuse her friends; a story that started out as a risqué anecdote, told over and over, in time became accepted as fact even by Ava herself. "Is that true, Ava," I asked her after one of her booze-fueled late-night recollections about an incident involving a young actor with whom she'd reputedly had a torrid affair. "Probably." She shrugged indifferently.

Since the 1940s, when she was getting started, and discovered her power over the opposite sex, she had only to snap her fingers for men to come running; there was Sinatra, of course, John Huston, Howard Hughes, Hemingway, bullfighters—an indication of how demanding she was can be judged in bullfighter Luis Miguel Dominguín's reply when asked, just before his death in 1996, whether he regretted not marrying her: "No. She would have left me no time for the bulls!"—and just about every movie star she had played opposite from Clark Gable to Robert Taylor and Bob Mitchum.

Naturally, I was dubious about some of her stories. Did she really turn down the role of the predatory Mrs. Robinson in *The Graduate*? I'd heard stories that director Mike Nichols never felt

that she was right for the role—it was said that he always saw Anne Bancroft in the part, which she finally played—and reluctantly agreed to meet with Ava at her hotel in New York only after she called him and announced peremptorily, "I want to see you. I want to talk about this *Graduate* thing."

When Nichols arrived at her hotel, the St. Regis, Ava was surrounded by a group of admiring young men whom she promptly dismissed (getting rid of lovers, she told me once with some pride, was a skill she had perfected at an early age). Nichols recounted, "Theatrical and over the top, she sat at a little French desk with a telephone, she went through every movie star cliché. She said, 'All right, let's talk about your movie. First of all, I strip for nobody.'"

It sounded right. It sounded exactly like Ava. "I never was one of those actresses whose clothes fell off all the time—at least not on camera, honey," she said. When I eventually asked her about the episode, she at first claimed not to remember it.

"You don't recall meeting Mike Nichols at all? At the St. Regis, in New York?"

"I might have done. It was a long time ago."

"It was 1966."

"Oh, I remember," she said, suddenly changing her tune. "He made me cry."

"Why did he make you cry, Ava?"

"He wasn't very . . . simpatico."

"Was that why you turned down the role of Mrs. Robinson?"

"I told him I couldn't act," she said. "That was the same thing as turning it down. I said I was no actress. Do you mind if I ask you a personal question?" she said, running the sentences together to avoid a response. It was a politician's trick, and made me smile.

"Go ahead."

"Are you gay?"

"I thought you said Dirk Bogarde told you I wasn't," I said.

"He said you weren't a faggot. There's a difference. I can't stand faggots, I get on well with gays."

"What's the difference?"

"Gays make the best 'walkers.' They are good company. You can tell them your secrets. They are useful to have around. They bathe a lot. A woman can even go to bed with a gay. At a pinch."

"But not with a faggot?"

"Faggots . . . they're something else. They are cruder."

"I've never heard that definition before."

"You have now. So, we've established you're not a faggot . . . are you gay?"

No woman had ever asked me that before. Was she softening me up for a confession? The idea offended my masculine pride, but I was curious. "Do you think I am?"

"You can never tell these days," she said. "You don't have to answer if you don't want to."

I didn't mind, I said. No, I was not gay.

Bisexual? she asked, playfully.

Not bisexual, either, I said.

"I've known plenty of guys who are, you'd be surprised," she said. "In Hollywood, a lot of guys don't know whether they're Arthur or Martha."

I didn't know it at the time, but later—in an interview published shortly after Ava's death in 1990—Artie Shaw recalled how she had showed up at his apartment in New York late one night saying she needed to ask him some questions. "When you and I were in bed together, was it okay?" Shaw assured her that he had no complaints. According to Shaw, "She heaved a sigh of relief and said, 'Well, then there's nothing wrong with me?'" Shaw said, No, of course not. What did she mean? He said she told him, "With Frank it's like being in bed with a woman. He's so gentle. It's as though he thinks I'll break, as though I'm a piece of Dresden china and he's gonna hurt me."

Shaw said he always thought Frank was a stud. Ava told him, "No . . . I just wanted to know that it's not my fault." But the episode probably affected the rest of her marriage to Sinatra. Though there may have been a touch of irony in her tone when, in 1966 when he married Mia Farrow, she said: "I always knew Frank would end up in bed with a boy," there was also perhaps a hint of justification, too.

"Anyway, I'm straight," I told her. I probably sounded stuffy but I didn't mean to. Did she really think I was gay?

The other night when I left, she said, she had kissed me on my mouth. Did I remember that? Of course, I remembered, I said. Wasn't I surprised? she asked. Who could forget it, I said. You didn't react, she said reproachfully. Well, I won't forget it, I assured her.

She had been standing with her back to the door as I prepared to leave. I'd leaned in to kiss her cheek, but she turned her face, meeting my lips with hers. Then she opened her mouth. I felt that kiss in every bone and fiber of my body. She must have been aware of it, too. Her breath was short and audible. The width of her mouth, the sensual fullness of her lower lip, that bold, feline stare and the assurance that came with her history—I was being kissed by a Hollywood sex goddess. How many thousands of men had fantasized about her as they made love to their wives or girlfriends?

But there were a dozen different reasons why I had not responded to her kiss. Ava had not kissed me out of love—though perhaps out of affection. I was certain that she was impelled by desire, but not for me. What Ava wanted was what she had once had: the adulation that came with stardom; her ability to incite men's lust; the admiration she aroused as, draped in furs, she descended the steps of a plane on the arm of Frank Sinatra, or stepped bejeweled from a limousine beside Howard Hughes. What Ava wanted was a reminder of the power she had relished then, a reassurance that even after two solitary, sexually barren years, she was still desirable. Ava past her prime was still something else.

So now when she said I hadn't reacted, there was no petulance, she was simply registering that it was unusual. "Weren't you excited? Men usually react when I kiss them."

"That would be a terrible mistake, Ava," I said. "We have a professional relationship that's far too valuable to complicate with . . . you know."

It was a lame finish. The look she gave me was wry—and amused.

"You're not afraid of comparisons, then?"

"No," I said.

"No hard feelings, then?"

"No hard feelings," I said.

That made her laugh. "Good. I want you to be happy," she said.

"You've made me very happy," I said. She had kissed me. But she did so out of loneliness and out of need, maybe nostalgia, too. And I think we both knew it.

Later, when she told Spoli Mills about the incident—she told Spoli *everything*—she changed the story sufficiently to protect her self-respect: I had made the move *on her*! She had told me it would be a mistake.

Her reputation and ego were intact.

25

We hadn't talked for a couple of days, not about the book anyway. On the third evening, she called and was all business: "We haven't talked about *Mogambo* yet, have we?" No, I said, we hadn't. "Well, that's important. I think we should talk about that. I got an Oscar nod for that one."

It was the first time she had mentioned her Academy Award nomination for her role—playing the original Jean Harlow part—in John Ford's remake of the 1932 *Red Dust*. There was I thought a hint of pride in her voice when she acknowledged her nomination, although she didn't dwell on it.

"What about the marriage to Frank?" she hurried on. "We need to talk about that, don't we? We've covered most of the other Frank stuff, but I don't think we've dealt with the actual wedding in Philly, have we? We don't have to dwell on it but we should at least mention it."

"We must."

"It was a circus. We went to Philadelphia to keep it quiet. The press found out, of course. My God, it was a circus." After a thoughtful pause she said, "What else? I suppose we'll also have to talk about the abortion, too."

"I think so," I said, although the question surprised me. She had mentioned it once before but not in any detail. I knew she had probably had a couple of abortions, but this must have been the one she had in London during the making of *Mogambo.* The one she'd told me John Ford, a curmudgeonly Catholic, had tried desperately to talk her out of.

"*Okay.* Wedding, *Mogambo,* abortion," she said briskly, like a chairperson setting an agenda. Her serious tone amused me, and surprised me, too. Her sense of commitment had been . . . well, coquettish to say the least, and I told her how pleased I was that she was determined to get on with it.

"Sometimes I don't know whether I want to get on with it or not, honey. That's the God's truth. I'm tired of remembering. I'm sick of trying to remember what he said, what I said. What he did, what I did. I'm sick of trying to explain myself all the time. Don't you get tired of asking the same fucking questions all the time?"

"It's my job," I said.

"Are we nearly there, do you think?"

"I told you writing a book isn't easy or quick."

"Thank God I didn't have kids."

We hadn't discussed her feelings about not having had a family, although she had now put her abortions on the agenda, so I knew it was on her mind. "Do you regret not having had kids?" I said casually, suspecting it would still be a touchy subject.

"Oh Christ, Peter," she said wearily. "More fucking questions. What do you want me to tell you? I regret not having had a family? I'm sorry I partied too much? Is that what you want me to tell you?"

"That wasn't—" I started to say.

"How many people do you know who haven't made mistakes in their lives, who've lived completely without vices, baby?" she said fiercely before I could answer, then immediately apologized: "I had a lousy night," she said. "I nearly called you."

"Why didn't you?"

After a moment of hesitation, she said, "Let me ask you something. What happens if we don't finish the book?"

"I don't get paid, for one thing," I said in what I hoped was an amused tone. But she wasn't amused.

"I have to tell you, honey, I'm at the lowest ebb of my life right now, and it's worse every day. It's been nearly a couple of years since I had those strokes. I'm a whole lot nearer to dying than living. I feel that. There's almost no corn left in Egypt, baby," she said grimly. It was the line she had used at one of our earliest interviews, and reminded me of how far we had come since then, and how much further we still had to go. "We must finish this fucking book before they put me to bed with a shovel," she said with sudden anger.

"I hope you're joking." I tried to assuage her worries. "Nobody's going to put you to bed with a shovel," I said.

"It doesn't sound like a joke to me," she said.

I felt rebuked.

THE FOLLOWING EVENING, WE had dinner at Ennismore Gardens, cooked by Ava's longtime housekeeper, Carmen Vargas, who ate with us. Ava, in bare feet, and wearing her familiar gray track suit, seemed in no hurry to start work in spite of her assurances the previous evening. She entertained us with stories about her friend Charles Gray, a notoriously camp and bibulous English actor who lived a few doors down. His aura of suave insincerity was eminently suited to villains—he played Ernst Stavro Blofeld, the boss of SPECTRE, in *Diamonds Are Forever*—and Ava adored him. Although one sensed that Carmen did not share her enthusiasm—he undoubtedly encouraged Ava's consumption of alcohol—and may have been responsible for banning him from the apartment. (They continued their relationship from their nearby balconies, often drinking into the night.)

"Did I ever tell you about the time Salvador Dali came calling in Madrid?" Ava eventually asked.

"I don't think so."

"The Surrealist painter, Salvador Dali. He must have been about fifty," she began contemplatively. "Although fuck's that got to do with anything. I was running away from Frank, we'd been married a year, and I was desperately trying to break up with him. I knew I just couldn't live with him anymore, I still loved him, Jesus, I loved him. But the marriage was never going to work. Financially, emotionally, physically, every fucking whichway it was never going to work. I told you about the time at the Hampshire House in New York? When he said he couldn't stand it any longer and was going to kill himself? I heard this fucking gun go off? Haven't I told you about that night?"

"Not yet," I said. She was off on a tangent. I didn't try to stop her. A word, a name, the mention of a place or a time, could open a whole new vein of memories and anecdotes. Scenes and conversations came back to her in short rushes of recall. Piecing her stories together was always a challenge.

"We were still waiting for his divorce to come through. Nancy kept changing her mind about whether she wanted to go through with it or not. Meanwhile, her lawyers were trying to screw Frank for every penny he had. I was commuting between the studio in California and Frank in New York. It put a strain on both of us."

She had landed the part of Julie, the black girl who was passing for white, in Metro's remake of Jerome Kern's musical *Show Boat*. She collapsed during costume fittings and was rushed to the hospital in Santa Monica.

"I know some people said it was an abortion that time, too, but it wasn't, I promise you. To be honest, I don't know what the hell it was—a viral infection, a nervous breakdown, exhaustion—but it wasn't an abortion. All I know is that I was bloody sick. I was kept in for nearly a month. I must have been genuinely ill because I was in St.

John's and they don't fuck around. St. John's is the same joint I was in when I had the strokes thirty-odd years later. A small world, huh?

"Anyway, I heard this gun go off. We'd been fighting, of course. And drinking. Every single night, we would have three or four martinis, big ones, in big champagne glasses, then wine with dinner, then go to a nightclub and start drinking Scotch or bourbon.

"It was another one of those nights I ended up refusing to sleep with Frank. I was half asleep in my room across the suite and heard this gunshot. It scared the bejeezus out of me. I didn't know what I was going to find. His brains blown out? He was always threatening to do it. Instead, he was sitting on the bed in his underpants, a smoking gun in his hand, grinning like a goddamn drunken school kid. He'd fired the gun into the fucking pillow. What a night that was!"

She seemed amused at the memory. "At least his overdoses were quieter."

"Overdoses?" I pretended to be surprised, although the stories of Sinatra's mock suicides, now well documented, were familiar to me, along with the incident of his attempt to gas himself at record executive Manny Sachs' apartment in New York. My feigned ignorance on a subject could often encourage her to divulge an unexpected nugget of information. "You mean he tried it more than once?"

"All the fucking time. It was a cry for help. I always fell for it."

After a pause, she said: "Anyway, I was telling you about Mr. Dali."

"Yes," I said, grateful that she had remembered.

"I was running away from Frank again. I'd finished *Mogambo,* and was about to start *The Barefoot Contessa.* I was just hitting my stride career-wise, and making some decent money—despite the fact that MGM still pocketed most of it under the contract I signed when I was eighteen. I was looking for a house to buy in Madrid. I really loved Spain, the pace of the place, the climate; I thought I could put down roots there, at least for a year or two.

"I was staying at the Castellana Hilton. I was one of the few Americans living in the city at that time. Dali asked me to go to an exhibit with him. He came up to my room like a whirlwind in a cape. He was as mad as a fucking hatter. He had this silly waxed mustache like a string of licorice twirled up at the ends. He carried a rhinoceros horn with colored candies, which looked like violets, in the top of it.

"'Oh *chérie,* you must have one, you must have one.' They were about the only words I understood. If he'd been offering me a drink, I wouldn't have hesitated. But I thought, what the hell is this stuff? I didn't want to touch it. It could have been anything! He was gabbling away in Spanish, French, some Catalan, I think, but no English at all. I smiled and nodded. I had no idea what he was saying. The whole thing was fucking crazy . . . *surreal*, right?"

She ordered tea and cucumber sandwiches from room service, hoping that the plebeian English ritual would restore some sanity to the sense of madness. But something must have been lost in translation—there was clearly plenty of room for confusion, she admitted—for Dali seemed to take offense at the word *cucumber.*

"Perhaps it means something different in Catalan, I don't know. He swept his cloak over his shoulder and flounced out. Unfortunately he collided with the waiter arriving with the tea and cucumber sandwiches and went ass-over-head. The rhinoceros horn, colored candies, the whole kit and caboodle went flying."

She threw her napkin down on the table. "I could never take *Surrealism* seriously after that," she said. "Let's talk about the wedding in Philadelphia."

We took our drinks into the sitting room. She curled up on the sofa and took out a small notebook, in which she had scribbled pages of dates. "I'd been seeing Frank since the end of '49," she said thoughtfully. "I went to his birthday party in New York in December. That was on the 12th." She didn't open the notebook, which she played with like a talisman between her fingers. "His marriage was already on the rocks. Let's make sure we put that in, honey: the ball and chain was well and truly smashed before I came on the scene. But he was a good dad, I'll give him that."

"But it was hardly a sotto voce romance, was it?" I said.

"Frank moved in with me the day Nancy announced she was taking the bus to Reno. That was St. Valentine's Day, 1950," she said precisely, still not checking with the notebook. "I'd taken a house in Pacific Palisades that belonged to a dance director at Metro. It was a beautiful place on the ocean, but Frank couldn't settle. I've told you about that time, haven't I? He was constantly moving in and out, in and out. Never quietly either! He was picking fights with everyone. Especially with me. Things got so bad between us I felt sick the moment I heard his voice. Figure that out!

"Then I made the mistake of letting him con me into telling him about my affair with Mario Cabré when I was making *Pandora* [*and the Flying Dutchman*]. I still don't know if I told him to clear the air or to start another fight or simply to hurt him. He'd convinced himself I'd slept with Mario before I admitted it anyway. But I couldn't have chosen a worse time to come clean."

Sinatra's records had completely fallen off *Billboard*'s list of top tunes. His agent said it was all over for him: he could no longer draw flies, he said. In April, MGM had had enough and fired him.

"They were pissed off with his attitude. Louis Mayer was pissed at me for sticking with him. If I hadn't been making the studio such a barrel of dough on the crappy loan-out pictures they were putting me in, I'd have been out on my ass, too. He did a record with Harry James that was so bad, I cried when I heard it. I couldn't listen to it with him. Poor baby, I was the star in the ascendancy and he was on his ass. No matter what I did, his having to rely on a woman to foot some of the bills—most of them, actually—made it all so much worse."

Nancy got her divorce on October 31, 1951, charging her husband with mental cruelty; seven days later, November 7, Ava and Frank were married at the Philadelphia home of the brother of Manny Sachs, the head of Sinatra's record label, Columbia. It seemed a bit too soon to Ava but she went along with it.

Bappie said, "You haven't told Frank that Howard Greer made that dress for you, have you?"

"Why not?" Ava said absently. This was a couple of days before the wedding. The dress had just arrived from Hollywood and she was trying it on for the first time. "It was a simple little gray and pink number. Howard Greer was a wonderful designer but you usually couldn't wear a stitch under his things. He made quite a few things for me. They were often sheer at the top, no straps—you couldn't wear a bra. The whole thing was like a second skin. The dress he made for my wedding was a little more respectable than that, but it had Howard's distinctive cut."

Bappie said, "*Why not?* Are you fucking crazy, girl? Who introduced you to Howard Greer?"

"The penny dropped. Howard Hughes, I said, appalled. Howard Hughes was a great tit man and loved Greer's designs. He sent all his girls to him.

"'Exactly, *Howard Hughes.* Frank's going to love that when he finds out you're marrying him in one of Howard Hughes's blue-eyed boy's creations,' Bappie said.

"Frank hated Howard Hughes. He was jealous of all my previous lovers but especially of Howard. And Artie Shaw, of course.

"'Well, Frank's not going to find out, is he?' I said, although anyone who knew anything at all about fashion would recognize it as a Howard Greer design straight off.

"'Well done,' Bappie said sardonically."

26

"This conversation never happened, okay?"

It was Bill Edwards, vice president of marketing for MGM International, and a friend of Spoli and Paul Mills. Through them, he had become close to Ava. He thought she was one of the wittiest, most self-deprecating actresses he knew. He was an old friend of mine, too. We had been young reporters together, and I trusted him totally.

"What conversation?" I said.

"Have you ever invited Ava to dinner—to your place, I mean?"

"Not yet," I said, puzzled. She hated going out at night. Although it was less noticeable than she believed, she was conscious of the frozen look of her left profile as a result of the strokes. She never accepted dinner invitations.

"It would be pointless to ask. She just wouldn't come, to my place or to anywhere else," I protested.

"You should at least invite her. She's upset about it."

"How do you know that?"

"She told Spoli."

"Spoli has never mentioned it to me."

"Maybe Ava told her not to, but I'm mentioning it to you now. I really think you should ask her," he said again.

A former MGM publicist, Edwards had spent half a lifetime dealing with actresses. Like Greg Morrison, he knew them inside out, their vulnerabilities and idiosyncrasies; he especially loved Ava's down-to-earth take on life. He had first met her at the Millses' apartment in London shortly after she had completed *Mogambo* in Kenya when she was in London doing the post-sync work on the picture and seemed in no hurry to return to California—and Sinatra.

If he believed that I should invite her to dinner, there must have been a reason.

"Okay, I'll ask her," I said. Accompanied by Bill, Ava came to my place for dinner with me and my wife.

Ava didn't wait to be invited to sit at the table. She sat down where the light was to her advantage.

"The canvas behind you, Peter, is that the one you told me about? Your favorite guests are invited to sign?"

"Yes, do you want to sign it?"

"Let me think of something."

We had a lovely dinner, and Ava regaled us with her story of one night spent with four New York garbage collection men.

She was in New York for the premiere of one of her movies, followed by the customary party at one of the city's top hotels.

Naturally gifted with a low boredom threshold, she rapidly tired of the company. "It was like watching a drunk count his change," was her expert opinion, "and I soon went AWOL [Asleep With Open Lids], so I kicked off my shoes, made the usual powder room excuse, left the table and started walking back to my hotel."

She was walking along Fifth Avenue when The Barefoot Contessa was spotted weaving her way by the team of a city garbage truck doing its nightly round. "Hey, Ava!" shouted the driver in his familiar New York way, "you can't walk alone like that in a city like this. Hop in, we'll give you a lift." Which she did, squeezed between two sons of toil in the cab and guarded by two more riding shovel at the rear.

Arriving at the hotel and noting the night was still young, she invited them in. "Come on up boys and we'll tie one on." Which they did, the festivities reaching three in the morning when they were interrupted by a knock on the door and the night manager entered. "I think he was English," Ava recalled, "because he was very polite and apologized, profusely, I think is the word." He said there had been complaints. Not about the noise, but because the garbage truck had been parked in front of the hotel all night. "Not the sort of thing we are used to, you see," he concluded apologetically. So the truck was moved to another spot, and the party continued. One of the best she had ever hosted, recalled Ava.

Then Bill told us how after a particularly heavy night, he had found himself walking with Ava and Spoli through the streets of Kensington in search of "some fresh air." It was that period when London was teeming with coffee and burger bars all sporting pseudo-American titles on their shop fronts. They were approached by two young American tourists who asked if they knew where *The Great American Disaster* was. Ava was not looking her best but was on the ball. "You're looking at her, kid," she told them.

After midnight when Ava and Bill had left, I looked at the canvas on the wall to examine the new addition. It was a caricature of a chicken squeezed between Rex Harrison and David Hemmings with a speech bubble saying, "The chick got her corn tonight." It was signed "Ava."

Epilogue

BY ED VICTOR

Peter Evans sat down to write the final chapter of this book on Friday morning, August 31, 2012, with his notes in front of him on his desk. The manuscript was due the next day, and his goal—to finish the book he had begun writing with Ava Gardner a quarter of a century ago—was finally in sight. Sadly, he never got to write "The End," because at about 11:30 A.M., he had a massive heart attack and died.

These are the notes he left behind: Soon after the dinner party, during one of their phone conversations, Ava said to Peter:

"You never told me Frank sued you for a million dollars."

"In 1972, that's right. He sued the BBC, and me, for a million dollars but finally he settled for about a thousand pounds and an apology in the High Court. I had forgotten all about it."

"Well he hasn't. He doesn't forget a fucking thing. You should have told me, honey."

"I'm sorry, what has brought this up?"

"I told him you were writing my book. He wasn't happy about that. What did you say, fahcrissake?"

"Not much, I was on the TV program *24 Hours*. I said it was rumored that the Mafia helped get him the Maggio role in *From Here to Eternity*. I never said there was any truth in it. I simply didn't know. Although it was widely acknowledged that Mario Puzo used Frank Sinatra as the model for singer Johnny Fontane in *The Godfather*. But the BBC program suggested that he was in London ducking a subpoena to appear before the House of Representatives' Select Committee on Organized Crime. Kitty Kelley said as much in her book. Frank didn't sue her."

That conversation was the beginning of the end of Peter's relationship with Ava and her book. He called me right afterward and told me he saw, all too clearly, the writing on the wall. Ava had always had her doubts about the book, constantly complaining to him that she was revealing far too much about her life for comfort. Frank Sinatra's condemnation of Peter was the final straw for her. We concluded that Sinatra had probably asked her how much money she expected to make from the book and offered to pay her that amount not to write it. Whatever the case, Peter's work with Ava ceased shortly thereafter. She eventually went ahead with another writer and produced a bland, sanitized version of her story, which was published after her death.

Many years later, in May 2009, Peter asked me to lunch with him, saying he had an interesting proposition to put to me. Over that lunch, he proposed writing a book about his adventures with Ava, incorporating into it the approximately forty thousand words of Ava's that he had on tape. I agreed this was a marvelous idea, because I knew just how revelatory and fascinating those words were. I told Peter that we had to get permission from the estate of Ava Gardner to print the transcripts of those tapes verbatim—which we duly did. Ava's manager, the venerable Jess Morgan, enthusiastically gave the estate's blessing to the project, and Peter began to write the book.

Peter's widow, Pamela Evans, remembers that sometime after the collaboration ended, Peter called Ava and said that he hadn't heard from her for a while and jokingly said he didn't know whether she was alive or dead. Ava promised him that she would send a sign when she died. On the afternoon Ava died, the promised sign was delivered. It was the day of the European Great Storm of January 25, 1990. A two-hundred-year-old oak tree crashed through the roof of Peter's writing room. Fortunately Peter was at the gym at the time.

Ava always said to Peter that maybe one day, when she was "pushing clouds around," the book she was working on with him could be published. Now they are both pushing clouds around and her amazing life story can finally be told properly.

Acknowledgments

Peter always enjoyed writing acknowledgments thanking all those who'd helped him. Sadly, with *The Secret Conversations* this undertaking has been left to me.

I probably don't know all of the people who helped Peter, so if I haven't mentioned you below, please forgive me, but on Peter's behalf you have his heartfelt thanks.

My thanks to:

David Patrick Columbia, *New York Social Diary,* where it all started when he published Peter's original Ava article.

Margo Howard, who read the article and pushed Peter to pick up his Ava Gardner book again.

Bob Bender, who worked closely with Peter on the manuscript.

The late Jess Morgan, Todd Johnson, Maggie Phillips, Bill Edwards, Eric and Marcelle Clark, Brian Wells, Richard Kahn, Greg Morrison, Michael Baumohl, Myrna and Jeffrey Blyth, Norma Quine, Jeanne Hunter, Penny Bianchi, Kitty Kelley, David and Nancy Aukin, Matt Warren, Paulene Stone Burns, Rev. Michael Kingston, Pat and Roy Bailey, Maggie and Jeff Tetlow, Jerry and Sheridan Lewis, Duncan and Rachel Clark, Helene Gaillet de Neergaard, Phillip Kurland. All supported Peter with wise counsel and friendly encouragement.

Ed Victor, Peter's agent and friend, who supported Peter

throughout the original Ava venture as well as *The Secret Conversations.*

Also: William Pratt, Christine Walker, Mark Saunders, and Michael Evans.

My children, Lisa and Mark, and granddaughters, Camilla and Clementine, who have always been very supportive of Peter and me.

Finally, I spent the late eighties living with Peter and Ava, and the last couple of years of Peter's life again living with them. While I was reading the manuscript of *The Secret Conversations,* I could hear Peter's voice on every page. To relive those memories was both a delight and sadness in equal measure.

So to Peter, my love always and thank you for being my companion, friend, and husband.

–Pamela Evans

Index